The Compassion Switch

Carl Semmelroth   PhD

DEDICATION

For Sara

TABLE OF CONTENTS

ACKNOWLEDGMENTS I

CHAPTER 1: COMPASSIONATE COMPANIONSHIP KEEPS OUR COMMUNITIES AND OUR SELVES WHOLE 1

Compassionate companionship is more than having caring feelings and actions..2

Compassionate companionship creates a whole entity out of individual members. 2

Self-compassionate companionship creates a whole self. 3

Sometimes we expel others from our compassionate companionship. 5

CHAPTER 2: WHY CONTROL SWITCHES OFF COMPASSION8

What does it mean to control people? 9

Control requires constant monitoring. 11

Threats and compassion don't mix. 11

We cannot switch compassion on by telling ourselves to be compassionate. 14

Why are we so wedded to control? 16

The belief that people in general deserve what they get. 18

CHAPTER 3: WHY ARE WE SO WILLING TO PUNISH?....... 21

The awakening of simple goodness (constructiveness) and simple badness (destructiveness) 21

Our "touch" can be gentle and constructive OR rough and destructive. 27

But what about children's innocence?..28

The end of innocence...30

CHAPTER 4: DESTRUCTIVENESS IS EASY 33

Altruistic Destructiveness: 33

Control with compassionless and destructive threats is the easiest path for changing behavior of someone whether they like it or not............................37

Control attempts by threat switch off compassion because they are grounded in our simple capacity for destruction. 40

CHAPTER 5: GOOD-ENOUGH CONTROL VS. ABSOLUTE CONTROL KEEPS COMPASSION ALIVE 42

Attempts to turn words into magic...42

Language can aid in either cooperation or control; not both at the same time. 44

Good-enough control of one another, not absolute control, is the basis of cooperation. 45

Good-enough control is required in our lives in order to remain a person.....47

CHAPTER 6: COMPANIONSHIP IN THE SERVICE OF DESTRUCTIVENESS 51

Cooperation can be used for well-being of insiders and control of outsiders.52

Janus gets a taste of his family's relationships with family outsiders.............56

People who cooperate in order to control suffer from doing so. 57

CHAPTER 7: SOLDIERS FOR CONTROL IDEOLOGIES— INTRODUCING FEAR INTO FAILING TO COUNT.............. 61

Who counts? **61**

Ideologies loaded with "could" vs. ideologies loaded with "should" **62**

When we are patriots for a should-loaded ideology, we become fearful.......**63**

Control communities reveal themselves by exercising control. **64**

Introducing fear into failure: **68**

CHAPTER 8: USING CONTROL TO RESIST CONTROL: LOSS OF COMPASSION ALL AROUND 71

Elitism entails hierarchies of entitlement which destroy cooperation. **74**

Sometimes we find soldiers for the community in unexpected places...........**75**

CHAPTER 9: CONTROL BY GOSSIP 77

Gossip polices the community..**77**

When gossip is used to establish trust, it doesn't necessarily switch off compassion. **80**

Control of large numbers of people requires individual by individual control. **81**

Gossip like gravity is one force that governs all **83**

Shoulds of a feather flock together. **84**

Evangelizing helps control communities control................................**84**

The value of hypocrisy..**85**

The good which I would, I do not...87

CHAPTER 10: NOT-CARING BY OTHERS IN OUR COMMUNITIES CAN SWITCH OUR COMPASSION OFF..... 91

Can individual freedom be an ideology?.................................91

The illuminating case of the incidental conformist who didn't care about conforming. 92

Caring about the rules is important in control communities; not just being compliant with them. 93

Requiring a person to care about rules amounts to requiring them to gossip in the correct way...96

The psychology of the gossip of caring was alive over 300 years ago. 97

CHAPTER 11: SQUANDERING SIMPLE GOODNESS WITH IDEOLOGIES OF CHILDHOOD AND ADULTHOOD 101

Learning to care about obedience—the key to the should-loaded ideology of childhood. 101

Cooperative play vs. playing for clout: On being an Adult in Control Communities 104

Young people can be adults in control communities if they have clout........108

The origins of effective threat...109

Recognizing the position of the compassion switch is a two-way street. 109

Our awareness of other's compassion switch triggers self-blaming gossip. .111

Joining the control game. 113

CHAPTER 12: WAKE UP: YOU'RE BETTER THAN YOU THINK

.... 117

Simple compassion and voluntary living: A valuable goal 117

Caring for others is done for others' sake. 123

We are better human beings than we think. 125

Simple compassion is marginally effective without careful and competent execution. 126

The "shoulds" involved in careful compassion do not switch it off 127

CHAPTER 13: HOW OUR SIMPLE GOODNESS IS HIDDEN FROM US WITH A LITTLE HELP FROM PSYCHOLOGISTS. 130

Teaching children to punish themselves in control communities 130

Simple compassion is hidden under a pile of shoulds. 132

The details of how two meanings of "should" are made into one. 134

One should feed hunger; True or False? 137

Crowding out simple compassion in favor of rules, passes as the psychology of moral development. 138

The search for rules is taken as morality in a control community. 140

CHAPTER 14: LIVING IN UNSAFE PLACES LEAVES LITTLE ROOM FOR COMPASSION 142

The stockade mentality 143

Maintaining a Stockade is a tough job. 145

Janus builds a stockade, a place where anxiety about others replaces compassion toward them. 145

CHAPTER 15: LEAVING THE STOCKADE.......................... 152

Janus discovers what he's been up to. 153

We need beliefs in the form of helpful habits. 158

Thanks to our simple goodness, we can avoid switching off our compassion and still have beliefs. 160

Gossips are soldiers for community beliefs, not necessarily their own. 161

Janus resigns from soldiering. 162

CHAPTER 16—DEPRESSION, MORAL DELUSIONS, AND THE COMPASSION SWITCH.. 163

Two kinds of delusional belief. 164

Acting out the delusion of moral inferiority--depression 165

Depression impairs our vivacity and our sense of goodness. 167

The opposite of depression: A voluntary life that we experienced as youngsters. 168

Depression is self-control that drives out compassion and vivacity. 169

We serve control community interests even when they don't serve us. 169

CHAPTER 17: GRIEF IS DIFFERENT (WHEN WE DON'T MIX IT WITH DEPRESSION) 173

There are two kinds of grief—compassionate grief and destructive grief. ...173

Caring grief leaves us with compassion that has no place to go. 174

Hanging on to enemies: Destructive grief leaves us with anger and hate that have no place to go. 176

Why we fail to recognize the selfless nature of our caring and hating. 180

Our misunderstanding of loss shows up as trouble in grief and depression. 182

Self-control is at the heart of depressive pain. 183

CHAPTER 18: THE JOY TEST FOR DISCOVERING GOALS THAT KEEP COMPASSION ALIVE 187

Whither goes thou? 187

Finding right directions for ourselves 188

Rules only rule when they require obedience. 190

Janus finds a rule that doesn't rule: Teaching clients to consult their simple goodness. 191

The Joy Test for our intentions. 195

Being Joyful encourages Self-Gratitude. 197

CHAPTER 19: CULTIVATING COMPASSION TOWARD OTHERS AND OUR SELVES 200

We tend to view those for whom we feel compassion as children. 201

The competencies required for acting on compassion are like imagination-fed ideologies. 204

Being able to help ourselves is an important part of well-being. 205

Displaying helplessness in order to get help precludes self-help in control communities...207

Bridging the gap in time between initiating self-help and reaping the benefit of self-help. 207

CHAPTER 20: CHANGING OUR SELF-BLAMING GOSSIP WITH THE GLAD GAME.. 211

The glad game instead of the sad game. 212

Gratitude limits unpleasantness and keeps compassion alive. 216

Adding disapproval of pain to pain is a membership requirement in a control community. 218

The stubborn myth that loss always results from bad choices. 219

Labeling our discomforts allows us to interact with them. 221

CHAPTER 21: INDIVIDUAL FREEDOM............................... 223

Sometimes bad things are the best things that can happen to us. 226

One's lowly place in a control community requires one's assent. 228

Sherman finds a real person buried under the ideology of childhood. 229

CHAPTER 22: OUTING CONTROL COMMUNITIES' BIGGEST SECRET: FREEDOM EXISTS 236

Three secrets that must be kept in control communities. 236

A note to a behavioral psychologist in the year 2112....................................239

Choices make us whole...240

CHAPTER 23: MOVING THE CONTROL COMMUNITY CULTURE TOWARD VOLUNTARY LIVING 243

Cooperative individuality (without joy) 244

What does joy look like and does it really accompany compassion? 245

The enhancement of joy is the business of individuals and cultures, not governments. 249

Is it possible for compassion to spread within a control community? 250

ABOUT THE AUTHOR: 254

ACKNOWLEDGMENTS

Many companions have contributed to this work over the twenty years that the ideas evolved concerning interrelationships among compassion, control, gossip, individual well-being, and individual freedom. Notably, members of the Sunday group who meet monthly to discuss and present our current ideas and writings have read, commented, and contributed to the evolution of many of the ideas contained here. Over the years Terry Shaffer, Bill Courter, Charlotte Courter, Jo DeShon, David DeShon, Sara Semmelroth, Katherine Von Moltke, Melissa Semmelroth have made important contributions to the book's final formulation. David Semmelroth has been a sounding board and offered many cogent suggestions over several years. The experimental philosopher Joshua Knobe kindly read the chapter that draws upon his work and was supportive of the idea that gossip might be an alternate explanation of the "Knobe Effect." A large debt concerning the notions of cooperative individuality and the penalty our well-being pays in obedience cultures, is owed to another philosopher, the late Canadian philosopher and author Will Crichton.

My largest debt is to my life partner, Sara, who has been the first to read every paper, book chapter and revision along with every misdirected exploratory effort I have written over the last 50 years. It is to her that I also dedicate this work.

Chapter 1: Compassionate Companionship Keeps Our Communities and Our Selves Whole

As you begin reading *The Compassion Switch* you may wish to take a moment and think of what you mean by the word compassion. Probably you associate the meaning of compassion with feelings of understanding or sympathy for others who are suffering in some way, as well as actions related to caring about them. We feel bad and may even weep in sympathy with a suffering child whose mother dies. We attempt to comfort her and may even attempt to provide financial or other aid to her and her grieving family.

This book uses compassion in that sense but also in a more inclusive sense, a sense captured by two words in the *Oxford English Dictionary's* first definition of compassion: fellow feeling.[1] This sense of compassion might be referred to as compassionate fellowship. A more inclusive synonym of "fellow" is the word "companion." So we will refer to this sense of compassion as "compassionate companionship.

Compassionate companionship is more than having caring feelings and actions.

Compassionate companionship covers more territory than feelings of sympathy for those who suffer, and our actions that flow from it consist of more than attempts to care for those who are in need. Our feeling of companionship actively affirms someone as a another member of some group to which we also belong. Our companions may include anyone with whom we feel a community connection—our family members, our classmates, our townspeople, our country's citizens, human beings, and sentient creatures in general. Companionships may also include those with whom we worship, work, play sports, club members, and members of common interest groups.

In addition to affirming common membership in a community, our compassionate feelings of companionship also include feelings of mutual respect, feelings of mutual equality, and feelings of shared joy.

Our feelings of compassionate companionship make us patriots for the well-being of others, caring for and protecting those whom we affirm as members of our kind. That membership which we affirm can be as limited as the various parts of what we perceive to be our selves— that confused child we may have been when we were five together with the person we are today. Or it can be as broad as human kind or even all sentient creatures.

Compassionate companionship creates a whole entity out of individual members.

The feeling of companionship brings us closer to others. But compassionate companionship recognizes more than just feelings or outlooks in common with others. It creates something that wasn't there before. Where there was just you and another person before, there is now you, another person, and a relationship. Your companionship isn't just a collection in the sense of a membership list. Compassionate companionship, like mortar between bricks, exists as something in addition to the people involved. It transforms our outlook toward the individuals involved into something new, into a wholeness that transcends its parts.

The wholeness of a compassionate companionship may be as small and fleeting as that bond between you and a stranger, created upon discovering you both grew up in the same area. You may immediately feel a sense of familiarity, but more than that, a sense of being together as parts of one thing, Michiganians or Ann Arborites. A temporary island can be created in a strange, maybe even threatening sea far from home. With companionship may come a sense of trust. A stranger sitting nearby while waiting to make an international call from a country ruled by a military dictatorship speaks to us in a language we understand. We quickly discover we went to the same school in the States. A quickly formed sense of companionship temporarily relieves both of us from our tension. It also reduces to some degree the reticence we may have felt toward that person who a few minutes before we saw as a stranger.

Or compassionate companionship may form a stronger and more permanent wholeness. It may be as meaningful and important in our lives as our companionship with a life partner with whom we have shared struggles toward common goals and with whom we have experienced both accomplishments and disappointments.

Self-compassionate companionship creates a whole self.

As we proceed we will also discover the role compassionate companionship plays in self-compassion and how it contributes a sense of wholeness and oneness to ourselves as individuals. Our personal journeys encounter many and varied, even contradictory, experiences which accumulate as memories about how we have acted and felt and thought. Feeling satisfaction and pride toward ourselves sometimes and irritation, even revulsion, toward ourselves other times can fractionate our idea of our selves. "Who are we?" becomes unanswerable. Am I that person who sometimes has mistreated others and felt good about it because they "deserved" it? Or am I that person who sometimes feels bad when we mistreat others? Or am I that person who thinks of ways to help people? Or am I that person who has sometimes tried to profit from our relationships? Am I that person who sometimes pretends to be interested in other people or am I the person who I am pretending to be? Or am I just a mixed bag full of a bunch of different persons?

Even more problematic are life experiences of failure and shame. Am I that failure that lost all my money and/or a job? Am I the person who was successful in school or am I the person who couldn't cut the mustard in the adult world? Am I the dutiful family person, or am I the hypocrite who talks trash to others about my spouse?

Compassionate companionship, when directed at all of these self-stories, cements them together with compassionate companionship. This process is much the same as that occurring when a parent expresses to a child things like "No matter what you do and how much I disapprove things you may do or how long it takes for you to be the person you can be, I will always love you and I will always continue to expect you to do better."

Self-compassion, when it includes a sense of companionship, can bring our "self-parts" together within a whole being, one whole but complicated self. Just as compassionate companionship creates a wholeness of individuals in relationship with each other, it can bring us personal wholeness, albeit a wholeness made up of individual pieces. Self-compassionate companionship creates one self. Out of self-compassionate companionship comes one person, I, that experiences all my experiences and does all that I do. All of my life stories are cemented together with an "I" that claims them all.

When "I" think of what I'm doing, and "I" consider how it feels to do it, and "I" think about how it will seem to me to have done it, and welcome all of these experiences under one tent, one "I," a self, has been created. A whole person is created out of act, thought, and feeling.

The most incredibly valuable product of self-compassion is that the one self we discover, is itself capable of generating ever-new stories on our life's journey. If we are willing to build that one tent which shelters our whole self at any one point in our life, the product, a unified self, becomes the fountainhead of future journeys. Our individual freedom is unchained—the origin of personal sovereignty. We will attend more extensively to the topic of self-compassion and freedom later.[2]

Sometimes we expel others from our compassionate companionship.

Compassionate companionship is sometimes switched off when we interact with those whom we at other times recognize as companion human beings. We switch from companionship to indifference to their suffering, joy, and well-being. Our child, our spouse, our neighbor, our fellow platoon member, the child of another human being, any one of whom we would give our lives to protect at some other time if needed, somehow become objects of disrespect; they can even become those we threaten with harm or worse.

Our child becomes our "naughty child" and we at least temporarily expel her/him from our heart. Our life partner becomes an obstacle to our wishes and we expel her/him from our partnership. Our fellow platoon member seems tiresome and we expel him/her from our "band of brothers."

What switches compassion off? What enables loving parents or teachers to turn off compassionate regard for fellow beings in their charge and instead feel indifference toward children's fearful or even traumatic experiences while they threaten or hit them? Or as happened in a famous psychological experiment concerning obedience,[3] at which we will be looking later in the book, what enabled willingness by ordinarily amiable college students to torture other students with electric shocks as punishment for making mistakes? And most puzzling, what enables us to switch off self-compassion, often to the point of allowing us to administer the merciless self-blame that accompanies serious depressions?

As tragic as they are for individual lives, these are relatively mild examples of compassion being switched off. History as well as current events are full of examples of people who normally value human life, whose compassion turns off long enough to blow up or incinerate innocent children and civilians, incidents that often lead to self-annihilation.

This book examines the complexities of that process which turns our human compassion switch on and off. The process is partly depicted by excerpts from the life story of Janus, a fictitious person. His quest for becoming a fully human being is chronicled in a series of stories we will view as a life journey, the "Janus Journey". His search takes him through various doorways which sometimes contribute to his humanity and sometimes injure his humanity. We borrow his name, Janus, from the Roman God who watches over doorways with two faces, one looking in each direction. As you the reader follow his journey you may find some surprising territory. In particular his discovery of the part that his attempts to control others and achieve success in the eyes of his community, play in switching compassion on and off. Perhaps you will find his later doorways leading to paths toward joy and freedom suggestive for those stories that remain for you to write with your own life. So, what switches off our compassion?

Notes

[1] "compassion, n.". 1. Suffering together with another, participation in suffering; fellow-feeling, sympathy.
OED Online. December 2013. Oxford University Press.

[2] Kristin Neff's beautiful book—Neff, K (2011). *Self-compassion: stop beating yourself up and leave insecurity behind.* New York: HarperCollins.—presents

much of her influential work on self-compassion. She views self-compassion as being kind to both oneself and others, as well as *not* being indifferent to others feelings and *not* being judgmental. Her work differs in many ways from the approach presented here. Most significant, we do not view compassion or lack of compassion toward others as a trait that is something present or not present in our personality and therefore shows up in a personality assessment. We take the view that the great majority of us are quite capable of sometimes displaying compassion and sometimes displaying indifference toward our own and others' well-being. Our target here is an examination of what leads most of us to switch compassion on and off.

[3] The work and line of research on obedience inspired by Stanley Milgram.

Chapter 2: Why Control Switches Off Compassion

When people get in our way and frustrate our attempts to control, our compassion switches off.[4] We commonly feel that those who frustrate our intentions are being bad and need punishing. We can therefore punish in order to have our way with a clear conscience. Our belief in control by painful punishment for "bad" behavior is such that when bad things happen to people, we feel diminished compassion toward them. They are hungry and their children are needy. They must have made bad choices We even experience satisfaction from knowing of their suffering. "Actions have consequences."

Our beliefs about control and our beliefs about punishment are close allies. When children aren't controlled by parents or other authorities, we feel they lack discipline. Most parents and teachers mean punishment when they use the word "discipline." This author's experience, answering daily questions on *Child Magazine's* web site as their "expert" on child behavior and discipline, was eye-opening. Ninety percent of the questions about child discipline concerned how to punish more effectively. "I give 5 minute time outs. Should I give 10 minutes?" This implies that at least ninety percent of those who sought help with child discipline took for granted that discipline means punishing effectively.

Many company managers believe their jobs are to control those who report to them. Their typical management techniques revolve around making their "reports" fearful—management by control—which means to them, management by threat and fear.

But is control as simple as punishing people or rewarding them? What is it we think teachers are doing when they are "in control" of a class? What is it that a family court is referring to when it rules that parents aren't controlling their children? What is it that people thought Alexander Haig meant when he said to the press, "I'm in control here" at the White House after an assassination attempt on President Reagan in 1981?

What does it mean to control people?

The concept of human control, as used in this work, refers to a very special way of interacting with others. The nature of control is discussed in a previous book *The Anger Habit.* In that book[5], a therapist explains control to Leslie, her fictionalized client.

> "What does it mean to control someone? It means more than just to cause them to do something. If you drive your car over the speed limit, you may cause a police officer to give you a ticket, but you wouldn't say you controlled the officer's behavior. If you fix a good meal, your daughter Sally may enjoy it, but you wouldn't be in control of her enjoyment. We interact with dozens of people every day, which is to say, we do things which cause them to behave in certain ways and they, in turn, do things which affect our behavior. We influence each other. But we don't control them and they don't control us. So what does it mean to control?
>
> "To control someone means that we cause someone to do something which we want him to do whether he wants to or not. Thus, he has no

way to counter our attempt to make him do something. He must do as we wish or suffer bad consequences which he will not be willing to accept. Like: "your money or your life."

"... If we tell someone, "Your house is on fire," we are causing his behavior to change, i.e., he takes [some sort of] action immediately. But we aren't controlling his behavior.

"If we tell someone that he can get a bargain on a CD player through a mail order house, then we are affecting his behavior: he may go and look at the price, etc., but his behavior isn't under our control.

"But what if we tell someone that, if he doesn't give us $10,000, we will set his house on fire? Then his subsequent behavior may or may not be controlled by us depending on what recourse he has. If he is able to get the police to stop us, or is able to restrain us in some way, then he was not controlled by us. However, notice that we still influenced his behavior. He struck back at us.

"So you see, Leslie, controlling others' behavior isn't the same thing as influencing it. Both influence and control involve giving others information which has an effect on their behavior. But control means that, not only does the behavior change, but the person has no way to forestall the (bad) consequences which our information predicted, other than to do as we demand."

In other words we are being controlled by someone else when they are able to engineer the contingencies of our behaviors so that our behavioral options are limited to those chosen by them.[6][7]

Control requires constant monitoring.

This excerpt shows us a crucial aspect of control: its cost. It requires the controller be on constant lookout for behaviors that deviate from those behaviors the controller prescribes. Children as well as adults are quite capable of finding ways to avoid punishment without actually doing what the teacher, parent, policeman, or other "behavior manager" wishes them to do.

Children learn to lie about what happened in order to avoid being blamed for a class disruption. "Johnny pulled her hair, not me." Drivers buy radar detectors to avoid being caught and fined for speeding. Competent employees stay away as much as they can from critical managers and spend time looking for another job while at work. (This incidentally tends to reduce the number of competent employees left behind in fearful and punishment-oriented organizations except in times of great economic disruption.)

Threats and compassion don't mix.

Control involves threat, i.e. showing a willingness to attack as well as carrying out actual attacks. Being prepared to attack someone and compassion toward them don't mix. The presumed exception—"this hurts me more than you" — reeks of a hypocrisy that is instinctively understood by anyone on the receiving end of the hurt: "If hurting is supposed to stop me from doing something, and it is hurting you to do it, why isn't it stopping you?"

Yet parents often do have feelings of sympathy for their children when disciplining them in ways that don't involve threats. Discipline is possible and effective without attempting to control their children. One can have rules and enforce them with consistent consequences, where the consequence consists of persisting in the expectation that children will abide by the rules.

For example: The parent says, "It's bedtime, time to pick up the toys." When the child continues playing, the parent continues to stand there and repeats the rule and continues to do so as long as necessary, ignoring temper tantrums or any other diversion attempt. This gets easier and easier.

Continuing to be present with the expectation that a rule will be followed is an alternative consequence to punishment for rule enforcement. But again, this is a difference that proves the rule that attempts to control someone switches off compassion toward them. This method leaves the "enforcer" with their compassion. Enforcing rules doesn't have to involve punishment. Rule enforcement is a very different process when it involves compassion than when it involves threats and punishment. It leaves children with their personhood.

If you are a parent, consider how you feel when you are merely enforcing a rule versus how you feel when you are punishing. If you think about the difference between rule enforcement and punishing you will recognize that when you yell or ground a child "for life," you feel like *you* are taking charge of their behavior, *you* are "stamping out" their propensity to do what they shouldn't do. Your feeling is one of exerting power, rather than compassion, at that moment.

But when you merely enforce rules, it feels different. For example, consider how you would feel while saying things like "You may not go out tonight because it is a school night," or "This paper you wrote is a start. Now I'm giving it back to you to make it better. And I will continue to give it back until it is a good paper." You are likely to feel like you are helping *them* change their behavior. Your child is the one who you want to be in charge of his or her own behavior. In other words you are teaching. You will only be in the position of continuing to say what you expect from them as long as needed.[8] The bottom line is that you maintain a sense of compassion when you are trying to teach people to behave differently. But your compassion, even toward your children, switches off when you try to assume control over their behavior. And as we shall see in later chapters, self-control attempts anchored in self-threats also turn off self-compassion.

Similarly, managers who enforce rules with punishment and threats feel, or would like to feel, they are "in charge" of employees' behavior. Obedience to what the manager says is a prime requisite in this form of management. Other managers who think of their job as helping employees do their jobs have a different experience while enforcing rules. The rules are there to make their jobs easier to accomplish, to encourage and support productive performance. The rules are not there to establish or test obedience. An "information manager" (as opposed to a "control manager") sees rule enforcement as an opportunity to show the employee how following the rule will help performance. "Your timely reports help me see if there is anything you need, to do your job." If that can't be done, then the rule is pointless. The "information manager" keeps compassion while enforcing rules by continuing to demonstrate to employees what is expected despite failures along the way.

A way of thinking about what does and doesn't turn off compassion is to think about two meanings of "you should" as well as "you shouldn't." Suppose we honk our car horn loudly at someone who "shouldn't" be driving the way they are and we are in control mode. We feel a sense of control projected through the horn. The more "powerful" the horn is, the more power we feel we are emitting. We are unlikely to feel compassion for another driver we are honking at in this fashion. For example, we lack any feeling of concern for their safety which might be endangered by driving in that manner.

Suppose we honk our car horn loudly at someone who "shouldn't" be driving the way they are and we are NOT in control mode. Suppose a truck is weaving back and forth in such a way that we are concerned that the driver is falling asleep. When we lean on the horn, we don't feel a sense of power. The driver shouldn't fall asleep because he might have an accident. We feel concern as to whether the truck driver will hear it. We are likely to feel concern and compassion toward this unknown driver.

Another example is the difference between control *shoulds* and information *shoulds*: Suppose someone asks for directions and we point out to them several ways to reach their destination and add, "But you shouldn't go that way because there is construction going on." We are saying they shouldn't do something, but we don't feel we are attempting to control them. The educational or informational use of "should" or "shouldn't" doesn't turn off our compassion. We feel we are merely contributing information that may help someone change their voluntary behavior; we aren't controlling their behavior.

The lack of human compassion we see around us is related to the use of attempts to control behaviors. We can try to influence behaviors by attempting to control them with threatening *shoulds* and should *nots* and switch off our compassion. Or we can attempt to influence behavior with information and remain compassionate and keep a sense of companionship.

We have the same choice to make in our attempts to manage our own behaviors. If we choose to manage ourselves with threats, the resulting lack of compassion toward ourselves gets expressed by our willingness to sentence ourselves to depressive sickness and self-blame. Given the prevalence of angry threats and depressive unhappiness and the lack of human compassion that is present in our culture, there are many choices for us to make between control and compassionate companionship. But finding our way to compassionate companionship isn't that easy.

We cannot switch compassion on by telling ourselves to be compassionate.

Most of us would prefer that we be more compassionate. We idealize compassion as a human characteristic. Eulogies tell us about the deceased's helpful actions toward others and the community and how much care was bestowed on family and strangers alike. We don't hear about how the deceased treated others badly with the exception of accounts of the lives of "great" warriors and strong leaders. Then the ability to harness power and project control over our enemies is admired and eulogized. Murder of enemies is admired assuming the enemy is everyone's enemy. Otherwise eulogies are about how caring and compassionate the person was.

But we cannot just switch compassion on by telling ourselves to be compassionate. We cannot be compassionate on command. Despite the critical role compassion plays in peaceful living with one another, and the destructive role non-compassion plays in widespread inhuman treatment of others, we cannot just turn compassion on at will or on command.

Authoritative leaders and religious teachings have told us forever to love one another and be kind to one another. Yet no one is fooled by an apology or a show of concern that was given due to a command by an authority. "Tell her you are sorry, Johnny!" does not produce a sorrowful or compassionate Johnny. At best it produces well-performed obedience—a well-acted show of obedience. This sort of "show" is easily detected by the target of the effort. " Do Gooders" are easily detected by members of needy communities. There is no such thing as obedient compassion.

The capacity for feeling compassionate companionship is clearly there in most people. Regardless of the state of her real-life relationships, a good movie actress playing a part that calls for being caught up in the suffering of a young child dying from cancer, weeps real tears. The audience follows suit. The capacity for compassionate companionship is clearly there both on stage and in the audience. But very few of those who cry at the movies or in them, show up at oncology wards offering to read fairy tales to the children and/or adults there, although perhaps I might tempt you to try it. A friend of the author reads Fairy Tales regularly to children and adults on oncology wards in hospitals and assures me that they love hearing them. But I can only tempt you. Telling you to do it isn't going to get you there unless your imagination awakens within you the possibility of compassion expressed in that way.

This is not to say that in performing an obedience-driven show of compassion, one cannot get caught up in the "drama" of the moment and actually start to "feel the part." In real life situations what starts as an acting job can sometimes unleash in actors the emotions of the characters they are playing.

Gentle parents and teachers can sometimes elicit compassionate emotional companionship in children who have hurt others. They may give a child a gentle push toward interacting with their victim as a person: "Talk to her about what you did to her. Tell her you are sorry" But this is an exception that proves the rule—it shows that the compassion must come from within. And it comes much easier when we see someone as a human being. Trying to follow an instruction that says "Love your brother" doesn't produce love. It may produce the appearance of love and concern when it is spoken by an authority that we fear or wish to please. The words and actions may be there, but the music is missing. Or perhaps a better metaphor is that the words are compassion, but the music is control.

Why are we so wedded to control?

A revealing clue to what makes control stick to us so tightly and so early in our lives is that children, as well as adults, more often than not respond defiantly to the request for compassion toward *enemies of our friends and loved ones*. As an example, we will utilize an early experience of our fellow guide in this journey about compassion, our first story in *The Janus Journey*.

The Janus Journey: At four, Janus tries to protect his big brother.

Not yet quite five years old, Janus started kindergarten in a small town near his family's farm. He was an afternoon kindergartner, so he wasn't able to accompany his fifth grade older brother on the bus ride to school in the morning. But his mother took him to the school at noon and instructed him to wait in front of the school with his brother for the school bus after school.

The afternoon wasn't nearly as exciting as he had expected. He had been looking forward to this for a long time. This was going to be full time learning. At home he had a lot of lessons from his parents and older sister, but it was only when they weren't busy. Now he expected non-stop answers to his "why" questions. Well, there were a lot of children there and they didn't seem to ask many questions. There were a lot of big wooden puzzles that smelled good, but were so simple he lost interest. Mainly he learned not to talk until the teacher called on him and to get in line when she asked students to line up. Maybe things would get better.

After school he went down the few steps to the front door and found his brother waiting outside along with several other older boys. His brother was arguing with one of the other big kids and they started pushing each other. Janus wasn't very concerned. He and his brother had many pushing matches. But then the other kid hit his brother in the mouth. Janus was stunned. They hit back and forth a few times but almost immediately they went down on the cement floor of the porch. His brother was on the bottom. Janus immediately ran over and started hitting at the kid sitting on his brother and yelling at him. Another big kid grabbed Janus and dragged him away and held on to him. By this time he was crying and struggling. He couldn't think what to do to get away.

The school bus appeared and the driver yelled at the kids to stop it. Nothing was said between Janus and his brother on their way home. Later his father asked Janus how he liked his first day at school. He said it was OK. He didn't tell him that the only things he could remember were the smell of the wooden puzzles and the sight of his brother being beaten on while he couldn't do anything to help him.

***

Janus shows us what many of us know from our earliest childhood memories when mixing with other yet-to-be-civilized children; we acquire enemies easily and early. We are apt to respond with anger toward anyone who hurts or threatens our family members. Too often an adult in the family is, or is seen to be, a threat to others in the family. They easily become enemies. Our anger easily results in behaviors that risk our own well-being in an attempt to punish those who are a danger to our parents, older and younger siblings—members of our families.

Here we find an early origin for our attempts to control others which makes compassion such a difficult pill for us to swallow: the bad guys, defined as those who threaten our families and communities. Few people feel sorry for "the guys in the black hats" when they are beaten or killed or die under gruesome circumstances in movies or in real life. The bad people deserve what they get.

The notion of bad people who deserve what they get, easily generalizes to the more general belief:

The belief that people in general deserve what they get.

We will have much to say about how this belief gets played out and eventually generalizes into "Bad things happen to bad people." For now the reader may notice common-place attitudes that reflect our willingness to be less that compassionate toward others. We may not be callous toward those who smoke and get lung cancer, but we are less sympathetic toward them than someone who never smoked and dies of lung cancer. Bad consequences are what bad behavior deserves. These commonly held beliefs lead us to observe that lack of compassion accompanies the delivery of punishment for bad behavior.

Our lack of compassion toward others is connected to our belief that they are bad or have done something bad. And further our lack of compassion can also enable us to punish them in some way for being bad, sometimes by merely withdrawing compassion.

We have seen in our description of control above that control over behaviors requires that we administer punishment, or threaten to do so. In other words, switching off compassion can sometimes be connected with our attempt to control behaviors.

This makes sense out of the fact that good people who may one moment feel love and compassion toward their families turn angry, unfeeling, and even destructive when they are trying to control them. Sometimes, the very person who is known to be a good neighbor and help out the family next door when they suffer a loss, is the person who puts out antifreeze that kills the neighbor's pet in a gruesome manner, albeit in secret, for the crime of coming onto their property. Sometimes at the movies, when we see "good people" commit gruesome acts against "guys in the black hats," we admire them—even envy them. The popular book and movie hero, James Bond, acts in nearly every way as a psychopath. He serially seduces and then either leaves or kills women and lies expertly with no anxiety in either case. The one way he is not like a psychopath is that he is unambiguously patriotic. We could never imagine him being a double agent and actually selling out his country. For that, he receives our admiration and backing for his total lack of compassionate companionship—for feeling nothing—toward others, both "good" and "bad." He is a weapon against those who are enemies of the community.

Our beliefs and attitudes involving suffering seem to be that causing suffering is a legitimate response to unwanted—bad—behavior. In the case of James Bond, we seem to identify him as good because he is patriotic, regardless of his lack of compassion toward others. His patriotism puts him on the right side even though his personality is basically criminal. We would cry for him if he were to be killed on screen even though he would never cry for the death of another human being unless they somehow had been serving his needs. Such a combination of psychopathy and patriotism doesn't exist in real life.

As we will see, these early defenses of our family and community are a drop in the bucket compared to our cultural training, especially in a culture that emphasizes obedience. But first we will discover, with Janus's help, the destructive fountainhead within ourselves that feeds controlling behaviors.

---

[4] The idea that frustration leads to aggression goes back a long way. Sigmund Freud incorporated the presence of frustration into his treatment of sadism. Later Freudian theory adopted Dollard and Miller's 1939 frustration-aggression hypothesis (Dollard, J., Doob, L., Miller, N., Mowrer, O., & Sears, R. (1939). *Frustration and aggression*. New Haven, CT: Yale University Press.) More recently this hypothesis has been modified and generalized by Berkowitz to mean "…frustrations produce aggressive reactions because they are unpleasant." See page 71 in Berkowitz, L. (1989). Frustration-aggression hypothesis: Examination and reformulation. *Psychological Bulletin, 106*(1), 59-73.

[5] See page 52 in Semmelroth, C. & Smith, D. E. P. (2004). *The anger habit: proven principles to calm the stormy mind*. Naperville, IL: Sourcebooks.

[6] James G Miller and many others since the 1950's have developed Living Systems Theory. (Miller, J. G. (1965). Living Systems: Basic Concepts. *Behavioral Science, 10*(3), 193-411. One of the crucial elements contained in any living system is the presence of what Miller calls a "decider." Our distinction here between influence and control is that control robs persons of their deciders. This is a monumental loss, extending even to loss of their personhood.

[7] Radical behaviorists such of B F Skinner take the view that all behavior is controlled and that environments can be engineered so that persons are reinforced for doing what we want them to do. They believe therefore that freedom is irrelevant, as well as being non-existent in any case. We take the view that being controlled is itself aversive, and that freedom does in fact exist. Much more on this later.

[8] For a more elaborate presentation of parenting with persistent expectations instead of punishment see Semmelroth, C. *The anger habit in parenting.* Naperville, IL: Sourcebooks. (2005).

Chapter 3: Why Are We So Willing to Punish?

In order to help answer this question we continue to follow the experiences and insights of a fictionalized life, which we refer to as *The Janus Journey*. We look at a couple of Janus's experiences that took place even earlier than his first day of Kindergarten depicted in the last chapter. His experiences represent the emergence of children's capacities for both simple destructiveness and simple constructiveness toward both people and things.

The awakening of simple goodness (constructiveness) and simple badness (destructiveness)

Neither simple constructiveness nor simple destructiveness originates in moral training or any other kind of training.[9] They are awakened in human and other social animals as result of interpersonal stimuli that trigger them.

Simple constructiveness refers to behaviors like one's impulse to run into a fire to save a person or an animal or an impulse to adopt a rescue animal. Or most universally, the willingness of parents to care for their children and children to care for their parents regardless of what sacrifices are required. Simple destructiveness shows up in examples as trivial as one's impulse to tip over the checker board when we are losing, or as non-trivial as an impulse to murder.

The Janus Journey: Janus's experiences on the floor awaken feelings he didn't know he had.

Eighteen-month-old Janus was still simply a child. He had a world to explore - the floor of the farmhouse where he lived. The floor was his. He knew how every table looked from underneath. It wasn't that he couldn't walk just fine. It was just that the floor was where he played and learned.

The floor he knew and loved best was the kitchen floor. He would park under the kitchen worktable while his mother was rolling dough for a pie or for a batch of cookies. The smells were terrific. His favorite was the smell of making donuts. His mother would put him up in his high chair while she was doing this. He didn't realize until he was older that she was afraid that the pot of boiling lard on the stove would spill and burn him if she left him on the floor.

From his high chair he could see her punch out the donut shaped circles of dough and carefully drop them into the pot boiling on the wood stove. They would quickly start to swell and turn from white to dark reddish brown. A trace of wood smoke together with the smell of donuts frying along with the sight and taste of their crispy shells melted together into one experience that he would love his whole life.

The kitchen floor was where his mother bathed him. She filled the big white enamel basin with warm water from the water reservoir that was attached to the end of the kitchen woodstove. The stove was hot and the heated air touched his skin along with his mother's hands and the washcloth. And then the best part. The towel, fresh from a couple of minutes in the oven, swallowed him as she picked him up from the washbasin.

The feeling of the towel's warmth and the strength of his mother's arms blended into how he felt when his parents sometimes hugged each other while standing on that same spot on the kitchen floor. He would *hang onto their legs until his father picked him up and folded him between his parents as they hugged, surrounding him with that same feeling that he had when his mother picked him up after his bath.*

Janus's mother never allowed any part of the farm animal world into the house. Boots that had been in the barn stayed outside along with all animals whose feet might have been in the barn. However, that spring, part of his father's world, the barn and the animals, was allowed to set foot in the kitchen. A spring lamb, probably a twin abandoned by its mother for some reason only known to mother sheep, was brought in together with its wooly intimate smell, and placed on a towel in a wooden box behind the kitchen stove just beside the door to the pantry. His father and mother and older sister and brother fed the voracious lamb from a bottle and even let Janus hold the bottle sometimes.

The lamb was still there when his mother next bathed Janus. Janus sat in his big enamel basin in front of the kitchen stove and the lamb lay in his wooden box behind the stove. They looked at each other, both content there on the floor on either side of the stove, seeing each other feeling the warmth from the same stove, the same kitchen, and the same family.

***

While we are simply children and have yet to learn how children are expected to behave and feel we, like Janus, feel attracted to others and to others' well-being. We do not yet know what sort of "animal" we are. But we naturally assume that all other creatures, including animals, have the same kinds of things going on within them that we do. Without this simple assumption, learning language would be impossible.

At eighteen months, Janus is a sponge waiting for learning language. This means he assumes that things that are said, and actions of others that occur, accompany an experience inside them that corresponds to the some kind of experience inside of him. This is the very heart of information transmission as depicted by modern information theory. Transmission of information means that there are several possible messages present. That is, uncertainty—information—is due to there being many possibilities. The uncertainty of which possibility is the message constitutes the amount of information present. No uncertainty; no information.[10] Notice that the uncertainty exists in the receiver, not the sender. Information theory, in this sense, reflects our human situation when we attempt to understand what someone else is communicating. We assume the other person or animal is "broadcasting" an experience they are having. And that experience is one of those experiences we have had and know about.

This principle of information transmission when turned upside down shows us what very young people are capable of feeling and imagining. We can conclude that because very young children understand that there are loving and destructive feelings in others, they must experience booth loving and destructive feelings themselves. When we are young children, we understand that others have loving as well as destructive feelings; therefore we must be capable of feeling them ourselves.

The Janus Journey: Janus likes to build and destroy at three.

Three-year-old Janus, like most boys his age, liked to play with blocks. His favorite block game consisted of piling block upon block into a tower of blocks. Sometimes the towers fell over by themselves. But sometimes Janus beat gravity to the punch, and he knocked a tower over with a sweep of his arm and a gleeful shout.

Sometimes his older brother played with him and they built more elaborate towers with larger bases and more elaborate attempts to interlock pieces. These changed his towers into buildings in Janus's eyes; but when it came time to stop playing, he still enjoyed knocking down the structures with grand swipes of his arms, scattering the carefully constructed buildings into their original state—just a bunch of wooden blocks.

On Janus's fourth birthday his mother invited a few of his friends over for play and a party. It is a beautiful September day outside, but they started off in the farmhouse with a birthday cake and homemade ice cream followed by a well supervised game of Blind Man's Bluff. This seemed boring and confusing to the boys and required constant intervention by one or more of their mothers to keep the confusion and complaints just back from the edge of chaos. The mothers finally tired of their unsuccessful effort to get the boys to like the game and gave into the boys' repeated requests to go outside and play. They fled out of the house to unsupervised play with the solemn promise that they would not go in the road.

In a corner of the large yard in front of Janus's farmhouse was a large roundish rock, perhaps three feet tall which Janus was used to climbing on. He led the screaming boys over to the rock and jumped up on it and declared "I'm King of the mountain." Another boy quickly attempted to jump up and push Janus off. He failed. Others tried and finally succeeded. Then bedlam broke out. The children were soon pushing and screaming and some were crying. The party ended badly.

***

From two to four years old, Janus's language learning had been blossoming. His understanding of behaviors around him depended upon the awakenings in his own experiential world. He clearly understood the feelings of destructiveness in his playmates playing King of the mountain. He understood them because they are awake in him and had been since an early age. He clearly understood the feelings of compassionate companionship in his parents and the animals he encountered. He understood them because they were awake in him.

At three Janus had never doubted that anything that he experienced inside him was also inside others. He knew that there was more to people and animals than he could see. Janus assumed that it was the person inside others that spoke to him just as it was his thoughts and feelings that originated what he said to them. He knew that his sister's dolls and his teddy bear didn't really have any feelings or thoughts inside them even though both he and his sister pretended that they did.

He couldn't see the person inside others, that person who chose what they did and said, and others couldn't see inside him the person who made his choices. But he had no doubt they were there. He had never doubted that he had companions in the world who felt, saw, and made choices as he did. He wasn't just surrounded by inanimate objects that, like dolls and teddy bears, experienced nothing. He was surrounded by people and animals, who like him, had a private self. He was his body; but he was also the unseen person in his body that communicated with and related to the unseen selves hidden within the bodies of persons and animals around him.

When Janus's mother picked him up and held him, it wasn't just her arms that he felt; he felt the loving person inside her and he experienced that person's choice to express her love toward him. And when one of his friends pushed him down, or his older brother pinned him down and sat on him until he cried, Janus experienced the persons inside his friend and brother. He experienced their desire to hurt him and their lack of positive feeling toward him. He experienced their "destructiveness" because he experienced those feelings sometimes.

When Rex, his father's sheep dog and Janus's friend, would "go nuts" in one of his frenzied phantom chases around the yard, he would sometimes smack into Janus with a glancing bump on the side of his leg as he went by. Janus felt Rex's choice to smack him, not just the bump of his body. It was no accident; it was how Rex often invited him to get excited along with him and join in play. It was an invitation. Just like Janus's invitation to Rex when he went out to play around in the yard.

When his father brought a spring lamb into the kitchen that had been disowned by its mother, Janus sensed the lamb's private feelings and thoughts. The lamb was choosing to look back at him from the box behind the kitchen stove from somewhere inside the wooly coat Janus could see and smell.

And it was the same private Janus, the inner Janus that chose to wrestle with his brother, fed the lamb, expressed loving feelings toward his family members, and anger toward his brother when he sat on him. He was all one person. The person who tended to feel and act and choose all the things he did and experienced all the things around him was all him.

And he assumed others were whole and "in there" just like him. It was his brother's private choice to sometimes not let Janus up, to frustrate him and make him mad; this was the same private self of his brother that chose to play with him and cared about him.

Like Janus, most of us start out assuming that others have feelings and thoughts that correspond to those we experience, even though we can't actually see "into" others, nor can they see directly into us and perceive our experiences. But we assume those comparable experiences between our and other's perceptual worlds are there from the beginning.

This assumption isn't as much of a leap as it might seem. Our experiences, even in the womb, include touching our own bodies. Self-touch, say touching your middle finger with your thumb, involves access to two experiences—you can feel your finger with your thumb; and you can feel your thumb with your finger. It's a short leap to assuming that when one touches another person, they are experiencing being touched. When you touch yourself you also feel yourself being touched. Why wouldn't someone else feel themselves being touched when you touch them? It's an even shorter leap to assume that in general, other people have all the same sorts of experiences going on privately that we have going on privately.[11]

Our communications with others are between what we think and feel privately, "inside us," and what others think and feel privately, "inside them." Much confusion and silliness in psychology and philosophy has arisen by using the language "inside us" and outside us." "Inside" merely means private. Other than our body sensations, our experiences aren't inside us. Stomach aches and babies are experienced inside us. Most of our experiences are literally outside our body. As I look out of the window beside me, I experience the trees "outside" along with the children playing among them "outside" who were once experienced by their mothers "inside."

Our "touch" can be gentle and constructive OR rough and destructive.

The game of King of the Hill played at Janus's birthday party wasn't between the children's bodies. It was between the children. They fought against each other's desires to achieve superiority, to be "King." And they were willing to knock each other down, just as Janus was willing and eager to knock down blocks and buildings.

Early *experiences of* destructiveness in both ourselves and others correspond to experiences of *capacities for* destructiveness both by ourselves and others. Our interactions are literally actions directed at one another. Children are quite capable of destructiveness just as are adults. Childhood innocence means something quite different than this.

But what about children's innocence?

When we are very young, we have no secrets. We refer to this characteristic in young children as their being "ingenuous." The ingenuousness of young children is more than honesty. It is an innocent form of honesty. "Mom, why is that lady so fat?" spoken loudly by a four-year old in the super-market may be embarrassing for the parent, but depending on how it is said, it is understood that the child means no harm to the lady. It is innocent curiosity.

The child's communications are not yet guarded. The child's mother may be thinking the same thing, but she thinks it would be wrong for her to say it out loud. Whether she feels that it is wrong to even think of the lady as being fat depends on the sort of ideologies to which she may subscribe. Some religions have taught that thinking bad thoughts is the same as doing them. In any case, for young persons, if they were unable to speak of whatever their experiences are, their mental development would be severely impaired.

We cannot grow psychologically without making honest contact with others. Without it we would be aliens from the beginning of our lives with no way of making the contact that informs us that we are people and belong with people.

Young humans operate, still unencumbered, on the Aristotelian principle that experinece is like a window pain that admits all colors. The mind admits all thoughts as well as their opposites.[12] We would not be capable of rationality if we could not think the opposite of everything we think, as well as any of its contraries. We can think "white," "black," "not white," and "green." Otherwise, we cannot decide which to believe we are seeing, and the use of reason would be fatally flawed. However, beliefs are quite different than thoughts and ideas. Charles Sanders Peirce, founder of pragmatism, and arguably America's greatest philosopher, made this crystal clear.[13] He viewed belief as the cessation of thought.

Our feelings would not be informative to us if we could not experience a wide variety of them as well as their variations in strength. If our minds were narrow filters of our thoughts and experiences, we would be unable to hear more than the notes of a musical scale. There would be no music; the music is made up of the notes, but it lies beyond them. Our experiences lie beyond the stimuli which produce them, just as music lies beyond the notes. We hear the music that composers heard when they wrote that music, just as we hear the message that people were experiencing when they composed the words they speak.

Because young human beings do not yet tend to keep private what they feel and think privately, they can "try out" anything and its opposite. They reach out to others as a whole person, unencumbered by taboo feelings and thoughts, ready to touch and acknowledge any experience they may find there that may correspond to their own experiences. They reach out to other human beings as human beings.

Without this "open-door" policy, human language learning would be impaired and thinking would be chaotic. We must learn names for our private feelings, and expressions for our private thoughts. Names for feelings and objects and adjectives that apply to them must be tried out. It is only then that our private lives become capable of blossoming privately and the open door of ingenuous expression can start to close. A private world populated with private self-talk can blossom. The original garden of thinking and imagination has been planted and it is bearing fruit ready to be tasted. Our whole inner self is ready to establish common borders with anyone we come across, or not, as we choose. Young human beings are free to imagine that other human beings experience a wide variety of their private experiences.

Our private selves are ready to find contact with all other thinking and feeling beings and in doing so they are enriched and become more distinctive.

Childhood innocence is made up of this openness of sharing thoughts and feelings. It does not mean that young children are incapable of destructive actions and thoughts.

The end of innocence.

Ready to take in a rich range of the thoughts, feelings, and actions of those humans around us, we are also ready to take in the stories that influence those around us. Between three and five, Janus's world was enriched with stories he heard while grownups chatted. Everything from hunting stories to stories concerning conflicts with neighbors over line fences interested him.

Some of these stories were more than stories. Some of them not only described ways people think, feel, and act, they also described how they ought or ought not to think, feel, and act. Stories about neighbors that didn't keep up their fences, or mow their yards, were like that. They should do these things because the township had a regulation that said they should. And people should obey regulations.

Janus would later call these "ideologies," literally meaning "sciences of ideas." This is because his parents and others in the community in which he grew up believed that good and bad behaviors, together with all behaviors, were the product of teaching. The Western origins of this point of view (in modern times) was British Empiricism, represented paradoxically by the Frenchman Condillac in his treatise on sensations.[14] [15] That the determinations of all our behaviors, public and private are sensations, is the point of view of modern radical behaviorism as represented by B F Skinner.[16]

Ideology is a word that described his parent's "science" of what made good people think, feel, and do what they did. Good people were good citizens who did what they did because they were taught to obey the rules that said what they should do. The rules they learned to subscribe to determined their thoughts, hence the rules formed their ideology.

We have already challenged this point of view with regard to questions concerning where the "decider" lies in living systems. We will cover many more questions in the pages ahead. But for now we may ask, "If children must learn to be good, why wouldn't they also need to learn to be bad?" And conversely, if sin can be original in children, why not good?"

---

[9] Moral training is in fact the origin of *seeming* to be moral. *Being* moral is found naturally occurring in "simple childhood." What happens later, when an obedience culture takes hold, is no longer simple, nor does it result in willingness to be moral. An obedience culture is quite different from a freedom culture—a distinction made clearly by the Canadian philosopher Will Crichton. Crichton, W. (2011). *Foundations for a new civilization: Structure, change, & tendency in Nature & Ourselves.* Kalamazoo, MI: Voluntary Living Press.

[10] Shannon, C, E. A Mathematical Theory of Communication. *Bell System Technical Journal*, 27, pp. 379–423 & 623–656, July & October, 1948.

[11] Try touching your middle finger with your thumb. Then attempt to feel your finger's finger print ridges with your thumb. And then try feeling your thumb print ridges with your middle finger. These are two distinct sets of experiences within the same person—you. This sort of self-body discovery is the foundation for our first experience of "fellow feeling." We have one body made up of experiences and experiences of being experienced.

[12] Aristotle, in De Anima, Book 3, Chapter 4 says "… since everything is a possible object of thought … to know, must be pure from all admixture;"

[13] Charles Sanders Peirce, the originator of Pragmatism, and perhaps the most original and notable American philosopher, maintained that thought and belief are not only NOT the same thing, but that belief is the cessation of thought. His

view was that doubt triggers thought that leads to beliefs which are made up of habits which take over when thought has stumbled on a trigger for action. Hence, once belief (habit) is triggered, thought ceases. Of course this can take place in a series of alternations between doubts that leads to thoughts that explore what's possible next, and habits which execute possibilities. A simple example would be playing a game of chess in which doubt over what to do leads one to spend time imagining possibilities (thoughts) interspersed with moving pieces on the board (habits). See How to make our ideas clear. In J. Buchler (Ed.) *Philosophical Writings of Peirce* (pp. 23-41). Dover, Oxford, 1955.

[14] Ideology definition from OED : "1. **a.** The science of ideas; that department of philosophy or psychology which deals with the origin and nature of ideas. **b.** *spec.* Applied to the system of the French philosopher Condillac, according to which all ideas are derived from sensations."

[15] Condillac, E; Aarsleff, H *Essay on the origin of human knowledge.* New York: Cambridge University Press, 2001.

[16] Skinner, B. F. *Science and human behavior.* New York: Macmillan, 1953.

Chapter 4: Destructiveness is Easy

Common sense tells us that we can't feel simple compassion toward someone whom we have targeted for destructive treatment. However, we *can* target someone for destructive treatment while being willing to sacrifice blood and treasure in order to hurt or destroy them. In other words, we can practice self-sacrifice for the sake of destruction in the same way that we can practice self-sacrifice for the sake of compassionate caring. The word "altruism" refers to behavior exhibited by a person (or animal) toward others which costs that person more than it gains them. We may as well call a spade a spade and call our willingness to sacrifice for the purpose of non-compassionate willingness to destroy "Altruistic Destructiveness."

Janus is about to observe a scene that confuses and scares him—the destructive behavior from a child which clearly doesn't payoff for the child but is nevertheless done willingly.

Altruistic Destructiveness:

The Janus Journey: Janus observes a confusing and scary scene.

At four, Janus was already bigger that his peers. He will continue to be bigger and stronger than his age for the next ten years or so which will complicate his role on the playground after he enters school.

But school was still to come. At four, while his brother and sister were in school, and his father was busy on the farm, his mother often took him along while shopping. Janus's mother was a careful shopper and often spent what seemed like hours looking at merchandize and asking the clerks endless questions. This was especially apt to be the case in the department store on the floor where they carried clothes. Janus would wander around, usually obeying his mother's instruction to remain where she could see him.

On one such occasion, Janus was hanging around close to the door of the elevator. It always fascinated him and he loved it when his mother used it. It had a gate which the elevator operator flung open or closed. The operator then would turn a device that looked like a wheel and the elevator would jerk into action. At the next floor they would stop, often not quite where they needed to be, in which case there would be some jerking up and down until they were at least close to being even with the outside floor. Then the elevator operator would fling open the door and the gate saying loudly "Watch your step!"

This particular day no one seemed to be using the elevator. So Janus just hung around the door waiting for some action. All of a sudden someone bumped into him from behind. He nearly fell down, but didn't. When he turned around he saw a child grinning at him who said, "Watch where you're going stupid!"

Janus thought the boy looked older than he, but not as big. Janus looked around to see if his mother was watching. She wasn't. Janus just shrugged and said "You're going to get in trouble." The boy didn't reply. He just tried to shove him. Janus reached out and just held him at arm's length and told him to stop it. The kid backed off, still smiling. Janus turned to go over by his mother. He got about two steps when the boy hit him from behind and this time knocked him down.

Now everyone was looking, including the boy's mother. She yelled at him and advanced on him. She slapped the boy really hard and then turned him over her knee and started pounding on him. The boy didn't whine or cry or make a noise. He just looked at Janus and smiled.

Janus was immediately full of confusion and alarm. He didn't understand. He would have been crying, like the time his father spanked him after he saw him hit his brother with a rotten limb in the front yard. Janus was crying before his father even touched him.

This was Janus's first experience with a smile that meant hate.

***

Just as our altruistic concern over the well-being of others can be awakened by our exposure to loving actions of those around us, our "altruistic" concern for damaging the well-being of others can also be awakened. We are capable as children or adults of seeking to damage or even destroy others' well-being without concern about what it will cost our own well-being. This phenomenon reaches the zenith of sheer destructiveness in what Jonathan Shay called "berserking" in his important book *Achilles in Vietnam*.[17] Under the right combination of recent rejection and loss, people can simply and coolly go berserk, attacking and murdering without emotion and with no regard for protecting themselves or avoiding enemy fire.

The human capacity for altruistic destructiveness in the form of "berserking," has slightly less severe, but more frequently seen versions. Incidents involving people who are willing to commit suicide along with homicide occur in the news regularly. In their attempt to simplify psychiatric classifications into a continuum of 5 levels of mental dyscontrol, Karl Menninger et. al. in *The Vital Balance* incorporates this possibility as a fifth and final level of mental dyscontrol. In their discussion of the 5th and ultimate level of dyscontrol they quote an early psychological contributor (1910) Wilhelm Stekel: "No one kills himself who did not want to kill another or, at least, wish death to another."[18] An obvious exception is suicide involved with terminal illness.

Ideologies can take advantage of their adherents' human capacity to willingly destroy, by fanning the flames of that destructive capacity, directing it toward non-members or violators of community standards. It is easy to see this happening in the modern world with wars and terrorist attacks committed by believers against unbelievers. Language such as "The God-less infidels" and "The axis of evil" excite destructive tendencies among particular ideologies toward human beings who adhere to other ideologies.

It is less easy to see this when practiced among members of a family or community where control of members' behaviors is an objective. There, naturally occurring human destructiveness can be tapped by making out that another person's behavior is blameworthy, that is, "He deserved what he got." Under cover of righteousness, an awakened capacity to destroy can become the fountainhead of discipline. "Tough love" becomes appealing to our destructive capacities when couched in language that justifies making someone hurt for their own good.

The mother of the little boy who attacked Janus in the department store when he was four-years-old, had no difficulty unleashing a destructive attack on her child. The little boy in turn, clearly had no difficulty unleashing a destructive attack on Janus for his crime of being in the way. Blame of others leads their way. No doubt both mother and child love their self-righteousness, but their blaming will circle around, sooner or later, and it will take a bite out of themselves. We will have much more on boomeranging blame as we proceed in our journey with Janus.

Destructive behavior, relative to constructive behavior, is easy and requires no talent. Therefore, children, being born ignorant, as well as being young people who have not yet learned constructive skills, are especially prone to destructive over constructive activities when something gets in their way.

Janus's early simple destructiveness required only a swipe of his hand to destroy a tower of wooden blocks. In general, we can be good at being destructive without much education.

On the other hand, Janus's constructive capacity, his "simple goodness," required not only his naturally awakened compassion; it required knowledge. One must learn *how* to care for a baby, not just apply one's natural inclination for caring. Loving care is an art that we must not only feel; we must also learn how to care for other's well-being effectively, no matter whom or what is the object of our

36

compassion.

Artists must spend a lifetime developing the craft necessary for expressing their love well, but the craft of destruction is simpler to learn. Simple destructiveness doesn't require much of a road map. Lighting a match, hitting with a brick, firing a gun, starting poison gossip, requires little learning. And with all this ready "talent" available, threats against others are easily communicated and used in the "art" of control.

Control with compassionless and destructive threats is the easiest path for changing behavior of someone whether they like it or not.

Three avenues for changing others *without their permission* are open to us.

1. Physically overpower their body. We can pick up a two-year-old who is in danger or imprison a person who is a danger to others.

2. Re-designing their physical environment. We can change the environment of people unwilling to exercise in order to change their weight. For example we can put locks on the elevators of a building, with keys only available to a certain few so that people working there must use stairways to get where they want to go.

3. Threaten them. We can threaten students who do not study with loss of sports eligibility and/or loss of privileges at home.

And one approach is available for helping people change *with their permission* is available. Provide information they lack.

We can supply students who wish to learn, but who are unwilling to study, with information about how to study effectively. Often they merely need to know how to study in such a way that they could learn. They never thought they could do it, and when they are shown how, they make the best of it, or not. Notice that helping people with their permission is by far the hardest to implement. Like any other constructive task, it requires careful attention. What are good study habits and how can they become more rewarding and easier? Changing others' behavior without their permission requires little more than the power and opportunity to threaten them. Like a three-year-old playing with blocks or playing King of the Hill, you don't have to know anything to knock a block tower down or push someone off their perch. But building a tower or teaching effective and appealing study habits requires careful effort.

The number 1 way of changing behaviors of others without their permission does not directly control the *behavior* of the person. It controls the *location* of the person's body. It is critical for keeping babies and small children safe and healthy. It is also critical for keeping us safe from people who, left to their own devices, would likely harm us or themselves. Physical confinement of people who are dangerous does not automatically switch off our compassion and it doesn't make them less dangerous people. It makes them less dangerous *to us.* However, if physical confinement is seen as punishment, doing it or advocating it *does* switch our compassion off.

Parents or other childcare givers of very young children sometimes go from control over the child's physical location to attempts to control the child. Their compassion switches off, resulting in child's arms being painfully yanked or being confined alone for long periods in cribs or tied to potty chairs.

The expectation that parents should control their children by threat and punishment originates to some degree in the fact that when children are young and small, good parenting does in fact require physical control over their bodies in order to keep them safe and healthy. Holding and carrying are in fact a necessary part of learning trust.

Unfortunately, this exercise of physical control over children's bodies continues into later development. Therefore number 1, physical control, often morphs into number 3, control by threat. Much more on this issue, not only concerning children, but with regard to its implications for meaning of morality as well as obedience, will be discussed later.

Number 2—overpowering a person's environment—is much easier than following them around with threats or treats. This is what is done in rat labs. The rat is put, and kept, in an environment where, for example, food is only available when a lever is pushed. That such "behavioral engineering" is carried out with unwilling subjects is shown by the fact that rats must be kept in cages. If they aren't, they simple flee the scene.

Some form of "keeping them in their cage" is also required for instituting so-called token economies. Token economies are settings in which people (or animals) are rewarded with tokens redeemable in things they want, when they perform "well." They are basically like economies that use money, except the tasks to be learned are chosen by others, and it is easier to flee the scene in the "real" world. A search of the social science literature in early 2014 using the subject heading "token economy" found over 800 articles. When listed by relevance, the first 40 articles concern token economies in either residential settings for mentally ill, or school class rooms, or group homes, or some other setting where "fleeing the scene" is not usually a viable option. One exception is an article concerning the successful self-application of the use of tokens by one person. This application would fall outside of control mythology and into our category of willing helpfulness because the person arranging it is the target of the procedure.

Weight Watchers also provides a similar methodology based on education and a token (point) system which is self-administered. One can "earn" helpings of desirable food by accumulating points by eating healthy food. Their system is entirely voluntary and can be "escaped" at any time.

Helping by providing a person with consistent and correct information about how to accomplish goals, includes how to find goals that awaken a person's willingness to pursue them, and preserves compassion. Helping others to find inspiring goals requires knowledge and experience. Wanting to do this is not enough. We can't tell someone how to get somewhere without knowing how to get there. Janus's brother couldn't teach Janus how to build a building out of blocks by just wanting to do it. Janus's father couldn't just tell Janus to go and plant a garden. They had to do it together.

Number 3—attempting to control by threatened punishment—has two big advantages over all the others when it comes to trying to change or manage behaviors. It's just so darn easy to criticize, hit, put down, frown, and show disgust. It requires little or no knowledge and it taps into a basic destructive appetite that we have had since early childhood. Just as Janus's four-year-old friends immediately bought into the game of King of the Hill, and energetically engaged in knocking each King down, we are all capable of buying into easy solutions to behavior problems that involve destructive threats and actions.

Control attempts by threat switch off compassion because they are grounded in our simple capacity for destruction.

Control attempts by threat of punishment or by actually attack are rampant. The criminal and compassionless behaviors they create are themselves treated as behaviors that ought to be punished. The Hatfield and McCoy effect of interactions of individuals—you hurt me and so I hurt you—is rampant among individuals, groups and countries. Aggression by others is answered by aggression meant to punish the aggression of the other party, leading to long term escalation. The parties are not only willing to hurt and destroy each other without compassion, they actively hate and seek to destroy each other.

Our examination of the compassion switch leads us to a consideration that we may not wish to entertain—our role in causing our own misery. Janus will spend most of a life time searching before he begins to own his complicity in causing his own suffering.

Our own natural capacity to destroy blinds us to our practice of self-control though self-blame. It deadens us to an alternative practice of careful and gentle self-care not to mention careful caring for others. This cannot be countered by merely doing what comes naturally. We are already doing what came naturally. We must choose to be different. "We have met the enemy and he is us."

Once entangled in a life that emphasizes control, finding our way back to a simpler, more childlike form of joy, becomes problematic. In order to choose a free life, we must be free; free from the web of control we have woven to ensnare others, but which too often catches ourselves in its compassionless embrace.

---

[17] Shay, Jonathan. *Achilles in Vietnam: Combat trauma and the undoing of character.* Simon and Schuster, 2010.

[18] Menninger, Karl, Mayman, Martin, and Pruyser, Paul. *The vital balance.* (p 268) New York: The Viking Press. 1963.

Chapter 5: Good-Enough Control vs. Absolute Control Keeps Compassion Alive

During the first four years of our lives, more and more of our interactions with parents and others are verbal (or signed in the case of deaf parents or children). As we begin to talk, we quickly learn that what we say can result in responses by others, and we learn that we are often expected to say certain things in response to others.

As a result it begins to look to us as if saying the right things can make people do things. It looks as if saying things can make them so. The notorious age of two and three-year-old negativism is an example of this phenomenon. The word "No!" is used as if it had the power to nullify others' demands. Of course, adults do in fact use "No!" in an attempt to control the demands of the child. Does either the adult or the child really understand that "no" is not magical? That is, do either adult or child realize that saying a magic word, or the right way of saying it, cannot absolutely make something happen?

Attempts to turn words into magic

The Janus Journey: Janus plays with the power of words.

As a three-year old Janus already loved to talk. Talking was almost more fun than playing in the yard with Rex, their Australian Shepherd, which his father used to herd sheep and cattle. Janus wasn't as fond of being talked to as he was of talking. He was allowed to play in most of the yard, but when he did, his mother spoke to him in a firm and even scary way—"You must not go near the road!"

Janus often played with Rex in the yard between the driveways, under the old pear and apple trees. But he stayed away from the big maple trees that lined the ditch by the road. Sometimes he tried to order Rex around, especially just after his mother checked on him and said to him again, "Don't go near the road!" Janus would say, "Rex, don't go near the road! Come here, Rex!" Rex didn't go near the road, but he hardly ever came when Janus told him to.

Janus talked to Rex the same way he talked to everyone else, including the young lambs in a pen over in the west yard on the other side of the house. He sometimes copied one of his father's chores, feeding the young lambs in the west yard. He opened the granary door out behind the barn, took a bucket that was about a third as tall as he was, and put some grain in it. He carried - mostly dragged - the bucket all the way out to the west yard to feed the lambs.

As he approached, he spoke to the lambs, although he needn't have bothered; they were already crowded up to the fence before he got there. Then, with a Herculean effort Janus attempted to boost the bucket with its small portion of grain, over the wire fence. Most of it spilled onto the ground, which eased his effort enough so that at least some of the grain made it over the fence. He was happy and the lambs were happy, and he knew they were feeling good just as he was. They were happy that he talked to them and fed them, and they thanked him in their high pitched voices.

Janus was still young enough to take for granted that he didn't need proof that animals have feelings, thoughts, and desires going on in them just as he experiences those private unspoken feelings and thoughts in himself. He assumed that was true of other people and animals show the same signs of thoughts and feelings and desires that other people do.

The thing about talking to people that was most fun for Janus was that it took little effort to make things happen. It wasn't like boosting the bucket over the fence or trying to get his older brother to get off him when he wrestled him to the ground in the front yard and sat on him. That was maddening when saying "Get off!" didn't work. Getting lambs fed and getting his brother off of him were both hard work. Words were easy and fun. They were most fun when they worked like magic and made other people respond. His parents and his older brother and sister would often stop what they were doing and listen when Janus talked. They would think what he was thinking. They would experience what he was experiencing. They often laughed and shook their heads in amazement, or perhaps it was amusement, at his chatter.

Even the animals would often stop what they were doing and listen and even mind, like his dog sometimes did when he called. But the magic of words didn't always work very well. Janus knew that to be the case both as a speaker and a listener. He didn't always pay attention to what others said to him; and they, especially his brother and sister, didn't always pay attention to what he said to them.

***

Language can aid in either cooperation or control; not both at the same time.

Despite the fact that words aren't magical, they are easy to use. Further, they often work better when we raise our voices which adds to the possibility that they might actually make people do what we intend for them to do. The Admiral says "Make it so" to his staff and can really make them jump. If needed he says "I told you to do that!" in a loud voice and they jump even higher. They hear the possibility of blame and punishment in the elevated voice and body language. Parents are often "trained" by their children to shout in this way. They first say "Stop that." When the child ignores the command, the parent says "Stop that!" in a louder voice and the child does in fact pause and look at the parent. Later the child resumes what he was told not to do and the parents shouts "I told you to stop that!!"

Clearly it is threat that is involved here; not magic. But parents and children continue on trying to use language as a way of commanding the world.

What is lost on both is that with their increased volume and body language, their attempts to use magic turn into angry threatening control attempts and with the transition from communication to control, their compassion switches off. And the more firmly compassion is switched off, the more real their threats become.

We are social creatures and we relate to each other as individual beings when we remain human. Communication is a gigantic facilitator for cooperation in play, work and bonding.

But it is also useful for intimidation, blaming, warning and other control agendas. The saying is "Talk is cheap." And when we try to take advantage of the low price of talk in order to use it to control other individuals, we switch off our feelings of compassionate companionship which ordinarily accompany play and cooperation.

Good-enough control of one another, not absolute control, is the basis of cooperation.

The Janus Journey: Janus doesn't know he knows about cooperation.

At three and four years old, Janus is puzzled by his efforts to "make" Rex obey him. Sometime Rex would come when he called him and other times it was as if Rex had gone deaf.

His experience with Rex contrasted sharply with how Rex behaved when his father was using Rex as a herd dog. Rex seemed downright eager to accompany Janus's father to a field to round up cattle or horses. Twice a year their entire flock of sheep was transferred between the home farm to a forty acre pasture down the road two miles. They were down at the pasture all summer after lambing and shearing, and back home in late fall. This required herding a hundred or more sheep down a gravel road where there were several other farms and some open fields along the way.

Rex was incredibly busy during this drive. He watched for sheep that strayed from the flock and immediately headed them back. He would immediately respond to a short whistle from Janus's father, looking to see what he wanted. His father would point ahead at an open driveway at the next farm and Rex would be off like a rocket moving ahead of the flock and ready where Janus's father had pointed, ready to head off any sheep who might try to move off the road.

When they neared the pasture gate, Janus's father would merely whistle and call out "Rex in" and Rex would position himself beyond the gate, ready to turn the flock into the open gate and the pasture they would occupy for the summer.

Janus failed to see the key difference between Rex's careful obedience to his father's hand signals, whistles, and words, and Rex's undependable obedience to Janus. Rex and his father were cooperating in a single effort. They were working together.

Janus's father and Rex were working together on the same goal. One was not fully in charge of the other. When Janus's father signaled for Rex that the sheep should turn into the open gate, Rex responded. But it was up to Rex to position himself and respond to whatever challenge the sheep presented. And vice versa, while Rex was occupied with preventing sheep from going up into a neighboring farmer's yard, it was up to Janus's father to drive the sheep past the yard. They were cooperating on the same task.

The dog and the man were obeying each other. Janus's father did not have absolute control over Rex. Neither had absolute control of the other.

Janus was not old enough yet to understand why his quest for absolute obedience was illusory. The prospect of magically being able to produce the behaviors he wanted was too attractive. Yet he knew how it felt when his father or mother asked him to help with something. He was always eager to cooperate. If his mother asked him to accompany her while she was hanging up newly washed cloths on the closes line, he gladly followed her along with a bag full of clothespins, handing her one at a time as she hung up the cloths. Or he helped her hold up an arm loaded with a wet sheet to keep it from getting on the ground. Janus, like Rex, liked to help out when it involved cooperation on a common project.

And Janus was well-aware at three and four of the presence of another person's agenda. He was especially reluctant to obey commands by others that were in a position of authority—namely older than he. His brother would try to order him around, especially when his brother had a friend over. He'd tell Janus to go away or he would tell him to go inside and get something for them. Janus sometimes did as he was asked, but often not.

Janus knew about cooperation and good-enough control and how it was different from absolute control, just like Rex did. He just didn't know he knew.

***

Knowing about good-enough control can make all the difference.

Good-enough control is required in our lives in order to remain a person.

Counselors get many questions from parents about their children's behaviors. Some are along the lines of Carl Sandburg's plaintive cries in *The People Yes.* "Why did the children put beans in their ears …?" "Why did the children pour molasses on the cat …?"[19]

Many years ago a mother and her reluctantly-present-14-year-old boy changed this author's way of thinking about questions like those posed by Sandburg. As a counselor I saw many families and children. I was used to parents dragging their children in with the hope that I could set their child straight from their wayward course.

One afternoon a worried and frustrated mother, with her fourteen-year-old son were in the office for a first session. She ended her angry and tearful tour de force of her son's deviant behaviors with, "And why does he wear that awful purple nail polish?" In one of those leaps to clarity that sometimes occurs when we don't know something is true until we hear ourselves say it, I replied, "He paints his nails purple because he can."

As I spoke, her son's eyes met my eyes, just for a moment, for the first time in the session. I was as surprised by what I said as he was. In that one-second contact, we both saw the same thing and saw each other see it. He was struggling for good-enough freedom to sustain the feeling of being a person instead of a robot, but had no inkling of it until that moment. Nor had I. It was an opening, a new beginning, for both my new young client and for myself and my practice as a counselor.

I was certainly familiar with parent-child struggles over rules and expectations and familiar with the box that many children feel they are in. The box is formed by their parents' and their teachers' promise of freedom if and when they can be counted on to do what their parents and teachers want them to do.

This interpretation of freedom is a sickly and harmful distortion of a fundamental truth for humans and all social species who care for their young. The truth is that because they are born without adequate tools to survive, they require some degree of behavior control until they have enough maturity and experience to rely on their own judgment. But this implies that more freedom should result from increased knowledge and ability, rather than more compliance with others' wishes. The sticky issue is who makes the judgment, the parent or the child? Growing up in a cooperative relationship between parent and child answers this question. Both. If they cooperate, their fellow feelings and their compassion for each other survives and serves them well.

Children are born helpless and ignorant. We take it for granted that children's behaviors must be restricted until they have the ability to keep themselves safe. This is the source of our universal concern for the well-being of young and helpless individuals.

What dawned on both that young person and myself is that his struggle for freedom to get out from under controlling adults, isn't really a search to be totally free. It's a search to be free enough. Or in the language of this work, it is a search for good-enough control to feel like a person instead of a robot.

Neither children nor adults are totally free to control everyone and everything. But we must feel in good-enough control of our own ship so that, even if we are not its captain, we are at least an officer. We must feel we are to some extent a contributing agent to our behavior. The feeling of "being some-thing" as opposed to feeling like "no-thing," as the French existentialists might put it, is more important than avoiding physical pain. Many children and adults will simply "take" any physical punishment handed out and continue to do the dangerous things they are warned to avoid doing, sometimes with tragic consequences. Surprisingly many teenagers and adults of all ages inflict cuts or burns upon themselves in an effort to validate the fact that they own the ability to decide their behavior; they are a living being.

Why do they do this? Why do children put beans in their ears when that is the very thing they are told not to do? Because being someone who is disobedient or in pain is preferable to being no one at all. Or again, calling on a French existential philosopher, as Jean Paul Sartre might put it, some-thingness is preferred to no-thingness.[20]

My young client and his mother, in the months that followed, were able to recognize, with relief, their options for cooperation in accomplishing both her attempts to keep him safe and his attempts to make his actions his own. All of us discovered we could learn from the other, even help one another. We discovered that to feel helpless and defeated in a struggle for control results in feeling a loss of being a person. I had long before known that rules could be enforced without anger and could be broken without defiance. I hadn't fully known why it was so important that we practice doing so. Attempts at absolute control or absolute obedience diminish both parent and child. Rules can be obeyed with a sense of cooperation with those interested in their well-being. Cooperative obedience costs their individualities nothing.

Fortunately, freedom and control good enough for validating our individualities are available, or can be made available, for both children and adults. It occurs when robotic obedience that serves a subservient agenda is replaced with cooperation through exchanges of voluntary obedience in a common cause, therefore also enhancing the cause of human individuality.

We can dance together in the common cause if and when we aim at cooperative steps that produce a good dance. In doing so, we sometime obey another person's direction and vice versa, both without ever becoming another's robotic tool.

Good-enough control of each other results in good-enough freedom for both. This requires us to be aware of what others intend, not just our own "music." Accordingly, beware of those who will not dance with you unless you submit to their choreography. Or as put by the Spanish novelist, Perez-Reverte, "Never trust a man who reads only one book.[21] You will lose your own music, and along with it, your own being.

---

[19] Sandburg, Carl. *The People, Yes.* Harcourt, Brace & Company, 1936.

[20] Sartre, Jean-Paul. *Being and Nothingness.* Philosophical Library,1956.

[21] Arturo Perez-Reverte. *Purity of Blood,* Plume, 1997.

Chapter 6: Companionship in the Service of Destructiveness

Our most ancient and universal community is the family. We as well as all social animals have families which to some degree involve compassionate companionships. As is the case for all social animals, our families are connected by common methods of communication and in-common experiences. We as well as other social creatures exhibit playful activity when we are young and we easily learn to share tasks with other family members. Family members usually look out for each other willingly. They construct a companionship with compassionate feelings. If this weren't true, animals that bear young who require care would have long ago disappeared, victims of evolutionary lack of fitness. After all, we aren't fit for survival when we are born without the aid of those who are willing to sacrifice for our well-being.

This isn't to say that we and other social animals who care for their young are not capable of destructive behaviors toward each other. But destructiveness within the family would soon destroy the family if it were allowed to outweigh simple constructive caring. We may ask why then does simple *destructiveness* survive as a natural attribute of human beings? What's it "good" for? Why do we retain a willingness to attack others without remorse? Why do we retain the compassion switch which can be switched off allowing ruthless destruction?

Cooperation can be used for well-being of insiders and control of outsiders.

The Janus Journey: A memorable story about cooperation and control.

The summer before Janus entered first grade was exciting. A newly married couple moved into the farmhouse across the road. They wanted Janus to call them by their first names, Harvey and Elsie. Calling grownups by their first names— that was something!

Janus loved to visit the couple. He would ask his mother for permission, sometimes several times a day, to cross the road and hang out with Elsie in the kitchen, or with Harvey in his workshop. He would follow them around eagerly waiting for ways to help them with what they were doing.

Sometimes Elsie would let him mix oleo margarine in a bowl with the little packet of coloring that came with it to make it look like real butter. And if he were there late in the afternoon, Harvey would let him go back through the lane into the pasture and bring the cows to the barn for milking.

Feeding the lambs in the pen in the West yard which he used to be eager to do, was now an assigned chore. He also was expected to keep the wood box full by the kitchen stove. Sometimes he forgot and had to be reminded to do his chores. Helping across the road was more fun.

At first Janus proudly told his parents what he had done at Elsie and Harvey's each day. As the summer went by his parents showed less interest in his descriptions. He stopped telling them about his days across the road after his father asked him one day why he was over there helping them and leaving his chores undone at home.

Janus felt his father's disapproval like a spanking. He turned away to hide his tears from his father and also to avoid seeing his father's disapproving expression. After that Janus felt he was doing something wrong when he helped Elsie or Harvey.

Despite feeling that he was doing something wrong, Janus still wanted to help the neighbors, so he sometimes crossed the road without *asking his mother for permission. He continued to go to the neighbors occasionally without telling his parents and his worry built that they would find out.*

Janus felt that his father and mother not only expected him to stay home and do his chores, but he should also want to be staying home and doing his chores instead of wanting to help the neighbors. That really didn't help him feel any different. Janus still wanted to help the neighbors and didn't really want to do his chores at home. He couldn't see why he didn't feel the way his father said he should feel about wanting to help them. He felt that there was something that he was missing.

One evening his father, after he was done reading the paper, asked Janus if he wanted to hear a story. Janus flew to his father's side and was picked up and put on his father's lap. His father proceeded to tell him a story about a group of children playing in the woods.

The children in the story had spent a summer afternoon in the woods making a fort out of dead sticks and grape vines that they cut down with a pocket knife that one of them, Jack, proudly possessed and shared as a common tool among them. When they got ready to go home, Jack couldn't find his knife. All the boys started looking around for the lost knife and each one looked wherever he thought he might find it. Jack saw that they were looking in the same places one after another and wandering around haphazardly and so he called them together.

Jack said, "It's going to be dark soon and we need to find my knife quickly. Why don't we split up the areas where we need to look? Bob, why don't you look around the bottom of the last tree where we cut grapevines? Joe, you look inside the fort. Carl, you look on the path over there. And I will look around the outside of the fort."

Janus's father finished the story by telling him that everyone agreed with Jack, and Joe soon found the knife among the shadows in the fort, and they all got home before dark.

His father paused and then said to him, "Janus, I know you don't like doing your chores. It might help you to think about your mother and I and your brother and sister and you like the boys together in the woods. We are all trying to do the same thing; take care of what needs doing on the farm. It works a lot better when someone is in charge and divides up the work to be done among us all. Your mother and I do this the way our parents did it. Your mother divides up the tasks for us that need to be done around the house. And I divide the things that need to be done around the barns and the fields.

When she asks one of us to bring in the wood for the kitchen stove, we do what she asks. When she asks me to fix the furnace or have it fixed, or help with canning, or fix a screen door, I do it. When I ask her to help with a newborn calf, she does it. Or when I ask her advice about buying a new cow or whether she thinks prices are right to sell some corn we will not need, she gives it.

When you get older, you will know more and you will be able to take over some of the responsibility of what needs to be done when we are doing something that you know as much or more about than the rest of us.

Janus's father finished what he had to say with a statement that Janus would never forget. "Even now, Janus, if you lost something in your room, like the boy and his jackknife in the story, your mother and I would expect you to run the show in a search for it, and tell us each where to search. After all, you know more about your room than we do. We are all a family and we help each other in whatever ways we can."

Many years later, whenever Janus would remember what his father said, it filled him with a sense of his father's humanity and his father's human concern for his well-being. Despite this good feeling, he also later remembered the point of his father telling the story—he was spending too much time helping the neighbors.

This was Janus's first lesson in patriotism—family first. His father left out any mention of the neighbors, but Janus got his point. He was already aware that conflicts arise among neighbors. One farmer's cattle would get into another farmer's corn. Farmers were supposed to keep up their fences and half of every line fence was the responsibility of each neighbor. He would soon learn much more about the relationships among neighbors.

But it would be many years before Janus saw a simple truth about *the formation and meaning of many communities, including his own family. They provided an incredibly valuable haven for individuals. Just as his father said, cooperation and willing mutual aid provides us with not only safety, but perhaps more important, an identity. However, their companionship can actually feed non-compassionate actions and feeling toward "outsiders."*

It was only later, when remembering his dog Rex, and how Rex bonded and joined with his father in herding, that Janus tumbled to an easily overlooked aspect of family cooperation. Although their relationship was cooperative and produced bonding between them, one use of their cooperative effort was to control. They cooperated in order to control in the most classic sense—threaten and harass all behavior that deviates from their wishes and expectations.

A herding dog barks, bears his teeth, nips, and places himself as an obstacle in the path that the sheep or cow or pig is attempting to travel. This is the very definition of being a good "header."

Janus's father and his dog formed a companionship of the sort that Janus and his father had. Rex was a member of the family. But despite Janus's feeling toward other animals on the farm, the sheep and the cattle and the horses and the pigs were not family members. His family was a compassionate companionship but the companionship ruled others who would be shorn and eventually slaughtered.

***

The compassion switch can remain ON among family members, including the family herding dog. However that very companionship, even though it involves compassion toward one another can be used in a common desire to control those who are not members of the family. This arrangement is very common as we shall see. It is nearly the definition of patriotism.

The story his father told him about cooperation didn't include the part about outsiders. Janus would not recognize this for many years. In the meantime he would have to deal with the consequences of viewing himself as a member of a special group that used outsiders—its price was confusion, blame, self-blame, and a senseless dalliance with elitism.

Janus gets a taste of his family's relationships with family outsiders.

The Janus Journey: Janus's sense of who he really is starts to unravel.

Five-year-old Janus loved to hang around his parents when they were talking to neighbors or each other. He had very "big ears." One conversation was indelibly tattooed in his memory. It was between his mother and an aunt. They were gossiping about a neighbor, who he knew and liked, concerning her apparent neglect of housekeeping. His mother's words that stuck with him were, "Her house is so dirty that if you pushed her up against the wall she would stick there. But she wouldn't care if she did. She wouldn't care what anyone thinks."

He felt an immediate surge of alarm when he heard her. Later he learned that his feeling was anxiety—fear without knowing what he was afraid of. That uncertainty was probably why Janus remembered it so well into adulthood.

He had no clear idea of why his memory of his mother's gossip about another neighbor frightened him until much later in life. At the time he somehow felt if being dirty was grounds for becoming an object of ridicule in the neighborhood, he was also a possible target. His mother was always accusing him of being dirty and telling him stuff like "Go wash up!" "Change your cloths!" He did get dirty a lot, and didn't really care about it. And he thought his mother saw dirt everywhere, even when there wasn't any. But he did what his mother told him. No big deal.

This was different. His mother and aunt were talking in a very unfriendly way about a neighbor, not just because she wasn't a good housekeeper, but because she didn't care. This was too close to home. Something about it frightened Janus. He didn't yet realize that in order to be accepted he had to learn to care about what others care about, or at least give an appearance of caring.

Although Janus didn't clearly understand why this bit of gossip alarmed him, he nevertheless started thinking to himself about whether *others viewed him as not caring about cleanliness. Occasionally his thinking, that is, his self-talk, used language remarkably similar to the language his mother and aunt had used in talking about their neighbor. When someone he disliked had dirty clothes or hands he would think, "People shouldn't get dirty. Don't they care?"*

Janus could even imagine himself talking to his friends about people who were dirty, even the neighbor his mother and aunt had gossiped about. Imagining himself gossiping like that about their neighbor troubled him with feelings of disloyalty. Janus didn't think he could face her if he talked about her like that. He didn't notice it, but he had been initiated into a control community.

***

Janus was beginning to experience the psychological effects of being a member of a cooperative effort that used their cooperation to control others. Having to face a neighbor with whom he had been friendly while at the same time having said things about her that were unfriendly and destructive involved being more than one person—one person with some people and another person with other people. And what a difference between those two people! One was constructive, drawing on his natural tendency to be helpful and nurturing to others and creative toward other objects. The other person was destructive, drawing on his natural tendency to be destructive to other people and destructive toward objects in general. He had never felt concern over his being a whole person. Now he was beginning to experience the anxiety, dread, and aloneness that accompany the deterioration of one's individuality.

People who cooperate in order to control suffer from doing so.

One of the most well-known psychological experiments of the 20th Century was published in 1963. Yale psychologist Stanley Milgram published a journal article titled "Behavioral Study of Obedience," which spawned a prolific line of research in Social Psychology that lasts to this day.[22] It involved asking student subjects to administer successively stronger electric shocks as punishment to other people who appeared to make mistakes on a learning task. They were urged on administering shocks (so far as they knew) by the experimenters with statements such as "Please go on. It is absolutely essential that you continue. You have no other choice, you must go on." The shocks weren't real, but the subjects thought they were actually causing pain to people as punishment for their mistakes. The strength of the shocks was steadily increased and the fake receivers of these fake shocks cried out and demonstrated convincingly that the shocks were causing them great pain. This resulted in increased badgering of the subject to continue to cause punishing pain for mistakes.

The fact that approximately two thirds of the subjects continued to "obey" the experimenters by causing pain to others was startling to the psychological community and much was written about it in the press. Memories of WW II and German atrocities were still fresh in the public mind and the prevalent belief was that they were the result of some evil streak in our enemies that allowed them to obey orders to commit atrocities. So at least some of the wide attention to this experiment on obedience was due to the fact that undergraduate students in a prestigious university would obey instructions to painfully shock others. They weren't strangers who were enemies in some foreign land. But of course, that was also true in Germany of the German Jews who were rounded up and eventually gassed. Their neighbors were often complicit.

Given the view of how control tends to reduce compassion, presented here, it is not that much of a surprise that students who were drawn into a cooperative endeavor with faculty (so they were led to believe) in order to investigate the effect of punishment on learning, would participate in that destructive cooperation.

But the experiment demonstrated something else. As they got deeper and deeper into the experiment, administering what they thought was more and more pain, they became more and more nervous. The subjects who did continue experienced very serious psychological symptoms. Extreme levels of nervous tension consisting of profuse sweating, trembling, and stuttering were exhibited. Subjects also demonstrated nervous laughter and some of them had uncontrollable seizures—one had a full blown convulsive seizure.

In other words, the complicit students cooperated in the use of electric shock to control the learning of other students, but they paid a sizable price. Given the view of altruistic destruction taken here, this is not surprising. The nature of the price paid by these students is, however, informative. Wrecking one's own self-regard and sense of well-being as a price for cooperating in destructive behaviors would have had a familiar ring to Janus.

Janus's early journey into cooperation with his mother and aunt in their destructive gossip about a neighbor brought him anxiety and the beginning uneasiness that comes with feeling less wholeness as an individual. The cooperation pitted his constructive and destructive capacities against each other and in so doing, the most important thing he owned, his identity, was put at some risk. It seems likely that Milgram's subjects suffered a more acute version of the consequences of being badgered into destructiveness, all for the sake of continued cooperation with elite members of their university community. Their capacities for simple destructiveness were awakened in a circumstance in which they were still aware of their simple caring so that the compassion switch was at least still partly on while they were practicing control by punishment. In this unusual example of the occurrence of human destructiveness while they were still experiencing compassion is a case where the compassion switch doesn't fully switch.

Cases similar to this sometimes occur for example when parents disagree about the use of punishment. If one of them "goes along" with what they consider to be inhumane punishment, not only by tolerating the other's use of it, but perhaps even engaging in it, that "cooperating parent" is likely to suffer severely. Similar circumstances most likely explain why military personnel suffer long after their military experiences due to actions they have taken or been involved with.

Even though the fact that our compassion switches off during our attempts to control others causes great harm to others, leaving it on while committing the same acts is acutely self-destructive. We are not built to be able to view with open eyes our capacity to destroy while we still feel caring. For these two engines to face off in front of our eyes is intolerable.

But despite the fact that the compassion switch protects us from the acute suffering that would occur if our destructive and caring capacities clashed head on in front of our eyes, it does not protect us from creeping concerns over who and what we are. Truly cooperative interactions require trust and that trust is undermined by the operation of control communities' use of destruction.

Statements such as "She is my friend; she would never talk like that about me." are easy to say about someone in a close circle of friends who care for each other dearly. But doubt inevitably creeps in when the facts are that "She" gaily reports gossip about someone else who wore out-of-fashion clothes or embarrassed herself in public, things you have been known to do. Like Janus listening to his mother and aunt talk about the neighbor who didn't care about cleanliness, one is bound to fear being seen as one of the victims who are attacked by our families, our "in groups," our neighborhoods, our religions, our countries.

---

[22] Milgram, Stanley. "Behavioral Study of Obedience." *The Journal of Abnormal and Social Psychology*, 67(4) (1963): 371-8.

Chapter 7: Soldiers for Control Ideologies—Introducing Fear into Failing to Count

Who counts?

Harry Bosch, a detective in several novels written by Michael Connelly, lives by the creed "Everybody counts or nobody counts." This creed is different from democracy. Simple democracies where everyone's vote is counted are easily led by a bare majority which can rule the minority with merciless oppression. Harry Bosch's creed—everybody counts or nobody counts—preserves everyone's humanity.

But who is everybody? If "everybody" is limited to our family or neighborhood or professional colleagues or gang or our town or region or country, then those outside of these communities don't count.

For example, you may be a teacher and feel a kinship with other teachers, but also feel a kinship with all human beings. In that case, just because your students aren't teachers, that doesn't mean they don't count. They count too.

Clearly we can feel we are members of one group where "everybody" is only a few people and yet we can also be a member of another group, say the human race, where "Everybody" really means everybody. One can be patriotic for one's family, one's town, one's country, or as Victor Hugo wrote in a letter "... as I advance in life, I grow more simple, and I become more and more patriotic for humanity."[23] But we don't know all humanity and we clearly aren't in a position to know who we are talking about. So the best we can do to become patriotic for humanity is to operate under the creed "Everybody could count." Individuals all count when we adopt ideologies of the sort that help us see what *could* be. Harry Bosch, in the proud tradition of all-powerful action heroes, was being just a tad grandiose.

Ideologies loaded with "could" vs. ideologies loaded with "should"

Consider the difference between subscribing to an ideology because it tells you what to do versus subscribing to it because it helps you to decide what you could do. This is a huge difference. Believing that you should follow the rules embodied in an ideology exports your decision making to the ideology. Its rules, rule you. On the other hand, believing that an ideology is helpful to you in making decisions keeps your decision making at home. *Your* decisions rule you.

We will distinguish between these two ways of being ideological with the terms "should-loaded ideologies" vs. "possibility-loaded ideologies." This distinction can be usefully made for all ideologies. Whether we are referring to political beliefs, religious beliefs, child rearing beliefs, educational beliefs, or whatever other kind of ideological beliefs that influence people's lives, the extent to which those beliefs govern people on the one hand, or help inform people on the other hand, has major effects on our lives. The extent to which we subscribe to should-loaded ideologies influences the extent to which we lose compassion in our interactions with others. It also affects the amount of anxiety in our lives.

When we are patriots for a should-loaded ideology, we become fearful.

Control communities of whatever size are dependent upon should-loaded ideologies. Suppose you are a member of a teaching community which subscribes to the view that students' behaviors must be controlled by teachers. Then, as a teacher, you count; but "counting" means your fellow members expect you to control students. You are a soldier for the teaching community, helping carry out control of outsiders (students who are not teachers) with the help of your teaching community. Preserving and protecting a should-loaded ideology that includes rules about how persons "should" behave, requires vigilance for deviants and misfits, among the membership. Seeing your mission as control, turns off your compassion switch toward students. Therefore, the creation of outsiders, the community creates fear among its members of *becoming an outsider*—a fear of not counting.

A teacher who gives too many good grades is the object of gossip and made to feel unwelcome. Such a teacher runs the risk of being viewed as "too friendly" with the students. Managers who reward those they manage are driven out of organizations that believe that fear is the correct tool of management. They are apt to feel fear of failing to live up to the party line. Police who are too soft on "civilians" risk being shunned by the police fraternity.

Persons have long lived with fear while attempting to work in places which included ideological expectations of gender, sexual orientation, color, or ethnicity. There were and still are should-loaded ideologies attached to gender such as "Men should run things" that make women misfits in many professions and jobs. Therefore, liking women in any other way than sexually became a taboo for any man who carried "manhood" as ideological baggage. There were and are should-loaded ideologies of skin color, sexual orientation and ethnicity that dictate where and under what conditions a person "counts" and "doesn't count."

Those who attempt to venture where should-loaded ideologies

exclude them suffer "stress" which is just another way of saying they feel unsafe. Examples are too numerous to mention of breaking color lines or breaking through glass ceilings. But what is overlooked is the fear involved for all members of such should-loaded ideological communities who constantly must prove that they are true believers. The practical result of such fear is often demonstrations of a controlling and punitive attitude in an effort to validate one's ideological credentials. Ordinary people become vicious in their pursuit of "violators" of the community should-loaded ideology, especially when they are in contact with each other, in order to validate for each other their beliefs. When control communities congregate, whether they are a junior high school clique or a clan meeting or a prison gang, the likelihood of some form of lynching is increased which has the effect of validating "true" membership.

Control communities reveal themselves by exercising control.

It is not until a companionship turns its attention to control that it reveals that it is a control community. And it is the treatment of outsiders that reveals the community's soldiers. Controlling others without their willingness, requires that they be threatened in some manner or be physically dominated. The point here is that just looking at how people talk and act doesn't reveal a control community until those people actually launch "corrective actions" toward others within or outside the community. Crusades against those who don't count reveal control communities.

Just looking at the relationship between Janus's father and his herding dog, Rex, one sees only cooperation and teaching. It is their relationship to other animals that reveals them to be a small control community. They cooperate in the use of threats to control others, in this case other animals. But it is usually people who are the objects of control communities.

Janus met up with a crusading soldier in a place he least expected it—school, and it affected him profoundly. He expected to count at school and feel safe there, just as he did at home. He didn't realize it at the time, but his early experiences there led him to also become a soldier in a crusade as well.

Janus Journey: Janus expects companionship but meets a soldier for control.

As a five-year-old, Janus became more verbally skilled and experienced. His conversations with his family members and others became more lengthy and involved. "Why does it rain?" he asked his father while he was sitting on his lap in the living room. His father patiently explained that there is water in the air that comes out and makes it rain. Janus thought that was amazing but his face looked doubtful.

His father sent him to the kitchen and told him to take the pickle jar out of the refrigerator and bring it to him. He ran to the kitchen thinking his father was just trying to end his questioning. But getting something out of the refrigerator was something he wasn't ordinarily allowed to do and he wasn't going to let the chance slip by.

He found the jar and returned with it triumphantly and handed it to his father. His father placed it on the copy of The Michigan Farmer magazine laying there on the side table and said, "Now watch." Puzzled, Janus fixed his eyes on the jar. What was supposed to happen? Magic? He kept watching for a minute or two and started getting a little bored. He kept asking, "What's going to happen?" His father finally said, "It's already happening. Don't you see it?"

Janus looked again. "I don't see anything happening." His father said "Don't you see the drops of water on the jar? Feel the jar. It's wet."

Janus felt the wet jar and looked at his father, confused. His father gently asked, "Where do you suppose the water came from?" Then Janus got it. "The air!" he shouted. His father said, "You made it rain. Look at the wet ring on the magazine."

Janus, despite the fact that Kindergarten had been disappointing, was looking forward to first grade, imagining what it would be like when learning things and getting questions answered was going to go on full time. He looked forward to it all summer.

Janus began 1st grade as he was about to turn six. The first day was terrific. The pleasant smelling rubber eraser, the untouched crayons with their perfect tips and paper sleeves in place, the sharpened pencils, workbooks full of mysterious new stories, were all carefully arranged in the private domain beneath his desk top. He was ready.

Janus was already familiar with numbers and how they worked. But he was eager to learn more. His teacher, Miss Box, started their arithmetic lessons with a window-shade-like roll attached above the chalk board. She pulled it down and it wasn't a window shade at all. It showed colored pictures of apples and grapes and little children all lined up in different rows with a number after each row. At first, Janus was just curious about this strange display. He already knew about addition and subtraction and multiplication, even with two-digit numbers. But he was curious about what numbers really were. It never even occurred to him that they could be real things like apples and even little children. He didn't see how this could be. But this was an attractive prospect. He had a penchant for searching for concrete explanations for what things are. Everything ought to be made out of something else, like the rain that came from moisture in the air.

One morning after Miss Box had pulled down the display containing the beautiful number pictures, Janus asked her if the "5" after the picture of the five little children meant that numbers could be children. Miss Box looked at him severely and said "I don't like a smart mouth. Do you want to spend some time in the corner?"

Janus panicked and couldn't think of what to say. Was this a question? He had seen her put a classmate in the corner the second day of school. Some of the kids in the class made fun of him. Miss Box asked again, more loudly, "Well? Do you want to go to the corner?" Janus was *barely able to answer no.*

"What was that?" Miss Box bellowed. Janus started to cry. Some snickers started in the class. Miss Box directed her wrath away from Janus with a loud, "Quiet!!"

With her eyes off him, traveling accusingly around the room, Janus was able to get himself together a little and when Miss Box's search light eyes came back to rest on him he managed to say "no" more loudly.

Janus felt like his head was in a cloud bank. He couldn't think. He didn't know what to do. Numbers had been good friends before. He enjoyed the rules for combining them and taking them apart. It was like doing a puzzle with rules. Now he felt a dread. He could hardly look at the display of little children in a line with the number five after it when Miss Box pulled down the display at the front of the room. He had an awful feeling that everyone else knew what numbers were except him. What was wrong with his head? He didn't see how those things pictured at the front of the room - the little children, the grapes, the apples – could be numbers. He didn't see how two grapes plus three apples could be anything other than two grapes and three apples. Maybe they could be five pieces of fruit? Could children and grapes and apples be made into numbers? Could he be made into a number?

Janus was confused about what numbers are. He did not yet know that many mathematicians are too. But at least he knew more about 1ˢᵗ grade. He needed to keep his mouth shut and hope Miss Box didn't ask him any questions. He now had a job. It was to figure out what she would want to hear if she did ask him. It was like a game. But it was a dangerous game. He was in the game, like a checker that his father might leap over, remove from the checker board, and pile up in the corner of the box, when they played checkers at home. Janus began dreading going to school.

If only Miss Box had just said, "No, numbers aren't anything you can touch. We use them to count things."

***

Janus began school with a bang—he didn't count in the education community. Miss Box was a teacher who belonged to a control community. She had transformed her membership in the teaching community to a control purpose. Control children. Janus had assumed that his teachers were like his family. They would care about him and he would care about them and want to do whatever he could do to help them. Miss Box had frightened him. She treated him like his father treated unruly sheep or horses. He didn't explain things to them. He just threatened them like Rex his dog threatened sheep by barking.

Introducing fear into failure:

Janus did not yet know that not all teachers are like Miss Box. But he had to reduce his fear somehow. He felt he had to prepare for their questioning in order to avoid the humiliation that might accompany failure. Fear of failure became a threatening companion.[24] It became a different reason to learn rather than joyful curiosity. He had begun a new journey to survive being the object of control in school while taking his native curiosity elsewhere.

Janus like most young children did not start out in life with a fear of failing. Miss Box introduced him to fear in failure. Learning all the things we have to learn as young children naturally involves failure. Children do not walk and talk without falling and failing to communicate. When Janus's father taught him things at home, he encouraged Janus to guess answers. Where does rain come from? Janus didn't know and his ignorance motivated his learning. He didn't hide his ignorance. He flaunted it with Why, Why, Why?

Now, Janus would go in a different direction. School, which he had thought was where he would get answers all day long, was going be something quite different. He had started on another journey, a journey to control his fear of failing by being the one who made others afraid. He would counter the attempts of others to control him with control of his own over them. And he had a teacher to teach him about turning the tables on fear. Miss Box would be his teacher along with other "authorities" he would encounter. He would build a model for threat out of his experiences with those who belonged to the "respected" community. Those where people who were in control because they held the reins of threat.

But Janus was not yet ready to challenge these people. It would take him a few years to learn their weapons and sharpen them for his own use. Their weapons: appearing to know everything, warning people off with a sharp tongue, or lying in wait and deliver a humiliating thrust to a self-important adversary, these would be his models. These weapons were still beyond his reach. But he had another weapon which he could employ for warding off fear—his attention to detail helped him stay a safe distance from his teachers' critical attentions.

---

[23] Victor Hugo's quote on patriotism for humanity appeared in his letter to M. Daelli, publisher of the Italian translation of *Les Miserables* in Milan. The letter was published along with an English translation by Isabel F. Hapgood, of *Les Miserables* in 1887 in New York by Thomas Y Crowell & Co. A more complete version of the quote is: "As for myself, I have written for all, with a profound love for my own country, but without being engrossed by France more than by any other nation. In proportion as I advance in life, I grow more simple, and I become more and more patriotic for humanity."

[24] The study of need for achievement (N ach) and fear of failure have a long history in psychological literature. McClelland and Atkinson's early work, McClelland, David C., et al. *The Achievement Motive*. Appleton-Century-Crofts, East Norwalk, CT, 1953 was followed by Atkinson's book (editor). *Motives in Fantasy, Action, and Society: A Method of Assessment and Study*. Van Nostrand, Oxford, 1958. Later Feather's work with Atkinson, Atkinson, J. W., & Feather, N.T. (1966). A Theory of Achievement Motivation (pp. 364-370). New York: Wiley. has been referenced 100's of times in the literature to the present time. The view taken here is that control practices utilized in educational and

parenting introduces performance and status into the learning which has the effect of marginalizing children's natural curiosity as a primary driver of learning. Janus's experience with Miss Box depicts the introduction of fear INTO failure.

Chapter 8: Using Control to Resist Control: Loss of Compassion all around

It would take Janus a major part of his life to realize he was making himself into another Miss Box, his first grade teacher, and others like her in his misguided attempt to avoid their control. He would later learn that there are other alternatives for escaping control. However, as a child he started down the path of trying to control controllers. Other's lack of compassionate companionship with him was to be matched with his lack of compassionate companionship with them. We join him a little later in grade school.

The Janus Journey: Janus learns to be a soldier for the community of victims.

Janus, who was large for his age all through grade school, played the part of defender for the little kids and often got into fights with bullies on the playground. His physical size and strength made this a natural role for him during recesses and after school while waiting for the bus. However, in the third grade he encountered a problem. A new student appeared who had recently moved into town, Dan. He not only was big because he was built that way. He was older. Dan had been held back two grades and although he was only in the third grade, he was twelve years old. And he was a bully on the playground!

Janus did what he could to intervene when Dan got physical and got a bloody nose for his trouble more than once. Janus just figured he would need to become a better fighter. So he started studying how fights went on the playground. He quickly discovered that most of the boys tried to fight like they do in the movies. They tried to fight with their fists.

That's the way Dan fought and that's why Janus was getting his nose bloodied. On the other hand some of kids tried to knock each other down and sit on them. This is how Janus's older brother had always fought with him.

Janus also started taking notice of what happened before most fights. Kids would talk and threaten and go through a whole song and dance. About this time, Janus and his brother were playing in the front yard and got in an argument. His brother started to walk around him and suddenly stuck out his leg behind Janus's knees and pushed him. Janus went down on the ground on his back and his brother jumped on top of him.

Well! Janus put together his plan. One really nasty November day, with wet snow on the ground, Dan pushed a friend of Janus down on the ground and made fun of him when he started crying. Janus approached Dan casually saying "why don't you pick on someone your own size?" The pre-fight threats and insults started. But Janus didn't just stand there. He started walking slowly clockwise around Dan. As he walked around him a second time, Janus stuck out his right leg behind Dan's legs about knee high and shoved him hard. Dan went down. Other kids who had drawn around started laughing. Dan was enraged and got up quickly. But he made the mistake of yelling obscenities at Janus and the other kids instead of just plowing into Janus. So Janus just started talking to him again and walking around him and after another round he stuck out his leg again and Dan went down again. Well, Dan was now beside himself. But Janus figured his trick was about to run out of steam. He tried it once more and Dan barely went to the ground, but this time Janus jumped on him and pinned his arms to the ground.

By this time Dan was thoroughly soaked with the icy ground water. But Janus held him there until the bell rang and the nearby door to the school house opened and offered an escape route. Dan and Janus had many altercations after that, but Dan was more wary and became somewhat more hesitant to push things too far on the playground. Janus now had allies, even followers among the smaller kids there.

Janus used his talents for observation and careful planning in class as well during elementary school. He quickly noticed most of the teachers weren't interested in answering his questions. They had their own agenda. He already knew how to spell and do arithmetic. But he was much better off if he just fit into their mold and let them think they were teaching him these things. Similarly, he learned to fend off controlling teachers by staying ahead of them, not doing what they assigned, but studying the teachers "tells" about what they would ask on tests. That was the real assignment.

He wouldn't have used the word, but he was on his way of being an elitist.[25]

He was to be an elite soldier in defense of learning, justice, and victims of any stripe. This was to cost him dearly as we will see as his story plays out. Being a soldier for any ideological community costs the individuals involved.

His early dealings with teachers who practiced control by arousing fear, were not his only early teachers. He met fear mongers in many places. His experiences on the playground pitted bullies against smaller children, country kids and farm boys like himself against city kids. Later, as we will see in Chapter 9 he learned that games were of two kinds; they were played for clout or for fun. For clout meant doing anything to win. Even breaking rules was okay if players could get away with it.

Playing for fun meant the players competed but took care of each other, including the opposing players. A runner heading for home plate avoided smashing into the catcher if he was a smaller kid, even if it meant being tagged out. Winners and losers both had fun.

Janus still knew what playing for fun was like. But he was learning fast how to play for clout—to play for membership among the elite. Playing for the means to control the controllers.

***

Elitism entails hierarchies of entitlement which destroy cooperation.

As pointed out by Janus's father in his story about cooperation, one can voluntarily obey a leader who is chosen merely to divide cooperative effort among members of a group. As a practical matter, the best candidate for leadership is someone who "knows the territory." But elitism entails a hierarchy of control based on more than just differences in expertise.

Elitists present themselves and are viewed as knowing about everything, and therefore they are presumably best at everything. They are therefore entitled to lead in every circumstance. They have all the answers and they are the strongest in every way. They are demigods who any sensible person would presumably be happy to have telling them what to do. But those unwilling to go along with this delusion had better be afraid for themselves if they show opposition.

This combination of providing safety for others alongside providing overwhelming power against their enemies is an exemplar for rulers historically. Believing one's self to be all knowing and all powerful is a wonderful awakener of simple destructive tendencies.

But being the best at everything is an insane illusion as is the belief in being the strongest match against any challenge. And as with all insanity, the person pays a huge price for believing a giant illusion—a delusional life that attempts to fit all life experience around one or two unbendable expectations. But what does not bend, breaks. When those who believe they can't lose, fail, they break in ways that we shall study in chapters on depression ahead. In Chapter 15, we will see that the delusion of absolute superiority has a moral quality. And when it crashes it is replaced by what Sigmund Freud referred to as a "delusion of mainly moral inferiority."[26] "I'm a terrible person and have always been bad."

The illusion of elitism forces one to explain how it is that one is always right, best, strongest, best informed, and smartest regardless of whatever happens. This delusion is validated by the deference of others. We humans have often been ruled by rulers whose insanity we have validated by submitting to their delusions of absolute superiority and power.

Sometimes we find soldiers for the community in unexpected places.

The Janus Journey: Janus's community obviously trained his friends too.

We jump ahead in Janus's life for a moment. Eighteen-year-old Janus was home from college for the first time since he began his freshman year. An old friend who was older, on leave from the army, was also home. They had spent the afternoon cruising around the small town where they both had grown up, talking about old times. Janus suggested that they stop at a party store and pick up a six-pack. Since he was underage, he needed his older friend to agree to buy the beer, which he did.

As they were walking out of the store, an empty beer can came rattling along the edge of the street as a car passed by. Janus's friend reacted with immediate anger, and ran to the curb to see if he could get the license plate of the offending car. As Janus tried to take in what had just happened, his friend continued to grumble about people who threw litter out of cars. Janus kept quiet, but he wondered what his friend thought about people who bought beer for minors.

Janus would be reminded of this incident later when he first saw the movie "Alice's Restaurant."[27] A young man in the movie was found unfit to be inducted into the army and go to Vietnam because he had once been convicted of littering. Apparently littering made him unfit for killing. Only later did Janus realize why. In control communities, littering is evidence of a failure to be a soldier for his community, much less a soldier for his country. Perhaps that was what Janus's friend had seen in the thrower of the beer can.

Janus didn't realize at that time that he, himself, was a soldier for his communities too.

***

---

[25] The Oxford English Dictionary Historical Thesaurus traces the word elite though the last few centuries as follows:

1623 choice

1823 The choice part or flower (of society, or of any body or class of persons).

1848 crème de la crème the élite, the very pick of society.

1884 corps d'élite In French phrases: corps d'armée /kɔr darme/, a main division of an army in the field, an army-corps; corps de bataille /kɔr də bɑtɑj/...

1939 sacred circle an exclusive company, an élite.

[26] This appears in Freud's *Mourning and Melancholia. See notes for Chapter 15.*

[27] A film released in 1969 somewhat based on Arlo Guthrie's 1968 song of the same name. Arlo Guthrie as well as folk singer Pete Seeger star in the film.

Chapter 9: Control by Gossip

Next we will examine what may be the most powerful means for community control of individual behavior ever invented by humankind—gossip.

Gossip polices the community

What is gossip? Sometimes understanding the meaning of a word that describes some human behavior tells us more about that behavior than psychologists have to offer. Gossip may be an example.

The Oxford English Dictionary tells us that Theodore Hook, in his 1850 autobiographic novel *Gilbert Gurney,* referred to "those meddling gossip-mongers, who invariably infest small country-town society."

Novelists don't usually use attributions that would leave their readership in the dark, so we may assume Gurney, a mid-nineteenth century novelist, knew that his readership in English towns were "infested" by the same sorts of meddlers as are today's work places, churches, and institutions. "Gossip" goes back a ways.

The word gossip originates, again according to the Oxford English Dictionary, from the Old English word "godsibb." "Godsibb" became "gossib" in Middle English which then evolved to the word "gossip." It originally referred to those who undertook the religious education of a newly baptized child - what we would call a godparent. What can be behind two such disparate meanings—acting as a godparent on the one hand and speaking nasty things behind someone's back on the other hand?

A connection between these meanings is given by understanding the role of godparents 400 years ago in Europe. Children, believed to be born evil, were thought to require the active intervention of the community to avoid sin. Today, a similar dynamic is demonstrated by people, who never gave all that much attention or time to religion, find it important to join churches when they have young children. Four hundred years ago, that intervention, especially by Godparents, was to drive the devil away from children. Martin Luther, for example, said that godparents needed "to take action against the devil and not only to drive him away from the little child but also to hang around the child's neck such a mighty, lifelong enemy."[28] The gossip's role was to drive away the devil. Not only that, but the gossip was to exercise vigilance toward evil during a children's whole lifetime.

Does this meaning relate in any way to our present use of the word gossip? You may remember sometimes gossiping while feeling a sense of righteousness. Try to capture how gossiping would feel if you were to tell a secret to a fellow employee about how the supervisor steals office materials. Isn't there a sense of striking a blow against something, something more than a rule infraction?

Your experience may include someone saying things like "Pastor Joseph's son was picked up for drug possession. I wonder if he is going to continue teaching the Sunday school class for teenagers." Imagine how saying such a thing feels to the person saying it. Isn't there a distinct ring of "People in the church community shouldn't be or act like that"? And a reason this is especially bad for church members or clergy is their should-loaded ideology makes doing drugs not just a poor life choice for legal and health reasons, but also a moral infraction.

But there is also a distinctive moral ring to all community gossip, not just gossip about church communities and their members. Imagine someone saying something like "Sally's husband lost another job. Well at least he lasted through the first week this time." Doesn't this ring of a moral judgment that not being successful at keeping jobs is not just bad financially, but morally bad? It is likely that if we talked confidentially to Sally's husband, he would not only say he feels bad about not keeping his job. He is feeling he has *been* bad. Both Sally's husband, and his community neighbors are acting as soldiers talking about an evil enemy—failure. Is there any enemy that we don't consider evil?

If you imagine the way real police feel when they talk to each other about their "enemy," you may catch the same accusatory tone. Imagine a police officer talking about "those liberals" who "allow dangerous criminals to roam free." "That kid was busted for possession again. He's going to graduate to selling drugs if somebody doesn't give him more than a slap on the wrist." But real police officers are charged by the community with protecting against harmful actions. When *we* civilians gossip we are self-appointed police with power to not only charge, but to punish. We are acting as if we are the police, prosecutor and court all rolled into one. If you doubt this, try thinking of why it is that you might have fears about how people in your community talk about you.

The CEO of a professional sports team recently declared "The only thing we all have in our life is our reputation ..." in bemoaning the damage done to the team-owner's reputation by presumably racist emails written by the team's owner himself. The notion that reputation is more important than who one really is was challenged by Plato around 380 BC in the lengthy Socratic dialogue, *The Republic*, and found to be wanting.[29] His arguments still make sense. He showed that being a just person (ethically good) makes us whole even if our reputation is bad. Being unjust (ethically bad) splinters us even if our reputation is good.

Any "talk" that is about people and conveys a sense of disapproval, and turns off your compassion switch toward those it describes, qualifies as gossip. This includes self-talk, the cornerstone topic of contemporary cognitive psychology.[30]

We spend a good bit of time listening to gossip in the form of news reporting. Broadcasters catch and keep viewers by framing the news to fit what interests people—the way they gossip. We as gossipers do the same thing. We give people the news knowing the marketplace. We give them the news that they love to hear because they are also police officers for community behaviors and will wish to pass it along to other willing participants in the process of policing the community. The World Wide Web has magnified gossiping on a monumental scale through so-called social networking.

TV and other news programming know this market well. Cable "reporters" pass on gossip about those who have done something disgusting. The nasty little story, repeated by one neighbor about another neighbor in a hushed voice along with a roll of the eyes that says "it's-beyond-belief," can have stadium-sized audiences on cable news. On TV, "news" of people, groups or countries being part of the "axis of evil" shares the stage with "The word is that the president was born in Africa and is Moslem." along with the shocking "news" of a lady in Cleveland who has a filthy house full of cats.

News stories, like other forms of gossip, can never be wiped out once they are promulgated. Their capacity to disgust assures their longevity, true or false. The news about an "axis of evil" is a fitting echo of the origin of the meaning of the word "gossip"—one who drives evil away. It will bounce around among us for a long time, assuring maximum effect of warning away the devil.

When gossip is used to establish trust, it doesn't necessarily switch off compassion.

Tidbits of self-gossip can be used as a preliminary test of whether someone is a candidate for personal trust. Since friendship is founded upon intimacy and intimacy requires trust, people tend to make friends utilizing a dance of intimacy which is remarkably universal. You have probably used it many times. First one offers a tiny secret to a potential friend that would be slightly embarrassing if it were made public. It is usually an offhand whispered remark, perhaps accompanied by brief eye contact and perhaps a quick smile. The process proceeds if that potential friend reciprocates by laughing or smiling and answers in kind, telling a secret of theirs. Sometimes these preliminaries are accomplished with the aid of jokes that may be off color or otherwise slightly offensive. The friendship blossoms as parties involved in the dance come to reveal more "secret" information to each other, thus adding to trust and a sense of intimacy.

Children can be quite naïve in carrying out this dance of intimacy and choose an untrustworthy or more often a careless child as a friendship candidate. A nine-year-old girl classmate of Janus in the third grade whispered a question one day. "Do you know how they take your temperature in the hospital?" Fortunately he did not share this with other boys in the class and snicker at her. They became close friends. But if he had talked openly to others of her "offer of intimacy," she would have been humiliated. His compassion switch would have been clearly in the off position. But if he had mentioned it out of carelessness, his compassion switch would have been on. He would have been mortified. Many budding friendships among children are terminated by careless gossipy recipients of attempts at intimacy.

Control of large numbers of people requires individual by individual control.

As we have seen, control of behavior requires constant monitoring. Control of even one person is a big job. Think of how individuals control their own behaviors. Self-control is like the self-control exhibited by a guided missile; it requires constant feedback of what is resulting from its actions. It continuously answers the questions "Where am I? Where am I headed? Where is my target?" And it makes "in course" corrections. Controlling our behavior without constant feedback is like trying to stand on one foot with your eyes closed.

Because we have constant access to our own behavior, self-control does not incur expensive monitoring of our behaviors and surroundings in the way that control of others requires. If cleanliness is important to you, you can easily monitor your body, your clothes, and your washing habits. If it is important to you that you obey the law, you can easily monitor your knowledge of the laws that are important to you and your deviations, or even tendencies to disobey those laws. But we can only use the experiences we have available for controlling our own behaviors. People in general, i.e., a family, a city, or a crowd, cannot be controlled except by individual consequences that are experienced by each person in that community. There is no discount in the cost of controlling large volumes of individuals.

One might think that the behaviors of mobs or herds are exceptions. Members tend to follow where a few leaders take them. But they are the exception that proves the rule. Herd animals are herd animals exactly because they stay in a herd. People are able to devolve into herd animals and when they do, they are less like people. We are persons to the extent that the decider for our behaviors stays home. We are quite capable of mob behavior. This just means that we *can* be herd animals. Luckily, we are also capable of resisting the controls imposed by others, herd or otherwise, a fact which makes controlling human beings more complicated than merely administering threats.

Control techniques go beyond threats against us for not conforming to the expectations of control communities. We must somehow be made to care about conforming to community expectations. We must not only be obedient, we must at least appear to want to be obedient. When Johnny is punished for pulling Sally's hair, he is expected to own the "fact" that this was wrong. If he doesn't show that he agrees with the fact that he did something bad, he is likely to be viewed as a scoundrel. He is likely to be treated as if he were a dangerous outsider. The compassion switch of others in the community goes off and stays off toward the unrepentant Johnny.

On the other hand, children, as well as adults who live in control communities such as classrooms and small towns, can get away with mischief for a long time, by always showing distress and remorse for their behaviors. Those who punish them lose their compassion only while carrying out the punishment. They as well as most of the community are likely to continue to treat them with compassionate companionship and continue to welcome them within the community.

When adults are convicted of crimes, they are expected to show remorse. A sentencing judge is very likely to go very hard on those who show indifference about the crime and their sentence. The metaphor, "throw away the key" reveals their expulsion from the community. We must show that we want to do that which we are expected to do, even if we don't always do it. Much more will be covered about what happens when individuals fail to show that they care about obedience to community expectations in the next chapter.

Gossip like gravity is one force that governs all

Direct control of large numbers of individuals by one controller does exist, but it takes a lot of power. For example, gravity counts as a constant controlling companion for all of us on earth, unless of course we escape earth's gravitational field. It therefore "observes us" at all times so that no one can avoid its negative consequences. For example if we were to choose to ignore it by jumping off the barn roof in the dark with no one watching, we would likely still suffer some punishment for our attempt to defy its control. No individual is exempt from the consequences of gravity as long as we are not perpetually falling. For example we can arrange to be in an earth orbit. Then the consequence of falling is just more falling.

This "escape" from the consequences of gravity is a tribute to human ingenuity when it comes to finding a way to avoid control, even a control that is as pervasive as gravity. We don't escape gravity while in orbit, but we escape the ordinary consequences of ignoring it. Pretty clever.

Totalitarian rulers attempt to mimic gravity by developing massive policing and observation of citizens tied with an ever-present fear. Following Machiavelli's handbook[31] for ruling, they orchestrate unpredictable mass purges of innocent and guilty alike to gin up fear and make sure that all citizens are either aware of or suspect the presence of police observation and informers. What they miss is that any species that is clever enough to nullify the negative consequences of gravity will almost surely find ways to nullify the power of a tyrant.

Gossip, like gravity and tyrannical rulers is a powerful master. Gossip controls people in general, i.e. a community, and is even more like the control of gravity than it is like the authoritarian control exercised by people over individuals. But the lack of compassion which is required by most gossip is not so easily abandoned by human beings as we shall see as we follow Janus's journey.

Shoulds of a feather flock together.

Gravity which causes material particles located in the same region to attract each other results in objects gathering more closely. Likewise, we find that once people are within "gossip distance," their similarities both shape each other and attract each other to the same region.[32] We are apt to find people in "should" communities actually living near each other in physical space—houses, towns, office buildings etc. Although now due to the World Wide Web, living in the same physical region is less a factor for gossip in control communities. We can live together in so-called virtual communities. A friend of the author who manages a university residence hall underlines this exception. He observes that students in the same room may sit back to back while each is actually socially interacting with others located elsewhere in the world. When they want to communicate with their roommate who is sitting three feet behind them, they message each other instead of turning around and holding a face to face conversation.

People who share gossip tend to stick together when they find each other. Like birds of a feather, their gossip sticks them together. Additionally, as they share more and more gossip, their gossip becomes more alike. Because they share the same "shoulds" and "should nots," they also share the same attempts to control behaviors of others, including each other and themselves.

Evangelizing helps control communities control

Controlling behavior, like simple herding, requires constant vigilance and the presence of threatening consequences.[33] Therefore success of control, by its very nature, improves by having many shepherds. The number of controllers counts, so it is important in "should" communities that participation be widespread. For this reason they tend to evangelize.

This is perhaps the most destructive factor of control communities. They tend to want other communities to be like them and view "outsider's behaviors" as an evil to be driven away from them for their own good. Religious and political soldiers against the "evil" ones are too widespread in recorded history to need citing.

Geometry tells us that for any given shaped object, as an object grows larger, the ratio of the perimeter size to the area enclosed grows smaller. In the same way, the larger the number of believers that band together in physical space, the lower the proportion of them that are exposed to "outside" competing should-loaded ideological beliefs.

Therefore they tend to recruit by whatever means is available. Like a swarm of bees collected in a ball in the winter hive, the larger the ball, the smaller the proportion of the bees in the swarm that are exposed to the "harmful" influence of the cold surroundings at any one time.

The value of hypocrisy

Many of us grew up with "should and should not" gossip and it wasn't just about cleanliness. We know what it's like whether we are personally surrounded with it or merely observe it. We hear gossip about others who have sexual misadventures, who mistreat others among their family or community, who cheat, who fail in business or academics or marriage. These are all examples of gossip in action in control communities.

Earlier, Janus got a whiff of the nature of the gossip that polices a control community and it triggered his anxiety. He experienced anxiety instead of fear because he didn't recognize what was really threatening him[34]—becoming an outsider to the community, or even being "cast out." What he was still to learn was that it really didn't matter so much whether he kept clean or not; what mattered was that he demonstrated the belief that he *should* be clean. All members of a control community are expected to be soldiers for community rules.

A few years later, Janus got another memorable lesson, again about control communities. When he was twelve, the same aunt was again involved in his education concerning "shoulds." The meaning of this lesson was also unclear to him until much later. But its emotional meaning left its mark on Janus.

The Janus Journey: Janus learns a little about hypocrisy.

Janus had been required to attend Sunday school in a local church for several years. He had objected, but his father had settled the issue with the promise that when Janus could give a good reason why he did not want to attend, he could stop attending. It hadn't gone well from the beginning. Early on, when he was six or so, the teacher had announced the lesson for the day in no uncertain words: God is everywhere.

Janus was stunned. He found that really confusing, and also very alarming. How could God be everywhere? Didn't other things fill up some spaces? Was God in the toilet looking up at his bottom? And that was only the beginning of Janus's travails in Sunday school.

He found over the years that he liked the stories, but he couldn't make sense out of many of the teachings beyond being kind to others, which he heard all the time anyway. Finally, after a few years, he told his parents that he didn't want to go to Sunday school because he didn't believe in most of what they taught there. He included the early lesson on the location of God, in the case he made to his parents, although he left out the part about the toilet.

His explanation was fine with his parents, but not with his aunt. She cornered him one Sunday at a family dinner and told him that he was getting old enough to join the church. He replied that if he joined the church, he would be a hypocrite. His aunt replied, without missing a beat, "Janus, one more hypocrite will not hurt the church." Once again, he was stunned.

***

As a child, Janus was very familiar with the advantage of giving the appearance to parents and teachers that he was a "good child," — obedient, helpful, etc. But he usually made it a practice to avoid deceit. Its discovery would hurt his parents in a way he dreaded. But this couldn't be what his aunt meant. Surely she wouldn't tell him that he should be deceitful. And that wasn't her message. But as it turns out, it was pretty close.

He later realized that she was telling him that it was much more important that he profess the should-loaded ideology of the church than live up to it. It was more important to talk like a church member than it was to act the way the talk implied one should act. It was a control community where it was more important to control what one did and said in public than what one thought or did in private. He should show his support for the should-loaded ideology of the church even if he didn't feel it.

The main lesson Janus learned, not from his aunt, but earlier from his older brother and sister and his experiences in school, was to at least pretend to give authority its due. In school, it was best to show that following the rules is important. Trying to be "good" at least got him credit for his extemporaneous efforts in class that substituted for doing his homework. Guessing often passed for knowing. Janus learned to do a lot of guessing with a little help from a reputation of respect for rules.

But Janus paid a price for his wayward strategy. The older he got, the less comfortable he was with only pretending to subscribe to authorities.

The good which I would, I do not.

Only much later in life did he realize that his aunt's message wasn't exactly about deceit. It was about her view of keeping order. Her view was that chaos will ensue if people are allowed to behave as they see fit. In order to be ruled, people must acknowledge they are being ruled. Therefore in order to keep order, the community must have informal laws that people acknowledge as laws, regardless of how well they are obeyed. His aunt had been a teacher who kept strict control of her classes.

Acknowledgement by individuals that they should do certain things is what makes it possible for them to punish themselves when they don't obey those "shoulds." Acknowledging authority makes disobedience blameworthy.[35] Guilt, together with a growing feeling of being counterfeit, was familiar to Janus long before he understood how those feelings are related to "giving authority its due."

Janus would see, later in life, a good measure of exposed hypocrisy is grist for the gossip mill in its mission of policing control communities. Excoriating hypocrites on a regular basis helps frighten members of the community and adds to their resolve to "keep up appearances." One might speculate that without the vulnerability produced by counterfeit selves, obedience to authority would be difficult to maintain. Janus's aunt would never have said it that way, but probably the reason she was comfortable with "one more hypocrite" in the church was that she understood that hypocrites not only didn't hurt the church, but were practically indispensable for maintaining its authority. Hypocrisy among the membership strengthens their desire to appear to be pious and loyal members

---

[28] Trigg, Jonathan D. <u>Baptism In the Theology of Martin Luther.</u> Leiden: E.J. Brill, 1994.

[29] Socrates was interested in whether "justice" (meaning goodness) was good in itself, or was good because it brought us something else. He sharpened the issue by looking at the life of a person (writ large as a city) who was known by all to be good, but was in fact evil vs. the life of a person (city) who was known to be bad by everyone else, but was in fact a good person. He concluded, 11 chapters later, that goodness, despite having a bad reputation, was to be preferred to badness with a good reputation. I know of no better demonstration of the importance for our well-being of actual integrity versus a reputation for integrity.

[30] Self-talk has become the mantra of contemporary cognitive psychology, but seems to have had a blind spot for the role of self-talk that attaches moral weight to status and power. Starting with Abraham Low in the 1930's (See Low, Abraham A. *Mental Health Through Will-training; a System of Self-help in*

Psychotherapy as Practiced by Recovery, Incorporated. Boston: Christopher Pub. House, 1950.), the way we talk to ourselves has been has been assigned blame for the way we feel. Low's early work was continued, albeit with different self-talk targets by Albert Ellis (See Ellis, Albert, and Robert Allan Harper. *A Guide to Rational Living.* Englewood Cliffs,N.J.,: Prentice-Hall, 1961. & Ellis, Albert. *Reason and Emotion in Psychotherapy.* Secaucus N.J.: L. Stuart, 1973.) Followed by Aron Beck (see Beck, Aaron T. *Cognitive Therapy and the Emotional Disorders.* New York: International Universities Press, 1976. & Beck, Aaron T. *Cognitive Therapy of Depression.* New York: Guilford Press, 1979.) More recently the torch has been passed to the Mindfulness approach to changing patient self-talk. (See for example Segal, Zindel V., and J. Mark G Williams. *Mindfulness-based Cognitive Therapy for Depression.* 2nd Ed. New York: Guilford Press, 2013.)

From the point of view taken here, a problem with cognitive psychotherapy in practice is that the role of moral self-castigation connected with status-changing events in people's lives has been overlooked. This is not a surprising blind spot because psychologists themselves tend to be highly invested in achievement and its attendant privileges of influence and good conscience. The present writer has been among those who suffered as a result of such a blind spot. A "tell" that this is the case is that the typical therapist-client relationship tends to resemble the priest-penitent relationship, or more generally the Shaman-community member relationship.

[31] Machiavelli, Niccolò. *The Prince.* Chicago: Published by H. Regnery for the Great Books Foundation, 1948.

[32] See for example Besnier, Niko. *Gossip and the Everyday Production of Politics.* Honolulu: University of Hawai'i Press, 2009. In the last chapter of Besnier's study of the Nukulaelae people, he writes "In its most simplified form, the argument I have develop in this book is that talk matters. In particular, talk

matters in the conduct of politics, the assertion of power and its contestation, the construction and destruction of reputations, the manipulation of truths, and the **formation of alliances** and conflicts among people and positions." Bold emphasis added because it supports the point made here. But the whole quote is supportive of our thesis that gossip is a tool for control.

[33] See description of control in the Chapter 1 quoted from *The Anger Habit*.

[34] Anxiety is made up of the same body responses as is fear, but the true stimulus that signals anxiety are not consciously known to the person, while the object triggering fear is known. This distinction becomes complex when persons think they know what they are afraid of, for example fear of failure, but there is actually a more fundamental, and unknown cause, fear of losing status and losing community standing. Thus the paradox of using test anxiety for measuring fear of failure (FF). Students are aware of their fear of tests, but they are unaware of their fear of loss of community standing. This lack of awareness of the fundamental source of their fear turns the fear of tests into test anxiety.

[35] Menninger points out that St. Paul's words "The good which I would I do not; but the evil which I would not, that I practice." vividly describe the psychological distress present in what he calls the "Second Order of Dycontrol." See Menninger, Karl, Mayman, Martin, and Pruyser, Paul. *The vital balance.* (p 176) New York: The Viking Press. 1963.

Chapter 10: Not-Caring By Others in Our Communities Can Switch Our Compassion Off

We are using the word "community" to mean a group with ownership of something in common, as its derivation from the French word meaning "joint ownership" implies.[36] Typically, common beliefs and or interests are what hold communities together. Any belief or set of beliefs or interests can cement individuals into a community. Belief that the earth is flat or ownership and interest in Australian Shepherds can draw individuals into membership in communities.

Can individual freedom be an ideology?

Groups of people who hold common should-loaded beliefs tend to restrict membership to those who have those beliefs. Another word for such a common belief is an ideology—a set of rules that govern behavior.[37] Communities not only restrict membership, but they actively monitor and control beliefs of their existing membership.

Because people in control communities share common should-loaded ideologies that prescribe how they should behave, we also refer to them as *should communities*. The operation of *should* and control in communities becomes transparent in communities such as teenagers who have in common a view of how teenagers should dress, or a group of teachers who have in common a belief of how teachers should teach, or a tribe that has in common a set of beliefs about how they should view their origins and how they should prepare each year for planting.

In all cases, where there are common *shoulds*, there are attempts to control. *Shoulds* provide the subject matter of control in communities.

This provides a paradox for the formation of communities based upon a belief in individual freedom. What should-loaded ideology can contain what one's beliefs concerning individual freedom *should* be? Are there fixed *shoulds* that govern freedom? How could this be? This is a serious issue which will be explored in later chapters. Hint: Some communities who proclaim a belief in individual freedom don't really practice that belief.

The illuminating case of the incidental conformist who didn't care about conforming.

As it turns out, we must care about what we do in order to get credit for our "good" behaviors. But this isn't true for our "bad" behaviors. Here are two examples of gossip that are nearly identical, but differ in a way that demonstrates the effects of gossip about caring.

❑ Gossip 1: "Have you heard about John Doe, president of DIG mining? A former executive there says that when Mr. Doe was told that the company's planned project in Nevada **would harm the surrounding environment**, he said, 'I don't care about that as long as it's profitable.' Sure enough, when they carried through with the project it did harm the environment."

❑ Gossip 2: "Have you heard about John Doe, president of DIG mining? A former executive there says that when Mr. Doe was told that their planned project in Nevada would not only make money, it **would also help the surrounding environment**, he said, 'I don't care about that as long as it's profitable.' Sure enough, when they carried through with the project it helped the environment."

These two "gossips" are the author's versions of those used by researcher Joshua Knobe for his doctoral dissertation[38] written about folk morality while he was at Princeton in 2006. He told similar stories to people he encountered in a city park, who would listen and respond. He asked those who heard the first story whether the company president intentionally hurt the environment and those who heard the second story whether the president had intentionally helped the environment.

Respondents generally said the president *intentionally harmed* the environment in story one. But those who heard story two, for the most part said the president *didn't intentionally help* the environment.

In other words, even though the fictional mining president was indifferent to either the helpful or harmful effects of a mining project, harmful effects were thought of as intentional but helpful effects were not thought of as intentional. (Knobe's work has led to what is now called the "Knobe Effect" although that effect is different from the interpretation of his study given below.)

Our point, not Knobe's, is that gossip in a control community consists of *shoulds* and *should nots* which are essentially rules prescribing the behaviors of community members and among the *shoulds* is the one that says members should care about the *shoulds*.

Our explanation of why gossip about the indifferent Mr. Doe blamed him for harming the environment, but didn't praise him for helping the environment is as follows:

Caring about the rules is important in control communities; not just being compliant with them.

A common rule that is enforced by gossip in control communities is that one should care about the harm done to others, including the environment. The gossip stories above were about President Doe's disregard for the environment. So why was he not given credit for helping the environment? How is it that disregard for a rule not only makes one responsible for a "bad" outcome, but also negates credit for a good outcome?

Community gossip is about control. Therefore it is about enforcing rules. Rule-governed behaviors are essentially games in which there are rules to be followed and results that follow the rule-governed behaviors. Chess, Go, and baseball are examples of such games; but arithmetic and logic are also rule-driven activities. All games that have rules require that all "players" acknowledge the same rules—the same *shoulds.* But players of most games with rules merely kick someone out of the game if they don't care about the rules. Communities have moral rules that everyone is expected to honor. Just as in games with rules, those who don't care about the rules get kicked out. But a community rejection is much more serious and frightening than merely being banned from playing a game. Rejection from a community leaves us alone in the world.

The key to understanding why Mr. Doe wasn't given credit for helping the environment lies in the fact that Doe said he didn't care. Janus's neighbor inspired gossip about her not caring about a dirty house. She was accused of not caring about her housework, but implicit in the accusation was also the charge that she was not caring about a community rule, cleanliness which for many Western communities is "next to Godliness." Presumably, given the result of Knobe's experiment, Janus's neighbor wouldn't have received credit for having a clean house either. Not as long as she was known as not caring about keeping a clean house. This was the same double whammy that President Doe was hit with—not caring about the environment also meant he didn't care about a moral community rule.

Doe disowned the moral rules of the control community by disavowing the super rule of all games—all players must agree to play by the same rules. If Doe were a real case, one can easily imagine that there would be much more gossip about him, perhaps like the stories that regularly appear in news media and gossip magazines concerning unpopular persons whose latest "bad behaviors" can be counted on to gin up reader's attention. The function of gossip is not just to control behavior through blame and disapproval; it is also to punish those who do not care about rules.

Caring about rules is much more important than following them. The "sentence" for not caring is more serious. If wrongdoers don't shape up and say they are sorry and convince the community they have experienced a conversion of mind and spirit, they can be cast out or shunned, not just punished. Those who commit crimes are on terribly dangerous ground if they demonstrate or say that they don't care. Their sentences are likely to be extraordinarily harsh.

But if you don't really care, changing what you care about is not easy. You may not even have a good idea of what you are supposed to care about. In other words you may not have a clear idea of what the rules are. When Miss Box, Janus's first grade teacher told him she didn't like a "smart mouth," he wasn't sure what that meant, but he was pretty sure he was supposed to care whether he had one. He cared about what numbers were. Was he not supposed to care about what he cared about? How could he do that? He cared about talking. Ah, perhaps that was the issue. Was asking the wrong question a violation of some rule? He could stop talking, but how was he supposed to stop caring about talking.

Superstitious avoidance is a common way of steering clear of something we recognize as dangerous, but don't completely understand. We invent a boogeyman. Janus had a lot of experience with boogeyman stories that kept him from doing things. The summer before he entered first grade, a group of Gypsies camped for a while under a big maple tree at the side of the narrow gravel road he used to walk to the creek to fish. His mother told him to stay away from them because they might kidnap him and put a spell on him, or turn him into a toad. This frightened him, but only enough to walk by the Gypsy camp on the other side of the road. The extra ten feet from them was his precaution against their magic. Miss Box was another boogeyman. He would have to give her distance also, although it wasn't clear how much distance was needed.

Requiring a person to care about rules amounts to requiring them to gossip in the correct way.

Let's revisit the case of Mr. Doe, the executive who didn't care and therefore was considered unworthy of credit for helping the environment. Notice that not only was the story that was read to some random person in a park a gossip item, but within the story there is a gossip item. It consists of what a former executive says he said to Mr. Doe and what he said Mr. Doe said to him.

"A former executive there says that when Mr. Doe was told that their planned project in Nevada would not only make money, it would also help the surrounding environment, he said, 'I don't care about that as long as it's profitable.'"

This is gossip about gossip. Mr. Doe is reported to have expressed a belief about the unimportance of the environment. That is what stuck in the craw of many of the gossip listeners and would likely have been the subject of their gossip if these gossips had been a news story instead of an experiment.

The requirement that members of a control community care about the community's rules comes down to a requirement that members participate correctly in gossip about the rules.

When Janus's mother and aunt were gossiping about the neighbor's lack of cleanliness, his mother said "She wouldn't care what anyone thinks." Her assertion amounted to saying that the neighbor would not talk about the importance of cleanliness in the way she "should." Janus took this to heart. It frightened him because he didn't care about cleanliness even though he washed when told to and changed his cloths when told to. He started thinking different "gossips" about "dirty people" and about himself when he got dirty. His gossip and particularly his self-gossip about the importance of cleanliness started to change.

If you stop a moment and consider what you care about you may begin to recognize that having the care is merely gossip about yourself. List something you care about. Ask yourself how you would feel if you weren't known to others to have that care. Would you feel alarm and perhaps guilty if others thought otherwise about you? Or would it merely mean that your caring would take place when and where appropriate regardless of how others thought about you.

Try these thoughts: "I care about children." Suppose others thought you don't care about children. Does that thought alarm you? Would you mind if someone thought you didn't care about children? Or would you be satisfied with the thought that given the circumstance where a child needed care you would respond whether others thought you would or not.

"I care about cleanliness." Suppose others thought you didn't care about being a cleanly person. Does that thought alarm you? Would you mind if someone talked to other people about the fact that you don't care about cleanliness. Or perhaps you are confident that you are as clean as you want to be regardless of what others may think. Or on the other hand, it might occur to you that if you actually cared less, you would spend less time cleaning your house and have time for something else.

If you hit upon a care of yours where the thought that others might think you don't care makes you uncomfortable then you have glimpsed the effect of community gossip on how you gossip, especially the effect on the way you gossip to yourself.

If you are a teenager who cares about the brand name on your cloths, your care isn't really about clothes. It's not even about the labels on the clothes. Your care is about what others think you care about.

The psychology of the gossip of caring was alive over 300 years ago.

Nearly four hundred years ago, the great French mathematician and essayist, Pascal, may have been on to the effect of gossip on caring. He was very religious, as well as being the inventor of probability theory, along with Fermat, another French mathematical genius. In one essay in his book of thoughts—*La Penses*—he combined his notions of rational gambling with his strong religious views. He proposed what has come to be called Pascal's wager.

Pacal's wager is the name given to his attempt to show that believing in the Christian God was a good bet. He proposed that it was a good bet to be a believer because the payoff for believing is so enormous that it far outweighs the cost of losing the wager. His argument was flawed by the fact that there are an endless number of alternative beliefs, not just Christianity vs. non-belief that might be posed in the same way. One could make the same argument by posing that even though it is highly unlikely, one might be able to achieve eternal life and avoid eternal damnation by eating Wheaties for breakfast.

Pascal, however, made a very modern recommendation for those who decided that they wanted to believe. He recognized that the result of making a decision to believe in the Christian God didn't result in a belief in that God. He recognized that just deciding to believe in something presents a problem. He proceeded to suggest a method for acquiring a belief in the Christian God if you should happen to want to believe, regardless of the reasons you might want to have this belief; put yourself in a situation which increases your interactions with those who believe what you want to believe.

He wrote[39] "You want to cure yourself of unbelief and you ask for the remedies? Learn from those who have been bound like you, and who now wager all they have. They are people who know the road you want to follow and have been cured of the affliction of which you want to be cured. Follow the way by which they began: by behaving just as if they believed, taking holy water, having masses said, etc. That will make you believe quite naturally, and according to your animal reactions."

In other words, if you act as if you believe and hang out with people who believe, pretty soon you will believe. This view is supported by psychological experiments over the last fifty years which have shown that our beliefs can be manipulated by manipulating what we say about them and the conversations we have with others about them.[40] If we get someone to just say the words that they like brown bread, they may very well later believe that they prefer brown bread; although they started out saying they preferred white bread. If a witness to a robbery is asked by a policeman to tell him the color of the robber's coat, the witness may believe that the robber had on a coat, regardless of whether that was what they saw or not. As a result of such experiments, concern over the effect of "good cop/bad cop," on changing what people think may have happened, has cast doubt on the reliability of eye witnesses, even personal confessions. After all, if you can change people's beliefs, you can change what they believe they have done or believe they have seen. The common thread of this modern research is that not only our beliefs in general, but also our beliefs about what we have believed before, are modifiable by the conversations we have with others. The changes in the nature of our beliefs tend toward those of people around us, especially those with whom we have friendly relationships.

Pascal's suggestion for changing beliefs recommends a method that is remarkably similar except he was assuming that you *want* to change what you believe. He suggested that you can become a believer in the Christian God if you want to by spending time with devout Christians. You need not want to. Otherwise his suggestion amounts to the instructions for changing what witnesses believe they saw. Today, we would say that the change in your belief might very well take place because you will begin to talk to yourself (read self-gossip) the way those around you talk (read gossip about beliefs), and the way they talk to you. Pretty soon your self-gossip has changed and it is what you believe. If you join the Chamber of Commerce, your beliefs concerning small business and government regulation are likely to tend toward those held by your fellow members. It you attend Democratic Party meetings; your beliefs are likely to drift toward your fellow party members. And if you say The Apostles' Creed regularly with others whom you trust and care about, you will tend toward believing it.

As it turns out, this not only works for individuals, but is basically a good explanation of the way communities control what their members care about through gossip, although Pascal didn't mention gossip so far as I know. In any case, whether you join The Chamber of Commerce, the Democratic party, or a Christian community, or a university psychology department, you are apt to learn to gossip, both with others and yourself, in such a way that you will care about the community's *shoulds,* and thereby avoid turning off compassion of other's toward you and your compassion toward yourself by thinking or saying heresies.

---

[36] See Oxford English Dictionary, Community, Etymology: Anglo-Norman and Middle French communité, comunité, joint ownership.

[37] As mentioned before, the word ideology literally mean the science of ideas. Following Condillac, the science of ideas adopted by British empiricists took the view that all ideas originate in sensation, meaning we are born an empty robot awaiting programming by our sensations. This is pretty much the view of radical behaviorism today. Our environment functions as our "control community."

[38] Knobe, J. M. Folk psychology, folk morality. Dissertation Abstracts International Section A: Humanities and Social Sciences, 2181.

[39] Pascal, Blaise. *Pensees and Other Writings.* New York: Oxford University Press. (1995) 155-156

[40] Confabulation—the confusion of memory with imagination—has been studied quite extensively. It is especially an issue in psychotherapy and in law enforcement. An entry into recent literature can be made through: Kassin, Saul M., and Katherine L. Kiechel. "The Social Psychology of False Confessions: Compliance, Internalization, and Confabulation." *Psychological Science* 7.3 (1996): 125-8. van Bergen, Saskia, Marko Jelicic, and Harald Merckelbach. "Interrogation Techniques and Memory Distrust." *Psychology, Crime & Law* 14.5 (2008): 425-34.

Chapter 11: Squandering Simple Goodness with Ideologies of Childhood and Adulthood

We raise newborn puppies to be dogs. We raise newborn colts to be horses. One would think that we would raise babies to be grownup persons. This is not always the case. In control communities, babies are raised to be children, not grownups.

Learning to care about obedience—the key to the should-loaded ideology of childhood.

In control communities the main thing a child has to learn is how to be what the control community expects of children. Like learning what it means to be a should-loaded Christian (as opposed to a imagination-fed Christian who learns the stories, music, practice of gratitude, and beauty of the church which are possible contributions to a joyful life), childhood is a should-loaded ideology that must be absorbed to the point where the habit of belief replaces thinking. The ideal "child" in a control community is a person, of whatever age, who obeys authorities without thinking. Childhood is a should-loaded ideology in control communities and like all should-loaded ideologies, the ideology of childhood tells one how to behave and what to think, in this case, about being a child.

In control communities, controllers must have the means to threaten and/or manipulate consequences of other people's behaviors. Here we use the terms "adult" and "child" in control communities to refer to those with and without the clout necessary to bring threat to bear on others. "Adult" and "child" are not necessarily age related. Even very young persons, say in a slave culture, may have the clout necessary to order older slaves around at will. And the slaves in a control culture are often treated and spoken to as children. "Come here, Boy" was a common way of addressing black men of any age in the United States until recently. In the 1942 movie *Casablanca*, the famous actress, Ingrid Bergman, asked a waiter to ask "the boy" playing the piano (Sam) to come over to her table. In other words, authorities are people who have clout over those they control, regardless of their age. They are the adults. Those who are ordered about are the children regardless of their age. They are people who don't have clout in control communities as a whole, although they may exercise clout in families or other small communities.

The important point here is that clout produces the ability to threaten without having to actually physically attack. In other words, clout has the ability to cause people to feel afraid. Clout is the currency that buys control over others. Clout is often called power or status in control cultures, and it is reflected in the culture's attitudes toward winning in any competitive situation. The difference between communities where cooperation and compassion are the norm on the one hand and communities where clout and control are a norm on the other hand, can perhaps be most readily seen in their games.

There are many, like Janus, who do not stop thinking and who don't really believe all of the should-loaded ideologies they are immersed in such as Childhood and Christianity etc. This becomes apparent if they struggle against the loss of compassion that accompanies the enforcement of ideological *shoulds*. They attempt to keep their humanity alive by softening the *shoulds* of their ideologies.

Some "Christians" maintain that compassion is the central tenet of their religion, not obedience and may call themselves by other names such as Christian Humanists. Some young people maintain the view that acting the way that they are supposed to act is meaningless unless it is done voluntarily, and unfortunately view themselves as alienated. Ditto with many other ideologies present in control communities. Still, what is present for all of these non-ideologues is an ever present awareness of the "rules" that they are *supposed* to care about.

The ideology of Childhood teaches young people, and people of all ages without clout, that the rules to be cared about are:

- Defer

- Be polite

- Follow instructions blindly (obedience)

- Refrain from making demands

These rules may be recognized also as the rules for servants, slaves, model employees, and those in need of help, whether in a doctor's office or in a welfare office. In fact, as we follow Janus on his journey through childhood, we will see that these rules continue to apply to many people of "adult" age. They remain children governed by these rules into adulthood or they revert to them if they lose their claim to adulthood if they fail or suffer reverses in their adulthood clout.

As with all control efforts, these rules involve threat and blame if they are not followed and therefore the compassion is shut off toward rule violators. They are the rules that Miss Box was attempting to instill in her first graders. She nailed Janus as a smart mouth. "Smart mouths" are in danger of violating just about all the rules of childhood ideology.

Janus's interactions with Miss Box and some other teachers and authorities startled him. He had never before come across those who were in charge of him whose compassion switch was always off. An awareness of the other's compassion or lack of compassion is important in control communities. The presence of compassion signals that "adults" are not in a control mode, which means "children" are seen as following the childhood rules. The relationship between learning the rules of childhood and our awareness of the compassion state of others is the topic of our next chapter.

Both childhood and adult ideologies are products of control communities. They are two sides of the same coin, obedience and authority. We have drawn a sharp distinction between cooperative human activity on the one hand, and human activity that is controlling by nature on the other hand. Cooperation with others can keep compassionate companionship alive which is incompatible with controlling others with threats.

Cooperative play vs. playing for clout: On being an Adult in Control Communities

There are two kinds of play. There is just fooling around like young colts playing in the pasture where there are no winners or losers. We can pleasantly interact, with give and take, mutual challenge, and friendly sharing. Whether it is physical, verbal, or sexual, playing well is measured by the pleasure and especially joy, we give as well as receive. Let's call this kind of play cooperative play. Sometimes cooperative play can extend to competitive games. Winning and losing may be involved, but they aren't the point of the play. People can play chess or bridge for the fun of playing, or even the fun of studying the game and its many variations.

Another kind of play consists of competitive games that involve winners and losers where winning means something much more than playing well. Playing these games well involves being good at deceptive plans and misdirection and therefore cannot include cooperation between sides except for obedience to the rules. Sometimes even skillful breaking of the rules can become part of the game. The nature of these games is betrayed not only by how they are played, but also by what happens when they end.

In some games, losing involves a kind of symbolic death played out as submission, as in Chess. Losers topple over their King on the board. They have lost their Head and are at the mercy of the decisions of their opponent. An even more ancient board game is Go, which is played with two colors of stones placed one at a time on intersections of a grid. It has as its goal the surrounding and killing of all of the opponent's "live" stones. To remain alive one's stones must remain in connection with "their own kind." These metaphors that end Chess and Go can become less metaphorical in games where the players are competing for clout— the ability to rule others. (Literally cutting off people's heads has returned as a show of clout, "I am now the decider.")

Athletic games can easily become games for clout. We can tell when this occurs because it raises fear of failure in the players who play only for clout. Like any other human activity, a game *can* be used to learn something, and losing simply means there is more that needs to be learned. Failing does not lead to fear; it leads to more attempts to learn. If failing, in and of itself, led to fear of failure, children would not try to walk until they could walk perfectly. Failed attempts to learn all you want to learn does not provoke fear. But when a game or any other sort of competition produces fear of failure, it's being played for clout, not learning.

Fear is a big motivator and it works well in athletic games for clout[41]. It leads to an urgent attempt for impeccable performance. This kind of game is also seen in school in the competition for grades in control communities. In schools, where teachers, students and parents use grades as the definition of success and failure (as opposed to using the mastery of tasks and skills as a signal that lets the student proceed to the next task for mastery), fear of failure motivates players to do better. Athletic games in which the final score is the only definition of success produces fear of failure as well. The legendary professional football coach Vince Lombardi is known for making famous what UCLA coach, Red Sanders, told his team in the 1950's. "Winning isn't the most important thing; it's the only thing." Perhaps no better synopsis exists of a belief in the control-community's ideology of rulers, "adults," who rule losers, "children."

All games of this sort end when one side has more of some valued commodity, usually points or positions, which allows them to have their way with the other side. Winners are impeccable and losers are "peckable."

In control communities we not only don't object to games that feature playing for clout, we pay large amounts of money to watch the games. Whole towns and institutions soak up the clout delivered by the athletic teams with whom they identify.

Schools and universities justify large investments in playing and winning these games on the presumption that they add to students' education by teaching teamwork, persistence, and hard work such as is required in winning at football and basketball. Most important, they add clout to the school in its effort to obtain superiority over other schools.

It is undeniable that persistence and hard work, even in the face of adversity, are valuable lessons for overcoming any obstacle. Increasing power through a team effort is also a valuable lesson. The power of our economic way of life is built on the advantage that accrues from a division of labor. These are all plausible justifications supporting these games. However, there is something terribly wrong about the way this case is made.

What are these "virtues" of cooperation, persistence, hard work, and increased power used for? Yes, benefits and advantages do accrue to individuals in the community when their adversaries are enemies of human existence - hunger, poverty, and sickness; not when the adversaries are each other. But games of clout, whether they are academic or athletic, aren't about using cooperation to overcome the *non-human adversaries of humans*. Rather, they teach the value of cooperation in overcoming *human adversaries*. The lesson for those who learn to play them well is that with persistence, hard work, and cooperation, some groups of people can gain the clout necessary to overcome other groups of people.[42]

Many of us played games for clout as children. It may take a lifetime to come to grips with that part of one's education. Basking in the reflected clout of teams fielded by our home town or alma mater is seductive. When watching our favorite team win we have a tendency to feel that we are part of some select group that is happily superior to a large group of inferiors, the vast majority of whom we don't know from Adam. When our teams lose, if we are not careful to view the games as a spectacle, like a circus, we feel a loss that must be mourned. The writer has counseled some clients who go further than mourning when a loss is suffered by a favorite team. They go into depression. A loss by the Detroit Lions over the weekend would throw one client into a state of inaction, social isolation, and loss of ability to experience anything pleasurable for the whole following week.

We will have much more to say in coming chapters about finding alternatives to living a life dependent upon clout. But here, in the context of athletes it is worth pointing out that it's never too late or too early to resist the nonsense of do or die games. Seeing games as spectacles or circuses helps counter our appetite for clout to some degree. Stories also help, especially children's fairy tales such as Snow White in which a young woman without clout is "discovered" by those who love her and a person with clout is made to suffer the truth about herself by looking in the mirror; or another young woman with no clout, Cinderella who, aided by the loving use of magic is discovered, lost, and re-discovered by a lover, and where those who do have clout are forced to see embarrassing gaps in their impeccability in the form of feet that are too large. In later life, Janus used stories that exposed the purpose of clout to help his clients turn their compassion switches back on.

The price we pay for seeking clout is the price that Janus paid. He tried to counter the clout of Miss Boxes of the world, who were attempting to make him subscribe to the rules of childhood. He may have defeated a Miss Box or two, but he subscribed to the should-loaded ideologies of childhood and adulthood in spades by his own use of clout. To the winners go the rights to control the losers. However, losing (failure) means we are on the receiving end of childhood ideology. To play the game of clout to begin with is to care about the should-loaded ideologies of childhood and adulthood. What else would we want to do with the power to rule except to rule with it?

Janus had already accepted the rules of childhood vs. adulthood, that having clout has perks, when he learned to play for clout. Winning and success give you the power to get what you want. But losing and failure lead you to Deference, Politeness, Obedience and Refraining from Demands. He was a believer.

In control communities childhood is the not just for children. All members who subscribe to "playing for clout" care about clout. They may very well be hypocrites about the way they behave. But they certainly aren't hypocrites about clout unless they pretend not to care about clout. When they suffer losses, they are fearful and when they win they feel like powerful deserving "big people."

Young people can be adults in control communities if they have clout.

If having clout depended on being able to physically threaten people, young children could not play for clout. But it doesn't depend on muscle in the modern era, although it more than likely did at one time in our evolutionary past. Today clout wouldn't work very well if its use depended on becoming some kind of action hero, although stories that involve that version of clout are obviously popular among children and adults. The vast majority of members of control communities who have clout are not physical bullies or particularly well-endowed physically. Even where the ability to physically triumph is used, say by police, threat works best when it is used sparingly.

The same is true in animal control communities. We see threat at work to control others in nature among all social animals. We count as social animals, animals and birds that rear their young. They rarely actually use physical force in their exercise of control over each other's behavior. Killing is a very poor way of teaching others to obey. A dead bird hasn't learned anything about submitting. At the bird feeder, even among separate species, threats without pecking, are enough to establish who backs off and who gets to eat first. In their everyday lives, if animals needed to actually fight in order to project control, wounds would likely kill both winners and losers, especially in wintery weather.

Similarly, a control community that encourages actual use of physical force to control each other becomes a very deadly place for all inhabitants. Arming citizens in order for them to enforce community rules, results in lots of dead citizens who haven't learned anything by becoming dead. Survivors have only learned to arm themselves. Imagine attempting to counter bullies on a playground by arming all the children.

The origins of effective threat

The origins of the effectiveness of clout in bringing about obedience lie in a surprising place, our early ability to recognize compassion and lack of compassion in others. It is our recognition of the switching off of other's compassion that serves as a threat.

Newborn children, like all newborns of social animals, are pretty much at the mercy of their caregiver's compassion. If compassion is there, they prosper. If it isn't there, they suffer and sometimes even die, not only for lack of physical care, but for lack of compassionate human attachment.[43] There isn't a lot they can do about it in the first months of life.

But as children grow and become self-mobile, and especially as they begin to communicate, they can do something about their caregivers' compassion or lack of compassion.

We, at any age, can zero in on the presence or absence of compassion in others. When we are young, much hinges on our awareness of whether our caregiver's compassion switch is on or off. Mother's smile and gentle tone of voice means green light, things are fine and I'm happy. Her frown and raised voice mean something else. Something is wrong and they attempt to find out what it is.

Recognizing the position of the compassion switch is a two-way street.

It is a mistake to attribute small children's concern about parental unhappiness to the child's selfish needs alone. Children display simple compassion toward their parents in the form of their concern about their parents' signs of happiness. It is the very definition of love and caring of children for their parents. We often miss the fact that children love and care for their parents as much as their parents love and care for their children. Our children are happy when we are happy and unhappy when we aren't happy. And they are often quite willing to sacrifice their own well-being in attempts to address the suffering they see in a parental figure. Small children will attempt to protect a parent or older sibling from physical attack by leaping into the fray. We saw an example of this in a five-year old when Janus attempted to intervene in his older brother's fight after school.

Of course children don't have the competence yet to do a lot of effective caring for their parents. However, children can, and routinely do, find some reason why they themselves might have caused their parents distress. When they see their parents frown and raise their voices and exhibit other signs of distress, young children can attempt to *take care* of their parents by removing themselves as a possible cause of their parent's distress.

A parent can of course take advantage of children's tendency to blame themselves for the parent's unhappiness and use their unhappiness to manipulate their children. The parent who exercises this kind of control can only do so with their compassion switch off which has the effect of doubling up the child's concern. These concerns are often missed by children of manipulative parents. Mom's misery is recognized as manipulative, but it still works because an awful fear is felt due to the threat presented by the threat posed by her lack of compassion. It's easier to just assume she might actually be miserable than to deal with the possibility that she's using you. This dilemma also occurs in reverse when children learn to use misery to manipulate parents.

Feeling that we are the cause of a loved one's suffering causes excruciating suffering whether we are children *or* adults. But because their compassion switch is off, it is common for parents and others who are concentrating on control of children, to miss this suffering in children who feel responsible for their parents' troubles.[44] Further, because children are apt to recognize their parent's attempts to control, they are themselves apt to switch off their own compassion in their attempts to control the parent's attempts to control. Parent says "You're grounded." Child replies "I don't care. Do what you want."

So children may quickly learn that most of their parent's shows of distress are signs that their parents are blaming them for something and they better look out. Their parents' compassion switch is in the off position.

Of course, parents can up the ante when children grow older and are less likely to be made miserable by parental misery. "You have no idea of how much I worry about you." "You are going to be the death of me." "I feel so ashamed of you that I can't face people." Older children respond to these efforts by trying to be "good," or at least make better provision for keeping their "bad" behavior secret, but not willingly and lovingly, at least not for long.

So smiles and gentle tones of voice are invitations to intimacy and free interaction for both children and adults. Frowns and harsh voices are indications of looming control and loss of freedom. We are aware, or think we are aware, of the state of other's compassion switch in our social interactions.

Our awareness of other's compassion switch triggers self-blaming gossip.

As adults our awareness of the state of others' compassion enters into the way we relate, especially in our closest relationships. We know friendly and unfriendly when we see them. A spouse knows when their partner is in a bad mood toward them. That is, when they are in a control mode with compassion turned off. Attempts of others to control us occurs when we have done something we weren't supposed to do. Therefore, when our partner turns quiet or morose, we may automatically feel like we have done something wrong. We may say to ourselves, "I said something wrong." or "She didn't like the way I dressed."

We learned this lesson in self-talk long before, as children. We learned that when another person's compassion switch turns off while relating to them, it means control is on its way. Our recognition of the lack of compassion is contained in the language we heard and learned to say to ourselves when we first learned about a parent or friend who was unhappy due to our behavior. The other person's "You make me unhappy" becomes our "I made him unhappy." Their "You make me ashamed" becomes our "I am making her ashamed." And of course, the consequences of talking to oneself like this is that you are either very unhappy because you are causing someone pain who you care for, or you are unhappy because the person you care for is trying to make you unhappy. Heads you lose, and tails you lose.

Our efforts to maintain loving relationships with others as equals is often sabotaged by our tendency to control by showing an absence of compassion. Marriages, partnerships and friendships work best when they are respectful relationships between equals—people respect one another as having equal rights and powers. The author's book on anger in relationships, *The Anger Habit in Relationships,* puts the problem in its most basic form. "You are not your partner's disciplinarian." This means that when a spouse drinks too much, or says something silly or stupid, one maintains a respectful distance. "He or she makes mistakes just as I do. In any case, they are responsible for what they do."

A large part of the effort to help one's relationships survive, is to stay away from control struggles. This is to say, keep the compassion switch on as much of the time as you can. Attempts to control are likely to stimulate counter attempts. Using unhappiness to control breeds counter displays of unhappiness, with learning to battle over who is most unhappy.

Perhaps because we are highly sensitive to the presence of compassion in others when we are very young, we find it easier to learn the effects of friendliness on others. Relating to others in a friendly way is not rocket science for young children. A delightful series of children's books about helping others feel good by being friendly uses the metaphor "Fill others buckets."[45] The writer, Carol McCloud, a widely sought out speaker, is known as "The Bucket Lady." The popularity of her books speaks to their effectiveness and appeal to children.

However, once we are drawn into the competition for clout with others who have or wish to have clout, going back to compassionate companionship with other cooperative persons becomes much more difficult. We have joined in the hunt for "success" that augments clout, and going back is likely to be viewed as giving up on that quest, which is tantamount to failure, that dreaded defeat which throws us into self-blame.

Back to Janus's encounter with the rules of childhood.

Joining the control game.

Janus ran headlong into the ideology of childhood in school. Prior to entering school, he certainly was familiar with its tenets—Deference, Politeness, Obedience and Refraining from Demands—but not as a religion. He thought these were the ways good people behaved. He thought his parents were just trying to teach him to behave in these ways because those were the ways they tried to behave and they wanted him to grow up like them. It was like teaching him how to take care of the lambs and plant potatoes. They were things adults knew how to do and were happy to teach to their children.

But behaving in Miss Box's class wasn't like that. Deference, Politeness, Obedience, and Refraining from demands, took on a whole different meaning under her lash.

The Janus Journey: Janus joins the control game.

There wasn't a doubt in Janus's mind that whatever she meant when she said he had a "smart mouth," Miss Box didn't worry about having one herself with him and the rest of the class. So this wasn't something he had to learn in order to be a good person. He was encountering something different than before. After recovering his composure, he distanced himself from her, like she was an alien being. This new and unfriendly being presented a challenging new game which he had to learn to play. It certainly seemed to have rules that would be enforced. And it was clearly a game in which children and adults played by very different rules, or at least they played with different pieces.

He wouldn't put it this way until many years later, but he knew for sure, right from the beginning, that some of the teachers had no compassion in their dealings with children. That is, they acted as if they didn't like children. Control was the only game they played. He was never going to feel close to them and they were never going to feel close to him. As he grew older and spent a lot of time on the playground he realized there were a lot of the other children, especially the older and larger children who didn't act as if they liked anyone. They played for clout, rather than for fun. Playing for clout was about shear control by whatever means available.

School became a different place for him. As he learned to keep his head down in class, he also learned that books were reliably friendly. Books were like his father. They told stories that he could learn from while exercising his imagination. He then discovered the town library. The library became his school.

Books and people in books became more and more important to Janus as he moved through the grades at school. School was increasingly boring. He thought someone must have made a fortune who sold clocks to schools that never moved. He spent most of the time in class fantasizing about the heroes in books he read. Robin Hood was an early favorite. Janus knew of a huge oak tree in the woods at the farm that had a large partially concealed hollow just above ground level. This became his home in his fantasies of Robin Hood adventures.

He discovered many other friendly books at the library. He mowed through author after author reading all the Mark Twain books the library had, and then Sherlock Holmes short stories. As he grew older he was attracted to more contemporary authors. He happened on a series of books by Philip Wiley and was impressed by Generation of Vipers. He couldn't believe that the library carried such books. Man invented God? Surely people in town didn't read much or they would be up in arms about some of the books in the library.

But there was a big downside to the library. As he grew into Junior High and High School age, his reading helped him develop a way to relate to unfriendly others that wasn't good for him. The books he read helped him develop a game for clout. When others threatened control over him his reading made it possible to relate to them by saying things that he knew would seem outrageous to them and sucker them into incredulity at his stupidity, and then lay on them the sense of perfect simplicity of what he said and how it was something that everyone should be expected to know.

Later in life Janus laughed when he thought of himself as having been then like a later favorite athlete, Mohammad Ali. He had invented the "rope-a-dope" before Ali ever thought of it. Lie on the ropes for a while and then let them have it.

Janus gained a kind of respect from others in the small community for his "deep" abilities, and more important, people laid off the judgments; they didn't quite know what to think of him. He had mostly been able to warn off those who he knew, even his friends, when they showed any sign of telling him what he should do or not do.

He was becoming an expert at switching his compassion switch to the off position when needed. He was becoming a Miss Box.

Janus poured over the classics and contemporary literature with an added purpose, not just to learn, not just to make friends with the authors and characters, but also to play games with his "knowledge," and especially to find ways to torture others before they could torture him. He learned to argue, not just to find convictions; he kept those to himself and a few close friends whom he trusted. But to find a winning argument. To get the drop on others.

Janus had developed an escape from the self-torturing self-gossip that says "I did something wrong." "I must have said the wrong thing." He was learning to put himself in the position of a Miss Box; someone who leads others to say these things to themselves. He had joined the adult ideology of a control community by finding ways to counter control with control.

***

Janus was well on his way to reducing his circle of compassionate companionship. Along with that loss, he would lose contact with his simple goodness, a morality that had supported his wholeness as a person from an early age. Next we will pay a visit to simple goodness and the gifts that Janus was leaving behind.

---

[41] Bélanger, Jocelyn J., et al. "Driven by Fear: The Effect of Success and Failure Information on Passionate Individuals' Performance." *Journal of personality and social psychology* 104.1 (2013): 180-95. They found that

" following failure information, obsessive passion predicted increases of performance through its effect on fear of failure. However, performance augmented only when the performance task was framed in such a way that failure would entail important negative consequences for the self and not when framed as inconsequential." In other words, fear works in athletics.

[42] Donahue, Eric G., Blanka Rip, and Robert J. Vallerand. "When Winning is Everything: On Passion, Identity, and Aggression in Sport." *Psychology of Sport and Exercise* 10.5 (2009): 526-34.

[43] Failure to thrive for non-organic reasons, that is, because of emotional neglect, was not recognized until fifty years ago. See an early study: Leonard, Martha F., Julina P. Rhymes, and Albert J. Solnit. "Failure to Thrive in Infants." *American Journal of Diseases of Children* 111.6 (1966): 600-12.

[44] For a detailed account on the problems incurred at all ages as a result of utilizing parental unhappiness and rejection as methods of discipline see: Semmelroth, C. *The Anger Habit in Parenting.* Naperville, IL: Sourcebooks. (2005).

[45] See for example: McCloud, C. *Have You Filled a Bucket Today?* Ferne Press. (2006)

Chapter 12: Wake up: You're Better than You Think

Most young children, before they have signed up for membership in control communities, live voluntary lives. *The Anger Habit* says this about Voluntary Living.[46]

"...what is voluntary living? It may be anything—and that's the point. It may mean living dangerously, if you wish, mindful of the consequences and being willing to accept them; or living conservatively, knowing what you're missing and being willing to miss it but deciding for yourself. It may or may not mean this - and that's the point."

Young children want to get up in the morning because the day in full of imagined possibilities. They live life willingly. The opposite of Voluntary Living is Involuntary Living which makes getting up a chore and which in its more severe renditions causes us to feel like we need to drag our way through each day, and maybe through life. We will have more to say on Involuntary Living when we look at the relationship between compassion and depression.

Simple compassion and voluntary living: A valuable goal

Ahead are some events in Janus's life which chronicle his struggle to release himself from practicing control in order to resist control by others. However, first we will make a temporary leap in Janus's journey to where he landed later in life. This will help us see where his struggles are headed and why they are worth it. After college and an academic career and some hard-won struggles to free himself, he landed in a private counseling practice. Here is an example of how he later attempted to aid others in their struggles.

The Janus Journey: Janus attempts to help Nancy see she is better than she thinks.

Janus didn't recognize the woman coming up the walk to his office a little before eleven o'clock. He wondered if he had made a mistake in scheduling. As she entered smiling, it hit him like a ton of bricks. She was indeed his eleven o'clock appointment—Nancy.

Janus had now been in full-time private practice for ten years since he had left university teaching. He had met and married a woman, who was on the same journey, back to well-being that came with a sense of voluntary living. They lived in a small town eighty miles from the university Janus had attended.

His practice occasionally included former students and colleagues from both his university days as a graduate student and as a faculty member. (Janus met Nancy earlier in a Janus story, we will review that earlier meeting in a later chapter.) *Nancy had called him the year before and asked if she could see him. She was now safely tenured in Janus's former department. Her husband, Jack, had failed to obtain tenure and was teaching where and when he could as an adjunct faculty member.*

But the safety of tenure had not brought satisfaction and happiness to Nancy's life. She felt that in most ways, her tenured university position had not improved her life at all.

Nancy had sought out Janus just for that reason. He had been embraced in the "safe" arms of tenure by their profession, just as she had been; but Janus had given it up and was now on his own. She thought Janus might very well have preceded her on her path of unhappiness and might have discovered something of value for her own journey.

This particular day, Janus had expected Nancy for his eleven o'clock appointment, but not this Nancy. She looked years younger than she had two weeks ago when Janus last saw her. She wore an attractive red jacket and black skirt. He had not seen a smile reflected in her eyes since she had been seeing him, nor had he seen her look like anyone other than a sort of "frumpy" person with a dour expression.

"You look different. I almost didn't recognize you as you came up the walk. I thought you were someone else."

Nancy's smile came back in a flash. "I feel like someone else. I'm beginning to feel like the person I remember long ago; the person you keep insisting that I can go home to."

They had been working toward this together for months. Due to the fact that Nancy was a psychologist, their work was easier in some ways, but more difficult in other ways.

Both Janus and Nancy were very familiar with therapeutic approaches that pointed out the "irrationality" of talking to oneself as if life "must" go a certain way. But early on in their counseling sessions, Janus had taken a quite different tack with Nancy. He suggested that her self-disapproving language and judgments weren't coming from irrationality. Yes, her language of disapproval had become a habit; but the habit of self-disapproval hadn't grown from irrationality. Rather, it had developed from her ideological conscience. She had bought into many of the same should-loaded ideologies as Janus had, and for similar reasons. Her self-disapproval was her conscience, punishing her for having been bad.

Because of her training, Nancy had easily identified what Janus was referring to as an ideological, or community conscience. This was essentially the same as Sigmund Freud's "Super Ego." She resisted his questions concerning her beliefs about right and wrong and where these beliefs came from. One day, in an angry outburst, she spit out at him, "So you want me to give up a whole developmental stage that helped me become a civilized person? You want to make me into a sociopath!"

Janus was ready for this and his response was quick and decisive. "Sociopaths have a kind of morality too. It's just that it applies only to others. They get upset when things don't go the way they think they should go, more so than you and me. You aren't a sociopath and will never become one. You are much better than you think and certainly much better than your conscience lets you believe. I view it as my job to help you find that out.

"And I think I can start by giving you an example of something about you that I was privileged to observe before you came to see me."

Nancy's anger quickly turned to curiosity and Janus continued.

"A year ago last spring, I attended a graduation at my alma mater with my brother and his wife. Their son was graduating. I spotted you sitting near us with Jack. I apologize to you now for spying on you, but you looked different—happier than I remembered you—and I was curious.

"As I watched, I recognized what I was seeing in you when I noticed the young woman in the graduating class you were looking at. I saw the way she was looking back at you. I knew that must have been your daughter Susan, you've told me about.

"Nancy, it was the goodness on your face that drew my stare. It must have been as apparent to anyone watching as it was to me. You looked like the mother in that Picasso print that hung on your office wall back at the university when we were colleagues."

Nancy answered quietly. "Picasso called it 'Maternity.' It's still there. "Jack used to say it was me and was why he loved me."

She looked at Janus, her eyes shining with tears she did not bother to wipe away.

Janus continued. "And then I was really blown away by your daughter Susan's face when she saw you looking at her. I saw your smile written on her face; or was it the other way?

"It doesn't matter. My point is that anyone watching you two would be able to see that your happiness was for each other, not for the diploma Susan had received.

"I watched the feelings spread across Susan's face as she spotted you. Her face changed from a smile to a mirror of your face. Your daughter's face glowed all the way as she walked to the back of the auditorium.

"As Susan turned away from the podium, college diploma in hand, I imagined you first seeing her when she was born. I could imagine you, like the mother in Picasso's 'Maternity,' looking at that infant in your arms, but also seeing the adult in the infant and feeling a devotion to that cause arise within you. I imagined you now reversing that image, seeing that infant once again, but now in the adult before you."

Nancy and Janus sat looking, not at each other, but into each other through the other's eyes. Tears were streaming down Nancy's face. Janus's eyes also glistened. They sat quietly for several minutes. And then Janus broke the spell.

"Let me ask you to look at yourself from my point of view on that day. I find it unimaginable that you learned to lovingly care for Susan and Jack from your moral teachings, most especially not from those that told you to love and care for others. Learned unselfishness hasn't motivated you to look out for Susan's well-being all these years with little regard to what it cost your own physical well-being.

Yes, I'm sure that you did a lot of learning about how to take care of her—when she should get her shots, what the signs of ear infection were, what the signs of drug use were, and so on. But you didn't take the trouble to learn how to do these things and actually do them because you were obedient to moral teachings that said you should.

"Nancy, you and I were both taught that what human beings do, they do because it satisfies some need. We are likely to believe that, so we believe ourselves to be essentially selfish people. Whether the reason for our behavior is Sigmund Freud's pleasure principle, or due to some motive that fits somewhere in a motivational psychologist's hypothesized hierarchy of needs, our behaviors seem to us to belong to our needful motives. And because our motivations are ours, and our behaviors satisfy them, it seems to us as if we must basically be selfish human beings.

"At the same time, long before our profession taught you about any of these psychological theories, you were probably taught, as was I, that your selfish motives were tempered by our so-called moral education, and that moral behaviors were the outcome of that education.

Essentially, we were taught that our selfish behaviors belong to us, and our unselfish behaviors belong to our moral training. We learned this every time we were taught we must do something or suffer the disapproval of others. Children, we learned, will be selfish if they are left to their own devices. Being told "You must love others" sent the message that you wouldn't naturally care for others' well-being unless you did as you were told and got rewarded for that love. The implication is clear, even to five-year-olds, that doing good is rewarded and doing bad is punished: therefore, we think that's why we do good.

"The Nancy I see is much better than that. The caring I saw that graduation day served your daughter's well-being, not necessarily your own. It certainly hadn't served any selfish motive during her upbringing. Your body sacrificed its well-being during your pregnancy in many ways. Your worries, the short nights during her first year, your financial sacrifices and your fears—I don't have to go on. You know there is no net profit in having children if you view the profit as selfishly yours. When viewed that way, even the experiences that you had, such as her graduation, would never make having a child a profitable investment. Your investment was for her, not for yourself. The profit you observed at her graduation belonged to your daughter Susan.

"Your caring for your daughter's well-being was awakened within you by her birth, perhaps even before her birth. And her love of you and Jack was in turn awakened within her by her awareness of you both as loving people. Consider the possibility that simple compassion did not need to be taught to any of you and that it is your real concern for each other that naturally motivates you all. You did not need to learn the meaning of simple compassion any more than you needed to learn the meaning of pain by being taught that you should avoid it. You may have been taught to avoid hot stoves, but you didn't have to be taught to avoid pain. You feel it—that's enough.

"Being reared on the Gospels, you might reconsider The New Testament command, "Love thy neighbor." Perhaps the translation should have been more in line with a historical Jesus whose message was to awaken others. Consider it, instead of a moral command, as a simple wake-up call: 'Wake up. Awaken to your love of your neighbor.' You and Nancy were certainly awake to simple compassion the day I saw *you.*

"Much of the presumably moral teaching you and I received wasn't moral teaching at all. It was the simple compassion that we already possessed in our conscience, co-opted by whatever ideological group with which we came into contact. It is a way of turning what you thought was a voluntary action into one that seems controlled by an ideology. When you accepted loving and caring for others as an obligation, you lost the sense of freedom that came with simple compassion. Instead, you became obedient, or not, to the community that graded you as a person according to your willing obedience to the community conscience. That should-loaded ideological or community conscience served to make you a moral police officer guarding yourself against disobedience. It's as if your moral phone, your simple compassion, was already ringing within you when you were a child, and your community said, "You know you should always answer your moral phone" You were made to think that you wouldn't naturally answer it unless you were told. If you bought into that, then what would have been freely done by you before would become controlled by a should-loaded ideology. As with the issue of goodness, telling you to answer the phone isn't really about getting phones answered. It's about control of your behavior and your participating in controlling other's behaviors according to the dictates of those who make the rules for the community."

***

Earlier meetings opened a series of explorations of Nancy's views of herself and her husband, Jack, and their relationship. It was Janus's attempt to spread out a map of the natural terrain of Nancy's family relationships for her use. Many months later Nancy appeared in Janus's office as described in this story—smiling and changed. We will rejoin that session in a later chapter, but here we will review some of what they discussed concerning simple compassion.

Caring for others is done for others' sake.

Simple compassion is about how we feel and act with regard to other persons' well-being without prompting by moral teachings. It is perhaps easiest to recognize in parents' spontaneous regard for their children's well-being. It is the heart of parenting in both senses of "heart."

However, even in the case of parenting, many fail to recognize its spontaneous nature. Believing themselves and others to be only capable of selfish behaviors that somehow pay off for *them*, they look for ulterior motives for why they want the best for their children. They assume that because they experience good feelings concerning their children's accomplishments they, themselves, must be benefiting from them. This reward takes the form of their having been "good parents." That is, they did their duty as prescribed by their moral beliefs. Their obituaries will be full of recounting how selfless and generous they were to their families and their communities. They may even receive a reward in heaven.

This parental self-misunderstanding extends to a more widespread mistake present in control-oriented cultures. Members of whole communities mistake their interest in the well-being of others in their community as being guided by some self-interest, some advantage that others' well-being will contribute to them. What we may call sociable love is no more driven by self-interest than parents' love of children, children's love of their parents, or children's love of puppies.

Our ordinary everyday psychologies—our explanations of why we and others do things—are part of our control community training, as are at least some of our need-based motivational academic and clinical psychologies. The belief in selfishness of children that must be overcome by authoritative paternalistic authority is helpful in selling the need for authoritative control and obedience on a community scale. The need to control people's morality sets up the job of controlling others just as the need to control other countries sets up the military industrial complex. This selling point is supported by gossip and gossipy media as well. Concern for others is seen as a "should," and is believed to only be exhibited by those who obey the command to act as if they are concerned, even as they punish those whose behaviors concern them.

We are better human beings than we think.

As Janus proposed, we are better than we think. Our simple compassion for others doesn't depend on what we get out of it. If one were to make a personal economic and health cost-benefit analysis of having children, and then use that profit/loss analysis to make one's decision about whether or not to have children, giving birth would be avoided like the plague. There is very little about having and caring for children, which would make it a good investment for us.

Our naturally occurring experience with children runs contrary to the idea of parenting as a self-serving act. A nearly universal abhorrence of mistreatment of a newborn baby betrays the presence of our simple compassion. No one needs to tell us or teach us what feelings to have toward the newborn, the young, and the helpless. Adults naturally hold children protectively, and children naturally attempt to hold and pet young animals caringly, although not necessarily with caring competence. Children also hold and protect their parents protectively.

A friend of the author who has gone through an awful time with a debilitating disease recounted her five-year-old son bringing a glass of water to her in bed to cool her "hot mouth." He needed no teacher for his act of simple compassion.

By the time we are adults it is less obvious to us that we have the same abhorrence of the mistreatment of all living beings as we do for our own families. Our should-loaded ideologies teach us people need controlling. By adulthood, these ideologies switch off our compassion switch toward others who we feel we must control. They unleash to some degree our capacity for self-less destructiveness and self-blame when we face losses and disappointments in our lives. If we lose, we feel we are to blame for that and require punishment in order to put us on the right track. Our self-blame is our way of punishing ourselves in an attempt to control *ourselves*.[47]

If we are Protestants we are less sympathetic to the well-being of a Catholic pope. Both of these faiths teach compassion, but feel the other one doesn't "do it" correctly. Many have died in attempts to correct each other. If we are Democrats we may even rejoice at the public humiliation of a Republican politician. Both preach the dignity of man, but both feel the other one doesn't "do it" correctly. We have been distanced from our simple compassion by our should-loaded ideological consciences. "They have it coming!" becomes the mentality. We are willing, even happy, to diminish the well-being of those violators of what we take to be our conscience, but is actually the conscience assigned to us by our ideologies.

Simple compassion is marginally effective without careful and competent execution.

We think of conscience as the self-monitoring of the moral aspect of our actions. A good community conscience is achieved when we have nothing to feel guilty about. Our simple compassion can also serve as a conscience. Here we use the phrase "careful and competent compassion" as self-monitoring of the effectiveness of our good intentions. If we are in touch with simple goodness, we feel good when someone else's well-being is actually enhanced.

Whether or not we experience the emotional component of simple compassion naturally, most of the knowledge and the skills necessary for *effectively acting* on our simple compassion must be learned. Much harm results from ignorant practices motivated by good intentions. Babies become unhealthy by being fed too much good-tasting food out of simple, but ignorant, love of their care-givers. Parents often say yes to their children out of concern for their children's feelings without a clear understanding of what enhances their children's well-being. Well-meaning counselors mistake their personal opinions as expert opinions about what enhances well-being of their clients. The very same opinions they acquired and have had since childhood are transformed into expert opinions once they've received their counseling degrees and licenses.[48] They take their childhood lessons about blame and guilt and turn them, unchanged, into expert opinions and therefore aim their clients toward finding ways to *express their anger*, or discover the *true source* of their guilt, with little or no understanding of what anger and guilt are about. These goals differ little from the aims their parents and teachers had when they were children.

Learning how to act upon our simple compassion means that we need to develop careful and competent compassion that guides us in our attempt to contribute to others' well-being.

Simple compassion, simple fellow feeling, by itself, without competence, is too big for us to act on. It is too big because we value much more in the world than we can possibly look after. There are too many causes for us to be able to look after them all. Cultivation of careful and competent compassion is our way out from under our overwhelmed and under-prepared simple compassion. We must look carefully for where and how we can effectively exercise our compassion.

The "shoulds" involved in careful compassion do not switch it off

Because caring carefully for an important value cannot consist of merely feeling and expressing our caring feelings, it requires the exercise of things that will contribute to the well-being of that valued object. But these *shoulds* do not switch off our compassion. When our child has a fever, we *should* take into account various possibilities, including waiting and observing, administering aspirin or cold medications, determining our child's discomfort and its location, determining availability of medical care and its competence, monitoring our child's state of alertness and so on. Our caring conscience requires understanding. It requires a map of the terrain of possible circumstances and the skills to act on the information contained in that map.

Our caring consciences contains *shoulds* and *musts* that are very different from those present in an obedient conscience. The *musts* and *shoulds* employed by our caring conscience are no different in character than any handbook or routing map. They don't say "You should go there!" They say, if you choose to help this person or a cause you value, then under these circumstances, it will or may be helpful for you to choose among these actions. Simple compassion *without* a caring conscience doesn't give us the knowledge to do good any more than wanting to protect the well-being of your car makes you an auto mechanic.

Simple compassion, left to its own devices, gives very limited knowledge and skill for helping others. This limited expertise is often mistaken for disregard for others, such as when a little boy who wants to establish a relationship with a little girl but doesn't know how, does as Charlie Brown did—he kicks her. His heart was in the right place, but his foot wasn't.

We may think of simple compassion as the parenting instinct writ large. Our natural reactions toward the young and helpless are the exemplars for our reactions toward others with whom we relate ethically. But it doesn't tell us what to do to help others. Albert Schweitzer was a very caring and moral person. But before he went to Africa to establish Lambaréné to exercise his simple compassion by establishing a hospital, he spent seven years preparing by studying medicine and raising money to buy supplies to take with him.[49]

Following Schweitzer's lead, children's moral education would be improved by being made more like what is taught in trade schools; teaching *how* to do something rather than teaching that one *should* do something.

Home economics can contribute to moral education of a caring conscience along with learning Bible stories that illustrate compassion, such as the story of the Good Samaritan. Home economics or nurses' training teach additional paths for *carefully caring* for others for whom one feels compassion other than leaving money for their care.

A caring conscience, taken as the *how* to care for others' well-being, can be taught without harm to voluntary living. Because it is like teaching children how to read a road map, the implications for failure are much different than the moral education of control communities. This way, failures are not the failures of caring and compassion that violate moral *shoulds*. They are honest mistakes born of gaps in one's knowledge. When mistakes are made, careful and competent compassion leads to sadness, regret, and corrective action. Regret, although painful, is very different than depressive self-blame because it serves a different purpose; changing one's approach to an important goal instead of self-blaming.

Caring and competent compassion allows self-improvement. A ruling conscience leads us elsewhere as we shall see in the next chapter.

---

[46] Semmelroth, C. & Smith, D. E. P. *The Anger Habit.* Naperville, IL: Sourcebooks. (2004) p 119.

[47] We will explore the relationship between depression and our community conscience later. However there is an intriguing suggestion in the neurological literature concerning compassion and our present culture. See O'Connor, L. E., Berry, J. W., Lewis, T., Mulherin, K., & Yi, E. (2007). Empathy and depression: the moral system on overdrive. In T. Farrow & P. Woodruff (Eds.), Empathy and mental illness (pp. 151-208). : Cambridge University Press. O'Connor's chapter, P152, says "While depression has been described as a 'disorder of the self,' it may be more accurately characterized as a disorder of 'concern for others.'" And again on P192-193 "The connection between depression and empathy is found in guilt, the moral emotion, the signal that makes us so uneasy when witnessing unfairness and inequity. The rapid rise in depression suggests that our current life style may be less than ideal for the social brain; assuming the human brain evolved for life in cooperative and empathic social unity, overcoming depression may require the development of social environments better suited to the nature of our species."

[48] Semmelroth, C. C., & Semmelroth, S. P. (1975). The need for better supervision among mental health professionals. *Improving Human Performance Quarterly, 4*(1), 37-42.

[49] Schweitzer, Albert, *Out of My Life and Thought: An Autobiography.* Translated by C.T. Campion. New York, Henry Holt, 1933.

Chapter 13: How Our Simple Goodness is Hidden from Us with a Little Help from Psychologists

Compassion can hardly be excluded from morality. Yet simple compassion may be hidden from us by what poses as morality in control communities. As we pointed out in the Introduction, one cannot successfully command someone, even ourselves, to be compassionate. Acting lovingly toward your neighbor because you are obeying a moral rule is an obedient act, not a compassionate act. Moral rules rule. They command. The decider for your behavior is the creator of the rule, not the person obeying the rule. It is not unusual to consider oneself a moral person if one is obedient to moral rules. I give to charity as I was taught to do. Therefore I am moral. Or is it just that I am obedient? This might seem to be a problem for morality in control communities where obedience is highly valued.

Teaching children to punish themselves in control communities

Control communities solve the problem of distinguishing between obedience and compassion by a two-step process of *moral education*. First, children are taught to obey rules by punishing them for deviating from them. Second, they are taught to punish themselves for deviating from the rules. This takes some time. The second step isn't usually accomplished before the ages of 9 or 10. This second step is considered to be the acquisition of a conscience.

For example, When Suzy falls down on the playground, Ruth laughs at her. But then Ruth looks up and sees a teacher watching her. She then comforts Suzy. The teacher scolds Ruth. Ruth tries to avoid punishment by claiming that she didn't realize at first that Suzy was hurt. And when she did realize it, she tried to help her. The teacher would have none of it and told her she was just trying to avoid being punished. Such experiences together with observing many cases where adults talked about children who are bad because they don't own up to the bad things they have done, will eventually train Ruth to blame herself when she violates community rules.

Psychologists have contributed to this view of moral training during the last fifty or so years. It flows seamlessly from a view of children as empty vessels except for reflexes. They are viewed as being born with no *internal deciders* that can possibly guide their behaviors. The psychological view of development implied by the following quotation from a current review of human developmental theory includes moral development as an extension of "simple reflexes."

"Many theories have been proposed to explain the cognitive, social, and emotional developmental processes that transform *the simple reflexive behaviors of the infant* into the complex informed behaviors of the adult."[50] Emphasis is added.

If today's school psychologists were asked about the Ruth/Suzy incident, and they were up to date on the literature concerning children's moral development, they might say something like: "Ruth is still in Stage Two of moral development—self-interest." In other words, Ruth was still only capable of selfish actions. More of how psychologists come to believe this about children and how children come to believe this about themselves later in this chapter; hint—gossip.

In order for us to successfully buy into the ideology of childhood and adulthood—of playing for clout over others—we must somehow hide our simple goodness from ourselves. If we were in touch with our simple goodness, games for clout would be offensive to us. Like Max, the seven-year-old chess genius in the movie, *Searching for Bobby Fischer*[51], we would likely offer a "draw" to an opponent who we knew would be hurt in a game our opponent was playing for clout. We would back away from causing discomfort, much less pain, to others. Experiments on obedience such as the ones done by Milgram and others that cause subjects acute discomfort would not be done by experimenters whose simple compassion was still available to them, even though they might be trying to play the game of "doing psychology" for clout. The students who participate as subjects, as well as the experimenters themselves, would have merely refused participation in the experiment. They would have rejected the experiments out of hand with "Using electric shock to punish people for their mistakes is not right." The fact that psychologists and social psychologists continue to perform endless variations on these experiments which are widely cited, speaks to how well we are able to hide our simple compassion.

How on earth can simple compassion be hidden from a whole community?

We look to Janus's experience to show us how the natural capacity for compassion can be suppressed by control communities by hiding it in a pile of *shoulds*.

Simple compassion is hidden under a pile of shoulds.

The Janus Journey: Janus's lessons in caring competence.

From an early age it had been clear to Janus that "caring" meant having cares, or "feeling caring" toward someone or something, as its derivation implies. It also meant to him to feel concern over someone or an animal that was hurt or injured. This was in fact the major derivation of the word as he would later find in The Oxford English Dictionary.

He also knew that this was a different meaning of the word than when his father would ask him, "Did you take care of the lambs?" The difference between caring about something or someone and being a care giver for them was unavoidable for a farm boy. He needed to know how to take care of animals or crops. He was acutely aware of the difference between caring about animals and people and crops on the one hand, and knowing enough or being able to go about taking care of them. In fact, a major part of his fantasy life concerned learning enough and being trusted enough to take care of things on his family's farm that he cared about so much.

His parents shared Janus's desire for him to grow in "caring competence." For example, on his eighth birthday his parents gave Janus a present of two small kid goats with the unoriginal names Billy and Nanny. His parents knew that helpless young animals are especially good at awakening children's caring feeling about the well-being of other creatures. They had no doubt that Janus's capacity for feeling care toward others was well-developed. They had observed the way Janus talked to some lambs that his father had rescued from mothers who had disowned them, as well as his concerns about their well-being. They counted on those natural caring feelings to make the goat kids a welcome gift for Janus. They knew that no matter how much he might have caring feelings about the well-being of others, it would make little difference in their well-being unless he learned how to actually take care of them. Caring is free. Taking care requires commitment and competence.

***

Despite his parents' attempts to teach the difference between caring and taking care and all it entailed, Janus had other "parents"—authorities in control communities at school, on the radio, and in his small town that taught him something deceptively similar, but tragically different in its effects. They taught him that caring about people was the same thing as caring for people, that compassion and carrying through with helping others were really the same thing.

Teaching this equivalence was a neat trick that depended on flashing around the word "should" like a card in a card trick. Now you see it and now you don't. "Why don't you do something? You should care what happens." The word should, meaning if one wants to take care of lambs one should feed them regularly, got used interchangeably with its meaning when they said one should always care. The community taught him simultaneously that one cares because one should care and that all the ways one takes care are included in caring. Feeling compassion meant the same thing as taking care of someone or something. Compassion turned into a giant rule that one should take care of everyone one cares about.

This simple sounding, even moral sounding, equivalence between two things that can't possibly be equivalent—caring about lambs and taking care of lambs—is impossible to carry out. One can't possibly know enough, nor have resources enough in order to be helpful to everyone or everything toward which they feel compassion. It ends up making all members of control communities into moral counterfeits (another way of saying "hypocrites"). Janus had grown up thinking that "caring about someone or something" and "taking care of someone or something" were two different things. Authorities in school, church and in other control communities in which he lived would now teach him that caring about someone meant being a care giver for them. And not taking care of them meant that he didn't care about them.

Learning that "caring about someone" means the same thing as "caring for someone" produces an avalanche of guilty failures. It is a process that ironically burdens those with the most guilt, who care the most about other people and sentient creatures. It provides them with the highest susceptibility to suffering caused by self-blame, even depressive illness.

The details of how two meanings of "should" are made into one.

We have pointed out that simple compassion isn't usually enough to actually be of help to others. Being helpful almost always requires some form of competence beyond a personal expression of caring feelings. Janus was acutely aware that helping his parents or helping Elsie and Harvey across the road required him to learn how to feed animals or drive a truck or chop wood. He had also been told many times by age six or seven that he should be kind to others, even love them. He didn't pay much attention to this advice other than to nod. He was still quite aware of how he really felt about people and animals in his life. He liked some a lot and as to others, not so much. But when it came to feeding the animals, as he learned how to feed them, he fed them all.

But learning how to do something involves following instructions or copying how others do it. Feeding the lambs in the west yard meant he should first remember to get the bucket from the milk house. Then he should carry it to the granary and open the door to the granary being careful to not let any cats in the door. (Cats were always after mice or rats which was good, but his father had warned him not to lock them in the granary or they might die in the heat without water in there.) Then he should fill the bucket only half full because that's all he could carry and manage to empty over the fence. Then he should carry the bucket from the granary to the west yard and dump it over the fence, being careful not to spill any more than necessary outside the fence. The lambs would surely try to push their way under the fence if he left any grain there, so he should clean up any grain he may have dropped. Then he should put the bucket back in the milk house, being careful to close the door after himself.

So learning to feed the lambs consisted of six shoulds:

1. He should remember to get the bucket from the milk house.

2. He should carry it to the granary and open the door to the granary being careful to not let any cats in the door.

3. He should fill the bucket only half full because that's all he could carry and manage to empty over the fence.

4. He should carry the bucket from the granary to the west yard and dump it over the fence, being careful not to spill any more than necessary outside the fence.

5. He should clean up any grain he may have dropped.

6. He should put the bucket back in the milk house, being
    careful to close the door after himself.

Except for #2—he should be careful about letting the cats in the granary or they might die there—these six *shoulds* have no moral import at all. Otherwise they are merely instructions, a recipe or a map of how Janus should proceed IF he were going to feed the lambs. They are no different than a map that his father might draw for him IF Janus were going to find a place back by the creek where he had found a stone axe head left their by Native Americans long ago when they probably used it as a camp ground. However that map might have a marking on it of a place to be careful because deer had only recently had their fawns and often "parked" their young fawns there. Janus should be careful in that area or he might run on to one of the fawns who wouldn't move until Janus almost stepped on him.

We have recipes for making dishes that we follow IF we want to make the dish; maps that we follow IF we want to go someplace; instructions that we follow IF we want to drive a truck or a tractor; and instructions to follow IF we want to use an axe to chop wood.

Janus wanted to do all of these things. He wanted to help out. He wanted to make his neighbors and his parents happy. He wanted to hunt for stone arrow heads and stone axes where his father had found them. He also knew that would make his parents smile and feel good. Their happiness was important, even if it cost him time and hard work. He was compassionate. He cared. But he wasn't born competent to care for any of these people whose well-being and happiness he cared about. He needed instructions of the sort he received regularly from his parents and neighbors.

But those instruction nearly always involved a "should" like "be careful you don't kill a cat by locking her in the granary" or " be careful you don't stumble on a fawn and frighten him" or later on "be careful when you are backing up the tractor that you don't run over someone."

So, even though this way of using the word "should" or "care" isn't intended to be "a moral rule to live by," still compassion toward others is mixed in as a should.

One should feed hunger; True or False?

Cooking is itself part of a recipe for caring for children and other loved ones, IF you want to care for them. That is, if you have compassion for your children and family, one of the ways you might want to become competent at actually contributing to their well-being is learning how to feed them. This is why the suggestion arises, without tongue in cheek, that perhaps classes in Home Economics and Cooking might be sensibly included in Sunday school as a contribution to children's compassionate competence.

But if the *shoulds* in cooking are understood to be compassion, *instead of tools* for compassion, then feeding people becomes a moral imperative *whether it contributes to their well-being or not.* Parents who feed their children at every turn, regularly asking them if they are hungry, no doubt feel they are helping them. They are following the moral command "One should feed the hungry." But there is nothing moral in itself about following the rules of food preparation. "Bake for one hour and serve." is not a moral precept. The only thing that makes it seem moral is the proviso that you want to help someone whose well-being would otherwise be diminished.

Parents who confuse the rules of providing food with rules for helping those in need, will indeed follow those rules with their children. Cooking or bringing in fast food becomes obedience to the rule "One should feed hunger." Unfortunately, this rule leads to 200 pound twelve-year-olds whose actual well-being has been greatly diminished, not enhanced, by following the rule.

The conversion of rules that guide, into rules that govern, provides fertile ground for the effectiveness of control in control communities. "Should" comes to have only one meaning. It is a moral command. It allows those with clout—the winners in the ideology of children and adults—to dictate by control of the rules of the community. Their *shoulds* become moral in nature. Those who are exempt from moral imperfection, or its appearance, have the "right" to rule. It is not a new concept in history that the right to rule is buttressed with a blessing to rule by religious institutions and individuals. The blessing of a tribal chief by the Shaman has much in common with the Divine Right of Kings conferred by the Pope on Charlemagne. All those who sin, which includes everyone else, must be ruled.

The history of the relationship between sin and the right to rule continues in modern psychology.

Crowding out simple compassion in favor of rules, passes as the psychology of moral development.

A major theme in the psychology of moral development over the last forty years is contributed by the work of the psychologist Lawrence Kohlberg. His work has been taken as a description of six levels of moral maturity based on how children and adults talk about (gossip about?) stories containing so-called moral dilemmas.

Kohlberg's work[52] is a brilliant and exhaustive compilation of how children come to view morality as a sort of calculus involving rules of conduct, although that is probably not how he views it. And it is certainly not the way others view it.

Interestingly, Kohlberg, like Knobe years later, used gossip as a way to gather data. He invited children and adults is listen to little stories about what he called moral dilemmas and then invited them to talk about whether the people involved should have done what they did and tell why or why not.

Here are a couple of the stories he used.

"Joe's father promised he could go to camp if he earned the $50 for it, and then changed his mind and asked Joe to give him the money he had earned. Joe lied and said he had only earned $10 and went to camp using the other $40 he had made. Before he went, he told his younger brother Alex about the money and about lying to their father. Should Alex tell their father?"

And the most famous story, the Heinz story, was used in many experiments over the years. Here we follow it with a sample interview with "Tommy":

"In Europe, a woman was near death from a special kind of cancer. There was one drug that the doctors thought might save her. It was a form of radium that a druggist in the same town had recently discovered. The drug was expensive to make, but the druggist was charging ten times what the drug cost him to make. He paid $200 for the radium and charged $2000 for a small dose of the drug. The sick woman's husband, Heinz, went to everyone he knew to borrow the money, but he could only get together about $1000 which is half of what it cost. He told the druggist that his wife was dying and asked him to sell it cheaper or let him pay later. But the druggist said: "No, I discovered the drug and I'm going to make money from it." So Heinz got desperate and broke into the man's store to steal the drug for his wife. Should the husband have done that?"

The interview with Tommy proceeded as follows:

"His wife was sick and if she didn't get the drug quickly, she might die. Maybe his wife is an important person and runs a store and the man buys stuff from her and can't get it any other place. The police would probably blame the owner that he didn't save the wife. That would be like killing with a gun or knife."

(Interviewer: Would it be all right to put the druggist in the electric chair for murder?)

"If she could be cured by the drug and they didn't give it to her, I think so, because she could be an important lady like Betsy Ross, she made the flag. And if it was President Eisenhower, he's important, and they'd probably put the man in the electric chair because that isn't fair." (Should the punishment be more if she's an important person?)

"If someone important is in a plane and is allergic to heights and the stewardess won't give him medicine because she's only got enough for one and she's got a sick one, a friend, in back, they'd probably put the stewardess in a lady's jail because she didn't help the important one."

(Is it better to save the life of one important person or a lot of unimportant people?)

"All the people that aren't important because one man just has one house, maybe a lot of furniture, but a whole bunch of people have an awful lot of furniture and some of these poor people might have a lot of money and it doesn't look it."

The search for rules is taken as morality in a control community.

Kohlberg comments on the above interview with Tommy as follows:

"On the one hand we notice Tommy's reasoning ability, his utilitarian calculation of the economics of the greater good. On the other hand we notice that the calculation of value is based on a "primitive" assumption as to the basis of moral values. A prosaic and commendable concern about the wife's life is eventually based on the notion that the value of a life is determined by its "importance" and that such importance is essentially a function of the amount of furniture owned."

That Kohlberg recognizes that the six stages of development of moral thought are related to gossip and self-gossip is shown by his statement: "Our six types of thought would represent six patterns of verbal morality in the adult culture which are successively absorbed as the child grows more verbally sophisticated."

We would add: They represent children's progress toward a morality based on finding *shoulds* to gossip about that emphasize obedience to community approved rules.

If morality is viewed as "verbal morality" then the obvious implication is that children have no pre-verbal morality. Perhaps no better modern view conforms better to the 16th Century view that children are born needing Godsibs to drive away the devil.

That very young children exhibit both altruistic interest in others' well-being, as well as altruistic interest in destruction of the well-being of others is somehow ignored entirely by these studies. Concern over family members or animals suffering is ignored as a foundation for morality.

In any case simple compassion does not enter into these studies either as a given in children's lives or a given in the stories presented. "Do you think this person cares about the other person?" is not asked. I don't know, but there may have been a moral dilemma presented somewhere in the voluminous studies along these lines that asked

"Should this person have cared about that person?" If so, it would have meant that even simple compassion is obedience to a rule.

In *Alice in Wonderland* when confronted with the Cheshire cat who disappears entirely except for his grin Alice remarks: "I have often seen a cat without a grin, but never a grin without a cat."

Likewise, young children often see simple compassion with a moral should, but never before visiting the wonderland of control communities do they see a moral should without simple compassion.

---

[50] Myers, Emily F., Forrest C. Bennett, and Hans O. Doerr. *Selected Theories of Development*. Hogrefe Publishing, Cambridge, MA, 2012.

[51] A 1993 movie in which Josh Watzkin, a very young boy played by Max Pomeranc, who is a chess prodigy, refuses to allow himself to become heartless. He is an exemplar for playing a game for fun that is often played for clout. This, even though he is surrounded by adults and parental figures who are grooming him to be the next Bobby Fischer.

[52] Kohlberg, Lawrence. *Kohlberg's Original Study of Moral Development*. Garland Publishing, New York, NY, 1994. This volume contains a compendium of all of Kohlberg's original doctoral research completed in 1958 at the University of Chicago.

Chapter 14: Living in Unsafe Places Leaves Little Room for Compassion

When you feel unsafe in the presence of others, which is the case? Do you feel unsafe because you fear you will make the wrong "move" and be punished or humiliated as a result? Test anxiety generated by fear of a bad grade is an example. Or do you feel unsafe because you are trying to be in in a position to hurt others and are not sure you are invulnerable to their counter attack? White occupation of Native American lands is an example.

Which story concerning your feelings of safety is part of your life? Perhaps both. Like Janus, we often attempt to get out from under controlling authority by seeking control over those who attempt to control us. We feel unsafe because we may be counter-attacked. And/or we may also feel unsafe because we might fail in our efforts to gain and maintain a position from which we can control them.

We build our "boxes" in an attempt to protect ourselves from failure and also in order to have a place from which we can launch punishing attacks on others. Appropriate words for this kind of "box" is "stockade" or "fortification."

Stockades, as we will call them, may sometimes be built as an attempt to feel safer. But contrary to common opinion, to the extent we actually take up residence in a stockade, our fear *increases*. It doesn't decrease it. And when stockades are easily breached, the result is chronic panic. You can never be safe enough in a stockade.

In any case, whether we call them boxes or stockades, when we live in them we are likely to feel that we are surrounded with potential enemies which leaves us without compassion for those "outside."

The stockade mentality

Control communities feature a struggle between those who succeed in winning the trappings of authority and the right to assert control over others on the one hand and on the other hand those who lose from the beginning or win for a while and then lose. Our focus here is on those who are playing the game for clout against others who are also playing for clout. In other words people who are competing for control against others who are competing for control or already are in a position of control.

The Anger Habit[53] introduces the notion of a Stockade Mentality with a letter written to a fictitious client, David, who suffered with a fairly severe panic disorder. The client had suffered from panic attacks.

Panic attack is something you don't want to experience. It feels like you might be about to die. Imagine you are in an automobile that is teetering on the edge of a mountain road with a thousand foot drop below you. You can't move because you might shift the weight just enough to tip you over. How would you feel? That's about the way a panic attack feels except there is no apparent danger. The only danger is your feeling of panic. Once you have one, you do indeed have something to fear—having another one. The letter to David includes a description of a "stockade mentality" as follows:

"David, you grew up in what may be called a 'stockade atmosphere.' It was your family against the world. You were the good guys and the rest of the world was populated liberally with 'the others.'

"There are three notable things about what it means to grow up in a stockade atmosphere. First, there is always danger 'out there.' Second, there is always the need to be in an impregnable situation. And third, family control gets exercised by the threat of your being thrown back 'out there.

"... David, given the view that you grew up with—that every place outside of the home stockade was a dangerous one—public places are particularly problematic. It is not clear to you in a public place whether you are intruding on someone else's domain or not.

"Suppose another shopper lays claim to your place in line. Suppose you are seen by this person to be acting inappropriately. You're not sure whether you are going to have to back off from another's claim to these territorial rights or whether you should be prepared to defend your own rights. Because public areas by nature belong to everyone communally and no one individually, the decision is hard to make. So you rush back to the stockade, where you know what your rights are and you know what to do—attack outsiders. The first thing to notice is that the world is made out to be a dangerous place where you must be prepared at all times to attack other people and defend against their attacks.

"The second thing to notice about growing up in a stockade environment is that it is very important to have the stockade be impregnable. This means that if you are going to be prepared to attack others, you must be unreachable by others. The situation requires lots of checking to see if you are vulnerable in any way. David, this is what is happening when you get the 'guilties.' You have a whole checklist of possible chinks in your stockade that would make you vulnerable to attack from others. Naturally, these chinks concern the taboos of the society in which you grew up. These are the faults people attack and make fun of, and over which they reject others. Your concern, when you go back over your guilty transgressions of past thoughts and deeds, is whether these guilty deeds make you vulnerable today. Your way of discovering your vulnerability is to think of your deeds and see if they make you feel bad. Each time your review provokes guilt. That is, it scares you. You "prove' each time that, yes, you are vulnerable. Your memories of what you did as a child still give you a jolt of fear. Others could therefore use this whole list of transgressions against you."

Maintaining a Stockade is a tough job.

You don't have to have a stockade unless and until you have enemies. In North America, when those of European ancestry first encountered Native Americans, it was mostly for trade. In Michigan, where Janus's father found stone axe heads and arrowheads, the Potawatomi and early traders merely traded and went their own ways. Not until people start trying to control what other people think, do, or where they live, do they start to need stockades. But the stockades have to do their job. They have to make you invulnerable to those with whom you are battling for control. And that's a continuing maintenance problem.

Imagine being the maintenance foreman for a stockade in the Michigan native forest surrounded by Native Americans who your settlers and your militia have attacked. You have a twenty-four hour a day job, seven days a week. You have to anticipate every possible way you might be attacked. Is it raining? Check for a wash out under the fence where people can crawl in. Is it windy? Check for any damage done to the fence. Are trees growing too close to the fence? And so on and so on. Any chink in the stockade is a threat.

In today's world, you might imagine what it would be like to live in Israel or in the Gaza, and experience attacks that murder your friends and family. Do you think that any amount of checking of your defenses would put you at ease? Would anything short of murdering all your enemies ever solve your fear problem? The latter is a solution that has often been implemented historically.

Janus builds a stockade, a place where anxiety about others replaces compassion toward them.

The excerpted letter above, concerning a stockade mentality, was written to David who grew up in a family that taught him how to maintain the stockade. Janus grew up feeling safe.

But as is the case of many who live in control communities, he built his own stockade beginning when he engaged in control games with others who also wished to play those games. By the time he was ten or eleven he was beginning to reap the harvest that control struggles sow.

Janus took an unfortunate path through his school years and into the early part of his adulthood. What he didn't realize was that he was building a box, an increasingly scary stockade, with his attempts to acquire clout.

He continued his earlier practice of trying to beat others to the draw by out smarting them with such strategies as his version of the rope-a-dope. Like Mohamed Ali did in the boxing ring, Janus pretended to be a dope on the rope and then slammed his intellectual opponents with some idiosyncratic fact that he had picked up in his reading and used for just that purpose—making an opponent feel dumb and inferior.

He found he wasn't the only one to use this strategy when he got to college. He learned that some students would show up for exams early and hang around others, throwing out odd facts as if they were part of what should have been studied for the exam. This had the effect of panicking their student competitors just as they were getting ready to take the exam. (Piece of advice for students: Don't go to exams early if you are in a highly competitive school.)

The problem for Janus, of which he was becoming well aware, was that he was becoming increasingly anxious. He was becoming more anxious in social situations. But he was especially anxious when having to present something in front of a group or was about to take an exam. He managed to appear to be the calmest person in the world while having these feelings. But his life was becoming increasingly miserable. Morning nausea, middle of night awakening, accompanied by imagined dire scenarios and regrets. These kept him awake for hours and were part of his normal life by the time he was twenty and attending university. His stockade was requiring more and more maintenance.

He was on his way to a stockade that required full time to defend. He had to anticipate anything and everything that might go wrong with the stockade. It was anything *BUT* safe.

Anticipation of danger is the hallmark of anxiety. All anxiety is anticipatory. When a danger is actually present, we either feel nothing because we are too busy acting or we feel fear, not anxiety. Janus was becoming one anxious puppy. He could get some relief at times by associating with others who shared some of his views about "stupid students" who didn't know anything and didn't want to know. Some of the teaching fellows clearly had that view, and they identified with Janus who seemed to be interested in original sources, not textbooks. But he couldn't really join their community. He was still a lowly undergraduate.

The Janus Journey: Janus interprets his first dream and misses the point. It was trying to help him, not humiliate him.

Janus, while an undergraduate, thought he wanted to be a college professor teaching and doing research in either philosophy or psychology. He launched upon a personal study program of carefully reading important original sources by great contributors to psychology as well as philosophy.

At one point, while he was painstakingly working his way through Sigmund Freud's Interpretation of Dreams, he started recording his own dreams for analysis. One of his first dreams contained images of a ladder and also the number 87. He took Freud's lead and assumed that the dream represented some kind of wish fulfillment. In attempting to interpret the dream he free-associated to the words he had first written down when he recorded his dream—the so-called "manifest content" of the dream.

He associated "success" for the ladder. His association for the number 87 was an All American football player at his school with that jersey number. He thought that his sleeping dream reflected his very conscious "day dreams" of what it would be like to achieve being a college professor. Both "dreams" involved an important element of achievement; a dream of fame and notoriety which involved people looking up at him like they literally do at people on ladders and figuratively do at famous athletes. This must be the "wish fulfillment" that Freud said would be there.

It wasn't pleasant for Janus to entertain this interpretation which made him more confident that it was correct. Actually his discomfort was more likely due to his long term reticence to share anything that would make him vulnerable to attack by others. And writing down these wishes was close to saying them out loud.

***

His interpretation of that first dream was inadequate. But Janus's unconscious didn't give up that easily. A few days later it tried again to let him know that he was on a track that was making him miserable. It was fortuitous that at that time Janus was taking an animal learning laboratory class. They were just then studying how to train animals with aversive stimuli, such as electric shock. They were using an apparatus called a shuttle box. It was a box divided in half by a line or a low barrier. Both sides had a metal floor. A laboratory rat, once introduced to the box, could be shocked on whichever side he happened to be, and escape the shock by moving over to the other side. One could turn a light on just before the rat was shocked and "teach" the rat to escape being shocked altogether by moving to the other side before he was shocked.

This is classic control as we are using the word "control" in this work. It's not surprising that it stirred something in Janus. He called his rat Mr. Silby, after a High School teacher whose nose seemed to resemble a rat nose. He had had more than one run in with Mr. Silby. Janus had never felt any compassion toward his teacher by that name. But he felt strangely identified with Mr. Silby, the rat.

The Janus Journey: Janus tries interpreting a second dream and almost gets it right.

The night following his lab experiment with Mr. Silby, Janus awakened from a dream and promptly wrote it down as the first step recommended by Freud for dream analysis.
His written dream was as follows:
"I'm in a big room filled with people. Something has happened and people are talking about it and looking, but I can't see what they are

looking at and can't understand them, but I feel afraid of what they might be looking at. Suddenly I'm in a shed that has a workbench with all kinds of tools. The workbench is covered with rats. I somehow know that there are 87. They swarm around something they are making, like ants. It looks like they are constructing some kind of model of a river and a dam."

The next morning, Janus eagerly proceeded to analyze the dream he had written down during the night. He followed Freud's directions, which consisted of sticking to the words he had written down and free-associating to those words. His associations are below with his interpretations in bold letters.

'I'm in a big room' – **the laboratory yesterday**

'filled with people' – **people as opposed to me? Am I the rat?**

'Something has happened – ' – **whole sentence seems to be me as Mr. Silby, not understanding what the students were saying and not seeing something they could see – the shock coming? But being fearful.**

'in a shed with - ' – **woodshed? Father spanking? Incident in childhood where I got taken behind the woodshed and spanked because of something my brother did – tools like board to spank with? Or tools I used as a child in my father's workshop to build a crystal radio.**

' workbench covered with 87 rats' – **There's that number again. 87 is the jersey # of Ron Kramer, Michigan football All-American. Famous? I want to be famous like him?**

Doesn't feel right.

'They swarm around something like ants' – **ant is aunt who was stern teacher? Always in control? Ah Ha I'm Mr. Silby trying to be in control of the laboratory instead of the other way around!**

'Constructing some kind of model of a river and a dam.' – **river= current? electric current, dam to stop the current but also to back it up and flood? I'm Mr. Silby constructing an apparatus that will shock humans who shock me. Teach them? Control them?**

'Dream – **I'm the rat in the experiment yesterday. I'm building an apparatus I can use to shock the experimenters when they shock me.**

I'm also me dreaming of being famous, like Ron Kramer, in order to be in a position where I'm above others so that I can control them rather than they controlling me. Others like my older brother, parents, teachers?

*Afterthought: **Could the ladder and #87 in my previous dream mean something else? Maybe the ladder was to get out of the stadium. Get out of the box that the rats were in—trying to shock their shockers?***

Janus was uncomfortable with the result of his analysis. He still did not like to think of himself as power or status seeking. For years after that the # 87 signified to him a "problem" with power, status, and fear. But it would be years before he could come to grips with this problem and realize that he almost had the right interpretation. But he nevertheless smiled every time he thought what it would be like to construct a shock avoidance experiment in which the rats could also shock the experimenter.

***

As it turned out, Janus didn't realize that Jung's approach to dream analysis would have helped him realize what his unconscious was trying to do for him. Chapter 1 of the book he had earlier put aside in High School—*Modern Man in Search of a Soul*—contained an analysis of a business man's dream that was very similar to the correct analysis of his own "87 rats" dream.

Simply put his unconscious was saying "You have a choice. You can get the hell out of the box. Or you can stay there and play for clout and be afraid of failing." He was placing himself more and more firmly in a stockade due to his attempts to play control games with others. It was costing him not only anxiety. It was costing him his human compassion toward those he began life relating to so closely—people and animals. The number 87 wasn't just Ron Kramer as a symbol of fame and success, it was the number of the rungs in the ladder needed to get out of the box (Michigan Stadium)—the 87 rows up to the top of the football stadium, the box where people played for clout on those Fall afternoons every year.

---

[53] Semmelroth, Carl, and Donald Smith. *Anger Habit: Proven Principles to Calm the Stormy Mind.* Sourcebooks, Inc., 2004. 110-111.

Chapter 15: Leaving the Stockade

Leaving the game of clout is very difficult, especially when we are good at it. This tends to make a stockade mentality a permanent fixture in our lives. When the possibility of success is right around the corner, of being a winner, of getting to the top of the class, of getting into the best school, of becoming a doctor or professor or a rich and powerful person or something else you or your family can gossip about, it's difficult to ask yourself serious questions about what you are really up to. Please don't misunderstand. Getting an education from the leaders in a field that is precious to you or becoming a physician in order to care for sick people, are not part of seeking clout. But when the game is on, it's very difficult to ask yourself why you're doing what you're doing.

The simplest question is "Is this something I love doing?" If the game takes the form of getting into med school it's hard to ask yourself "Am I really going to love practicing medicine?" It is easy to take for granted that liking to earn money and be respected by others means I will like medicine. Are my dreams of success about working at something I love doing? Or are they about winning against others in the competition it will take to get there? It's hard for us when we get a taste of winning some clout to ask questions like "When I am a success, will I love to get up in the morning? Will my life feel voluntary? Or will I love the status and money? Will I count the time until I get enough money to retire, to get away from doing it and still have what I wanted—reputation and money?"

Janus surely loved to teach. Anyone that liked to talk as much as Janus did is likely to love teaching. You ask him how to get somewhere and he'd gladly tell you at least four ways to get there. That would fit with being a college professor, or does it? Maybe some small college where you aren't expected to publish or perish?

In any case, Janus clearly wasn't in the game to become a teacher even though he loved teaching. He was in the game of success and clout. This should have been clear to him when, upon receiving his doctoral degree, he was asked by a former mentor and teacher, who was then chairman of the department of a small college, to come and teach there. Janus refused. He had a prestigious post-doctoral award to complete and then he was looking for "bigger fish to fry." So much for teaching. It was only afterward that he regretted his decision.

Despite his sense of being in the fast lane, Janus's anxiety continued. He completed his post-doctoral work and took a university job that looked promising. He was on a course to success. But his personal well-being was not getting better. It was getting worse.

Fortunately he never forgot his first attempts to analyze his dreams. He never really forgot that he was making a choice. But he hadn't realized the damage that his choice inflicted on his natural love of helping and relating to others. He had chosen a life that involved little simple compassion toward others. This opened the door for hurting others.

Janus discovers what he's been up to.

The Janus Journey: Janus finally sees the box he's placed himself in.

Janus, now in late twenties, had been hired as an assistant professor and was quickly promoted to associate professor with tenure in a university psychology department. Like most young professors he was expected to serve on various committees within the department and the university. His teaching duties were limited to two classes per term. But he was expected to bring in research money, 50% of which the university got off the top for overhead. He was also expected to use his share to help support his research assistant, a graduate student. He also paid his own summer salary out of his research account, spending the summer with no teaching duties.

One of his duties was to serve as chairperson of the university's committee on the human use of human subjects. This committee was charged with reviewing research projects originating from any university department that involved humans in order to make sure that they treated human subjects humanely. A major consideration was whether experimenters obtained what was called "informed consent" from those who volunteered to be subjects. Another consideration was whether the subjects used in their studies participated voluntarily.

Nancy and Jack were then promising young assistant professors in Janus' department who had been hired together. [We met Nancy before as a client of Janus after he left the university, and we will meet both Nancy and Jack again.] *They had met and married while they were in graduate school at another university. Now they were under pressure to publish. Faculty bi-laws said that assistant professors had 5 years after being hired to be promoted and tenured; otherwise they would have to leave.*

Nancy and Jack were in a unique position. If only one of them were to be promoted, it would leave the other who wasn't promoted without a job and without the option of leaving the area to find another job. They were under extraordinary pressure to publish.

They jointly wrote a grant proposal, which asked for funding for an extensive line of research. It concerned male vs. female responses to instructions to administer electric shock to others in experiments. Their proposed experiments were patterned after the original Milgram study on obedience. Janus was required to bring their grant proposal before the committee on human use of human subjects for review before they could submit it for funding to a government agency.

Janus was still playing the clout game that he started way back in elementary school. This produced pissing contests with other department members. Janus had already had run-ins with some in his department because he objected to the practice of giving students, enrolled in Introductory Psychology, credit toward their grades for participating in experiments. This practice was justified by the argument that being a subject in a psychology experiment would presumably give them experience in what psychology was about. Besides, a readily available pool of subjects was handy for department members.

Janus used his skill at argument to object that this wasn't really voluntary. It wasn't any different than justifying asking students to pay their professors $10 for extra credit in their courses because it broadened their psychological experience of cheating. Janus admitted this was a bit over the top, but he still felt there was something in the practice of offering students credit that they would otherwise have to earn by studying, when the faculty stood to gain by the arrangement. But the real argument was about misleading subjects about their presumed use of electric shock to "teach" others.

When Janus's committee considered Nancy and Jack's research proposal, most members of the committee agreed with their argument that the subjects to be used in the research weren't really going to cause anyone pain. Furthermore, misleading them about what they were doing was justified by the fact that it was impossible to do the research unless they misled the subjects. Furthermore, the original research had obviously passed muster at Yale, so that should indicate that there was nothing objectionable about it.

Janus had made his argument and lost, but he continued to ruminate about it. There was something about it that resonated with him. His concern went beyond just losing an argument. He was genuinely troubled by this research and with the arguments made for it.

Janus thought long and hard about why this research especially troubled him. His thoughts took him a direction that would soon after lead him to resign his position in university teaching and devote himself entirely to private practice.

When Janus finally took hold of what he had been grasping for, he suddenly came face to face with himself in a way that exceeded even his long hard work during his own psychotherapy while he was in graduate school.

He reached a painful but liberating insight when he took seriously the harm done to those naive subjects who participated in the study— those who were asked to shock other people. Long after they had every indication they were hurting another person by "shocking" them, they continued to do it at the experimenter's urging, suffered deep discomfort and agitation, even to the point of seizures.

It clicked with Janus that his early attempts at dream analysis had involved electric shock in order to teach rats to do something. He had thought his dreams meant that he liked success. Now he wondered. Milgram's subjects were trying to get away, not from electric shock, but from the university experimenters that urged them on to administer more and more shock.

The question that leaped up at Janus was how could the experimenters bring themselves to ask their subjects to do this? The answer finally burst into Janus's consciousness. They were using their status to control the student "volunteers" and they felt little or no compassion toward them.

Stepping back one more step, how could universities sanction experimenters to do this? Treating people as subjects in an experiment somehow insulated experimenters from the lives and feelings of those "subject/people." Not that the experimenters couldn't detect and record those feelings, thoughts, and actions; but that somehow they wore insulated gloves that prevented them from feeling the human emotional changes that they were measuring. What was that insulation?

The experimenters doing these experiments were suffering from the same problem with obedience that they were demonstrating in their subjects. They were soldiers for a should-loaded ideology. They were the winners of a game for clout. They were the adults in the should-loaded ideology of adult ideology. Their subjects were children who should follow the rules of childhood. Do as their betters told them. Obey.

The subjects in Milgram's experiment also believed in the ideologies of education and research, which meant to them that it was the right thing to obey researchers and teachers. They were the adults. More importantly they became soldiers for the belief that punishing people would make them learn. But many of them had trouble turning off their compassion. They suffered in the process of attempting to hurt people. But their professors, their betters, were oblivious to their actual suffering, describing it clinically as "interesting dynamics."

Janus's insight had been difficult for him to discover because he wore the same insulation as those who proposed what he took to be inhumane treatment of people in experiments – being a soldier for the ideology of scientific psychology.

But his should-loaded ideologies and their beliefs did not stop there. He was a soldier for his own beliefs fighting soldiers for other beliefs. Control, control, and more control. He was disapproving (read, he tried to punish) people left and right on the basis of whether they did the right thing or felt the right way or thought the right way. He criticized others without trouble because they had the wrong ideology; their religion, their teaching methods, their view of art, were all fair game for him. And in doing so, he wore the same gloves that insulated him against simple compassion toward the person's standing in front of him that experimenters did while urging college students to give others more and more electric shock.

He flashed back to Miss Box in the first grade who treated him like an object. She believed in a should-loaded ideology of education and was a soldier for it. That made it the right thing to do to treat him the way she had. Janus believed in somewhat different should-loaded ideology of education that made it all right to be critical of the way his colleagues taught. Was he any less insulated from his students or his colleagues than she had been? Was he any less disapproving of students who didn't behave the way he thought "real students" should behave? And most importantly, was he any less disapproving of Miss Box than she had been of him? Where was his compassion for her as a human being? Why after all these years did he still carry disapproval of her that made her into a non-human?

Didn't his attempts to enforce his own ideology of the human use of human subjects insulate him from the thoughts and feelings of Nancy and Jack, his department colleagues as he tried to enforce how "legitimate researchers" ought to behave?

But what ideologies was he obedient to that led him to be always so critical, both of others and himself? He thought of the story his father had told him about the children in the woods who decided to increase the effectiveness of their search for a lost knife by letting one of them tell the others where to search. That was the only story of obedience that ever made sense to him. He could see how he could be disapproving of another person who didn't carry through with an agreement to obey to do their share in searching. What if one of the boys in the story had just stood around, instead of searching the area he was assigned to after agreeing to search where he was told. That didn't seem to fit. Fit what? That was the point; it was a story of voluntary obedience, and here he was looking for yet another set of shoulds that said how people ought to behave while behaving voluntarily. What a contradiction!

He had always distrusted ideologies that tell people how they should behave. How could he have come to this point?

***

We need beliefs in the form of helpful habits.

As mentioned earlier,[54] Charles Sanders Peirce, the inventor of the philosophical system called Pragmatism, referred to belief as the cessation of thought." Peirce, as other people of note, was apt to say simple things in a provocative way, like Einstein saying "God doesn't play dice with the world" or Mark Twain saying "Go to Heaven for the climate, Hell for the company."

What Peirce meant by "belief is the cessation of thought" was simply that when we believe something, we no longer scrutinize that belief, at least not willingly. The comedian Steven Wright[55] used the same basic idea to get a laugh by observing "A conclusion is the place you reach when you get tired of thinking."

"I believe in Santa Claus" says you can assume I don't wonder how Santa is going to arrive at my house with presents on Christmas Eve. I don't know and don't question how the heck he's going to get down the 'chimney—we have a furnace—but I don't bother to question how he will pay me a visit.

Peirce was correct. Beliefs are habits. Like other habits we don't think about what they are made of anymore. They are just there as a habit, or a set of habits, all wrapped up in, yes, a belief. We learn habits piece by piece that are made up of several things like walking, or playing a C Major scale on a musical instrument. But once it become a habit we don't have to think about the parts anymore. We think "walk" and we walk. One foot just goes in front of the other. Ditto playing scale on the piano, or riding a bike.

Well it is also "ditto" for things we learn about the world. We learn where East is relative to where we live and we end up believing that the sun comes up over our neighbor's house. We learn the layout of a new house we live in and we believe the kitchen is just off the family room. These beliefs merely amount to the fact that without thinking, we expect the sun will come up "over there" without thinking about where east is, and when we want something in the kitchen we go there without thinking it's just off the family room.

Habits help us whether they are behaviors or conceptions of the world. Another provocative quote from an early psychologist is "Habits are the flywheel of society."[56] We don't have to decide every day whether we should brush our teeth, we just do it. We also don't have to figure out each day what to think about whether education is good or whether we are Christian or Moslem; we believe in one or the other or something else or we can believe there is no adequate religion. We have closed the book on "why this religion." If someone asks us why, we don't think about it, we just spew habitual answers. If we don't have any of these beliefs, it just means that religion is still an open question for us.

As pointed out by George Bernard Shaw's play *Pygmalion*, habits of speech can also have a downside for those attempting to take part in the world of clout. When we speak with awful grammar in a dialect spoken by "disrespected" people, we are unlikely to have a hard row to hoe in the world of clout. In Shaw's play, a rather self-important linguist, on a bet, takes on the retraining of the speech habits of a London flour girl, and is able to pass her off as royalty.

Thanks to our simple goodness, we can avoid switching off our compassion and still have beliefs.

Being a soldier for a belief is the source of our loss of human compassion, not just having a belief. When we are soldiers for a belief, like any sort of soldiering, stockades get built and compassion gets switched off. But we can transpose a favorite musical piece into C major on the fly and play it with love, even though we remain in the new key because of habit. No one is a soldier for C major. One can have religious beliefs and political beliefs and still have friends with other religious and political beliefs. But if you are a soldier for these beliefs or your friends are soldiers for their political or religious beliefs, watch out. The common advice applies—never discuss politics or religion with friends. You risk becoming enemies if either of you starts "soldiering" for your beliefs.

Janus was now beginning to understand this. He was beginning to understand where his disapproval of others and the anxiety that had become a life companion was coming from. He *did* adopt should-loaded ideological beliefs as a teenager and had become a soldier for them. In fact he had joined a war of ideologies. He battled "Onward Christian Soldiers" with Onward Philosophical and Scientific Reason." He battled "Love thy neighbor" with "Love thy neighbor spontaneously or forget it." He battled "People should be held accountable" with "People do what they are determined to do."

Now he realized that the should-loaded ideologies that he had adopted fed him not only beliefs that were at odds with others' ideologies and beliefs. He now was seeing that he was at odds with them as believers. He was a soldier fighting under a different flag than anyone who dared to raise their own flag. If someone attempted to "preach" to him, he often found a way to preach back. Any person or group of persons that was in the control business was apt to draw his fire.

Gossips are soldiers for community beliefs, not necessarily their own.

When he was young, Janus's aunt asked him why he didn't join the church and he told her he would just be a hypocrite if he did. Her reply was that one more hypocrite wouldn't hurt the church. Looking back now on what she said, he wondered if she was telling him that there were a lot more people like him than he realized.

Gossip was everywhere in the small town where he grew up. All it took was a traffic ticket, much less a drinking problem. God help the person whose business failed or got a divorce or got pregnant out of marriage. How could the gossips, so full of disapproval, not be afraid of their reputations?

He wondered how they felt when they woke up during the night worrying where "they stood" in the "community" because they couldn't be with the others checking out how they were talked about all the time. At three in the morning, they weren't there at the country club bar or the Elks club to check how people treated their reputations.

Janus's memory of the connection he had made between community beliefs and power led him to grasp what the motor was that drove all this willingness to obey community *shoulds*. Now Janus saw the point of joining up as soldiers with any of these beliefs. They presented an opportunity for power and control and status that was unimaginable without them. The "pillars" of the community were at least outwardly obedient to the community's beliefs and the instructions that went with them and "pillar-hood" was quickly lost without their "good" reputations.

Janus now understood how he had used his love of those friends he found in books in the city library. He had discovered could-loaded ideologies to join, that expanded his horizons and stimulated his imagination. But curiously, they gave power and status in another community – the higher education community. The library had introduced him to the community of scholarship that had its own *shoulds and should not's*, and which conferred status and power according to one's obedience to them. He realized now, that when he left that town years earlier, he had gone off to the hometown of his ideologies, the university community. He took the bait and sought status and power there. Otherwise, if he had been interested in his friends in the library books he read, he could more easily have simply stayed with his books and his friends that lived in them and with other real and living friends who also loved them and loved to learn and loved each other. He could have simply treated college as a preparation for a job that he could love doing without regard for clout. Fortunately, he still had such an alternative. But he needed to walk away from playing for clout and should-loaded ideologies.

Janus resigns from soldiering.

Janus soon resigned his tenured position over objections expressed as "friendly" advice by others there, that he was being stupid or crazy or both, and that he would never be able to "get back into" university teaching. Their advice strengthened his resolve to just walk away.

---

[54] See Chapter 2 discussion of how our thoughts include all ideas and their opposites, contraries, etc.

[55] You can get to Steven Wright's books and humor by starting here: http://www.goodreads.com/book/show/16070413-steven-wright-humor

[56] See the chapter titled "Habit" in James, William. *The Principles of Psychology, Vol I*. Henry Holt and Co, New York, NY, 1890.

Chapter 16—Depression, Moral Delusions, and the Compassion Switch

Because authority in control communities rests on obedience to control, and obedience to control in turn rests on punishment or threat of punishment of "bad" behaviors, it is inevitable that those who are "in control" view themselves as morally superior to those they control. After all, what right have I to punish another person unless they are doing something bad. Nowhere is this seen more clearly than in the should-loaded ideologies of childhood and adulthood. Parents and other authorities not only attempt to teach obedience in place of simple goodness, they lay claim to moral superiority. Those who wear the mantel of "adulthood" don't just punish bad behavior, they punish disobedience. They are the ones who know right from wrong. When they punish in the name of discipline, they are punishing *bad* behaviors, among which are disobedience.

Yet, compassion and simple goodness are present in very young persons. And the moral training of young people tends to overwhelm their naturally-occurring moral sense in a pile of rules. Are the "adult" beliefs in their moral superiority to "children," delusional in nature? How so?

Two kinds of delusional belief.

Sigmund Freud described the "talk" of depressed people as a "delusion of mainly moral inferiority" in his original venture into what was then called melancholia. As far as I know he never noticed the flip side of the coin, a delusion of moral superiority.

A person's moral development in control communities is measured by how far along they are in substituting the *shoulds* of the community for their own simple compassion, and the extent to which they blame themselves for not measuring up to them. This kind of moral education suits control. It teaches a morality that serves those who are in a position to command others.

Since control over others can't really take place without the acquiescence of the controlled party, control is a delusion and must be supported by delusional beliefs.

Delusion 1 is that controllers (the "adults" of control communities) have moral superiority which entitles them to the advantages they experience. For example if Sally, the High School Valedictorian, gets into Brown University, community gossip ascribes her success to being a "good girl" from a "good family." Lest the meaning of "success" in a control community be mistaken, it will read in the High School year book that she was voted Queen of home coming. Queen's and Kings are powerful.

Why is this delusional? This is a delusion because both Sally and her family are happy about all of this and repeat it to others at every opportunity even though none of this is good for Sally. She and they are soldiers for control which, sooner or later is likely to make them miserable.

Delusion 2 is that controlees (the young or old "children" of control communities) lack success at being controllers because they are morally inferior. Their moral inferiority entitles them to be blamed for lacking advantages or possessing the disadvantages that they experience. Susan gets pregnant in her junior year in high school and is kicked out. She keeps her child and gets a job at a grocery store and takes GED classes at night in an attempt to earn a high school diploma. She and her family are ashamed of her plight and she has bouts of depression and periods of feeling very much alone in the world. Concern about her child keeps her from attempting suicide.

Why is this delusional? This is a delusion because her pregnancy was due to something she did which she rightly regrets. Unprotected teenage sex is unwise and generally a bad idea. It is delusional for both her and her family to view her as *deserving* of a hard struggle in life and nasty gossip of the community. She would rightly regret what happened. But shame is much more and much different than regret. She and her family are doing the gossip work of the control community. Like Sally, who is going to Brown, Susan and her family are also soldiers for the control community, but unlike Sally, it is already making Susan and her family miserable.

Both gossip and self-gossip in control communities promulgates these delusions of moral superiority and moral inferiority.

Acting out the delusion of moral inferiority--depression

A Christmas Story

Nancy leans forward as she walks, her head preceding her body through the Christmas shopping crowd like the prow of a tug boat cutting through a packed harbor. She keeps hold of her husband's hand behind her, their arms forming a tow line. Jack is dead in the water every Christmas. Unable to make himself shop, he resigns himself to Nancy taking charge, towing him through the stores.

Jack's head is full of unpleasant thoughts about himself and his future and just about everyone else and their futures. He not only feels bad much of the time, he feels he is bad. He thinks that this is his real self—an incompetent pretender. To the extent that he is able to show any Christmas spirit, it is indeed a show, a "Christmas pretense," every year.

The rest of the year he more often than not feels he's faking his life, too. He does not feel like a grown-up with children. In fact, he feels that he's more of a child than his children. Pretense is a familiar feeling, pretending to know things he doesn't really know, attempting things with an enthusiasm that he doesn't feel—presenting pictures to others of someone he's not.

As Nancy stops to examine a price, Jack sees the determined look on his wife's face. He doesn't think she's going to take much more of this. He has told her about how he feels about himself. She sometimes tries to reassure him that what he thinks about himself just isn't true. He would like to convince her that she's wrong; he really is worthless. He imagines her leaving him. The prospect is frightening but the possibility of even more intense suffering somehow comforts him. It's as if being punished would be satisfying.

Jack's unpleasant thoughts, like pampered but rude guests, seem to enjoy being with him and will not leave. Why don't they let him alone? What's the point of staying around just to torture him? Or is that their purpose?

Jack, being self-absorbed, doesn't see a third member of their Christmas outing: Nancy's ghost of resolve ahead of her dragging both her and him along. The desperate trio, Nancy's determination dragging her, Nancy dragging Jack, and Jack, trudge on.

Nancy often feels pretty much the same as Jack does; but she takes some comfort in believing that she hasn't "given in" to her feelings like he seems to have done. She's feels she is not a quitter like he is. Her self-blame is more centered on her inability to help Jack.

To calm and discerning eyes, the stores are even more crowded than they seem. Many struggling, but determined ghosts, creatures made out of wisps of will, battle with each other over tiny spaces left between the joyful shoppers, dragging their reluctant creators behind them. The music, decorations, smiling children, & joyful families conceal the desperate expressions of depressed shoppers among them along with their private tugboats made from sheer willpower.

***

Depression impairs our vivacity and our sense of goodness.

The two self-inflicted wounds of depression:

1. We lose heart when we are depressed. We act and sometimes feel as if we are physically sick. In fact we act in many ways like animals act when they are sick and which veterinarians call "sickness behaviors."[57] That is, we lose interest in things that otherwise may motivate us and we feel we must make extra, even extraordinary effort to do ordinary tasks of living. Even light work, mental or physical, weighs us down.58 We live an involuntary life. In other words we must drag ourselves and/or be dragged through daily tasks.

2. We lose our sense of self-goodness and self-compassion when we are depressed. We think we don't measure up to other people. We feel and think of ourselves as a failure or at least not up to being what we want to be. We feel our true self has lived a failed, even immoral, life even if this failure is unseen by our family and/or community. In other words we heap blame upon ourselves. We have a delusion of moral inferiority[59] about ourselves, as well as a delusion of moral superiority about others.[60]

Jack, whose Christmas shopping is portrayed in the above vignette, is not the "reject" that he portrays himself to be. He surely sometimes pretends that he knows things he doesn't, but he is actually a smart guy whose is quite capable in many ways. We will see this in a later Janus story. Yet he treats himself as if he does everything wrong and is a total phony.

Jack is clearly living life involuntarily as well as possessing delusions of both in own moral inferiority and of others moral superiority. Counselors like Janus encounter large numbers of clients who, when asked, "Do you feel like you are having to drag yourself through life kicking and screaming?" reply that this is exactly how they feel. But they did not start out life feeling weighted down and feeling self-blame for being unlike what they felt they were supposed to be like.

The opposite of depression: A voluntary life that we experienced as youngsters.

Jack and many in the Christmas shopping crowd around him, who also suffer, did not start out with Christmases like this. When Jack was six years old, his mother held onto his hand while plowing through stores at holiday time. But her tether wasn't needed to pull him along. It was needed to keep him from sailing off into the sea of people.

Every year Jack aches with memories of his early Christmases. He remembers trying to drag his mother toward the toy trains and other goodies, unable to move her away from her conversation with friends in the very store in which he and Nancy are now shopping.

When we are young persons, our behaviors are energetic, fueled by possibilities that hold promise of satisfaction. Our play consists of acting out the possibilities presented by story lines. Some of those stories are of being like our parents or others we admire in our lives. A youngster growing up on a farm plants a tiny crop behind the chicken coop. Another young person spends hours arranging and feeding and changing a family of dolls and is delighted to be asked to help a parent with the household tasks.

As youngsters, our imaginations are tools for psychologically effortless movement in the search for satisfaction. Christmas is a time for us to restock the tools helpful for exercising our imaginations—dolls, building blocks, toy houses, trains, anything real or virtual that imagination can use to build stories.

Jack and Nancy had also played out possibilities presented by Christmas story lines when they were young. The possibilities of gifts and joyful people and the smells of Christmas trees brought inside the house in the winter, colored lights and food and music and shopping, all fed their imaginations. And their imaginations fed their behaviors.

Among Jack and Nancy's childhood imaginings were possible ways of making their parents joyful. Jack spent nearly an hour by himself (with his mother waiting at the door) when he was eight, looking around the department store floor that stocked knickknacks, looking for just the right thing for his mother's Christmas present, finally deciding on a jelly dish that cost thirteen cents, which was all he had to spend.

Depression is self-control that drives out compassion and vivacity.

The sense of living energetically with joyful possibilities extends to most young children's everyday lives. Perhaps you can remember awaking in the morning as a young child, immediately excited about the day ahead—excited not for any particular possibility that lay ahead that day, but for many possibilities that the day contained. If you still feel that way when you wake up in the morning, you still live a voluntary life. That sense of living life voluntarily, of being free to chase satisfaction, extends beyond youth for many people and at least to some days for most. It is what we miss most when we are depressed: our imaginations no longer serve voluntary living. Some or even a lot of the time our imaginations serve an involuntary life, because we imagine bad things happening or what might have been if we had done things differently.

We serve control community interests even when they don't serve us.

Control communities—families, cliques, small towns, churches, countries, cultures, etc.—each have within them commonly accepted disapproved behaviors and people. We hardly need to describe the name-calling that separates the winners from the losers of these groups—losers, riff raff, entitled, lazy. But they all have in common that losers are bad. Read obituaries for the good names, and listen over the back fence for the bad names.

But, both winners and losers share in common the willingness to police the community by remaining ready to disapprove of those who show signs of being losers, even if they the losers are themselves. The "American dream," where we are better than average at everything, where we are richer than most, and we are respected by all, may be shared by all, but it is impossible for all to accomplish. Even though it can only exist for all in the mythical boyhood home of Garrison Keillor,

Lake Woebegone, it is important that it seem possible to everyone in real control communities. We share a common dream even though the reality cannot be shared.

Consider those who have little to no worldly goods, those who lose their jobs, those who lose their life savings, those who are unpopular, those who are ugly according to community standards or become disfigured because of an accident, those who get average grades or even less than perfect grades, those who have children who are imperfect in any of these ways; suppose all of these "failures" were to let go of the community standards and gossip that defined them as failures. There would be no control community left.

It is imperative that losers stick around in control communities. If "losers" simply left or dropped out, there would be no people to look down on, no community to exploit, no community members to give deference and admiration to those who rose to the top. If losers in a beauty contest and those who had no hope of competing in them were to seek other values than beauty, who would be left to admire the winners?

Involuntary living keeps the relationship between status and authority alive. Involuntary living along with delusions of moral inferiority is the self-policing mechanism needed for control in an authoritarian family, community, or culture.

It is easy to see the importance of self-disapproval portrayed in the universal importance placed in confession of sins, both in religious practice as well as civil prosecution. Showing that one abhors one's failure is the most important thing a defendant or a petitioner for forgiveness can do to attempt to reduce their sentence and/or to obtain absolution. Children learn quickly to not only "take their punishment" but to show that they agree that they should have been punished in order to be accepted as a "good" child. Children who merely want to learn and have their questions answered, but don't care about "good grades" are considered disruptive "smart mouths" and expelled or given off-putting psychiatric diagnoses such as Antisocial Personality Disorder.

On the other hand, those who acknowledge that they want good grades and fail to get them are given a place in class, a lower one, but still a place, as well as much different and less off-putting diagnoses, even transparent euphemisms such as being "special." Their acknowledgements of failure validate their community membership, even if their behaviors don't. They must learn to blame themselves, and in the process their compassion for themselves is switched off.

When we experience a loss of status or money we tend to become less active, more withdrawn, sleep more, and ordinary pleasures seem less pleasurable and less attractive.

A technical name referring to loss of interest and pleasure, is anhedonia, a ten dollar word that just means "not being able to experience pleasure."

When losers in the game of clout, the competition for control, react to their loss by losing heart, and losing their taste for the prizes that the winners will "feast on," the winners become more secure. Their competition decreases. They take themselves out of competition.

In summary, loss of heart and hope is triggered by losses and failures in those areas that the control community holds dear—power and success in any area that bestows power useful for maintaining a delusion of moral superiority. Loss serves to grease the game of clout by keeping losers in the community, even though it does not serve their well-being; it also serves to reduce their interest in competing for success.

---

[57] Hart, B. L. (1988). "Biological basis of the behavior of sick animals." *Neurosci Biobehav Rev 12*(2): 123-137.

[58] See for example: Dantzer, R. (2006). Cytokine, sickness behavior, and depression. *Neurologic Clinics, 24*(3), 441-460. Also Dantzer, R., & Kelley, K. W. (2007). "Twenty years of research on cytokine-induced sickness behavior." *Brain, Behavior, and Immunity, 21*(2), 153-160.

[59] See Sigmund Freud's detailed description of melancholia detailing depressive self-condemnation far beyond anything that Freud could substantiate as being

justified by facts of the person's life, in the essay *Mourning and Melancholia* in Gay P. (Ed.), *The Freud Reader*. New York, NY, US: W W Norton & Co.

[60] Freud does not mention the depressive delusion that others are superior. This delusion, however, is implicit in the depressive willingness, even compulsion, to confess to others in authority. Therapists and other priest-like people often fulfill this role.

Chapter 17: Grief is Different (When We Don't Mix It with Depression)

Grief is produced by loss, just as is depression. But the loss involved is very different. Simple grief, that is, grief that is uncomplicated by the presence of depression is produced by the loss of a loved, or hated, object.

There are two kinds of grief—compassionate grief and destructive grief.

When one loses a loved one or friend or even finishes a loved project such a problem one has been working on, one's love then has no place to go. Like a dammed up river, one's actions can no longer reach their destination.

Likewise when one loses a hated person or someone who they are used to battling, one's destructive attempts toward that person have no place to go. Loss of people with whom one has had a control relationship involves some of both compassionate grief and destructive grief. The empty nest syndrome is experienced by parents regardless of the extent to which they are controlling or compassionate parents.[61]

Grief over the loss of loved ones and valued objects is a care package of feelings returned to sender. If we have caring compassion in our lives toward someone or something and we lose the object of our compassion, we can no longer deliver the compassion we are used to delivering. We are stuck with an inventory of compassion that at least temporarily, has no place to go. Unlike depression which switches compassionate caring off, caring continues when we grieve.

But destructive passion that regularly feeds our attempts to control others can also be part of our lives. When we are threatening others with our anger because they aren't behaving the way we want them to, we are exercising our capacity for hateful and destructive feelings, thoughts and actions. Just as love has objects, so do destructive feelings. When the objects of our threats and "soldiering" recede out of our reach or are lost altogether, we also grieve that loss. We are left with an inventory of blame and threat that has no place to go. Often it goes to whatever target is handy. When bombing targets are wiped out or recede, the bombs are sent to the descendants of those who are gone.

It may seem odd to think of grieving over the loss of an enemy. However, the loss of either the object of our caring or the object of our hate, disrupts our caring compassion or our hateful feelings and thoughts. But before examining grief due to our loss of the opportunity to threaten, blame, or destroy, we will look at what is commonly seen as grief, the loss of loved ones or valued objects, and then the common error we make about its nature.

Caring grief leaves us with compassion that has no place to go.

Grief is not over the loss of *getting* love or anything else. It is not selfish. It is a loss of opportunity for loving and caring for someone or something of value. It is caring compassion left without its object.

Yes, many loving relationships yield something in return. But return can be minimal or even non-existent. What is often mistakenly thought of as reciprocation of love, actually serves as an assurance that one's love has reached its mark. A child's smile, or the molding of a newborn's body to our body when we first pick her up, reassures us that our caring regard is being accepted. This does not mean that young children don't actually love us. It only means that children's love of their parents is shown by their spontaneous attempts to comfort parents, not necessarily by their acceptance of their parents' love. If we make progress on a painting of a sunset, the progress is proof that the work is worthwhile; the work begins to speak to us. It is telling us we are contributing to a valued object. This does not imply that it returns our love.

The Janus Journey: Janus learns how to help people who are grieving.

Janus loved to walk and did so every day, rain or shine. His walk often took him through an arboretum as well as a cemetery. One day, while walking through the cemetery, he noticed a young couple in the distance who seemed to leave something at a grave. This aroused his curiosity, so while returning that way, Janus investigated. He found the grave of an eight-year-old child. On the headstone was a McDonald's hamburger.

Janus, by then, a fairly seasoned counselor, was affected deeply by this poignant demonstration of grief. A grieving couple was continuing their attempt to care for their dead child. It opened a door for him to be more helpful to those of his clients who were suffering grief.

Sometime later, a young couple came to him for counseling. They also had lost a child a year before, during the third trimester of pregnancy, and were approaching the first year anniversary of that loss. The year before, they had named the child, prepared a room for her, and were preparing in every possible way to care for and love this unborn child. Now, a year later, the room remained. Their preparations for caring and loving remained. The child was gone. They were frozen in their preparations for giving to and loving someone who was not there.

Janus was able to tell them what he had imagined soon after he found the hamburger at a child's grave site.

Janus's imagined story was about how that couple finally came to terms with the mistake they had made about why they had to continue suffering—that their grief could never be resolved. He imagined that on one of their regular graveside visits they talked to their lost child. They told their dead child they had a great deal of love to give him, but could no longer express that love by taking care of him. They asked his permission to direct their love to another child. They felt that their child loved them and readily approved and applauded their idea.

Janus's young clients, after hearing the story, looked at each other in a way that said they had a lot to talk about. Two weeks later they reappeared in the office, looking like different people. They were beginning to be unstuck from their grief and were considering ways to find a home for their loving care.

***

Hanging on to enemies: Destructive grief leaves us with anger and hate that have no place to go.

We also have the capacity for voluntary living based on something very different from compassionate caring for others. The vivacity that comes with voluntary living can be supplied to our imaginations and actions from a very different inner source. From childhood, we are quite capable of energized and voluntary destructiveness. Sigmund Freud, after experiencing the terrible devastation perpetrated in WWI, explored man's destructive tendency, positing a self-destructive drive. He followed this with another conjecture, that to protect ourselves from our self-destructive tendencies we turn them outward, producing the raw material for destructive thoughts and actions aimed at others and other objects.[62] [63] The account given here does not agree with Freud's view in that there is evidence from the beginning of life that we enter the world readily equipped to attack and destroy. The evidence for our destructive capacity is found in the destructive behaviors of young children directed at others such as biting and hitting others, the destruction of toys, and the violent temper tantrums that erupt when the child's attempts to control others and events are taken out of their controlling reach.

Our destructively-driven thoughts and actions, although voluntary and sometimes performed at great personal expense as Freud observed, are by their nature for the sake of hurting another, not helping ourselves—they are selfless in the same way that altruistic actions are selfless—they take place without regard to the cost to one's own well-being. As we have seen, they form a way of living and acting that is the exemplar for what switches off the compassion switch when we are engaged in attempts to control other people.

We see examples of the compassion switch being switched off in everyday life when parents' caring attempts devolve into control attempts with threats, and sometimes into overt aggression toward the child for whom their intent was originally caring. Examples are also plentiful on the highway in the form of road rage. The road to control others and events is paved with selfless willingness to blame and punish without measure.

But when the objects of our blame and control recede from our capacity to deliver threat and harm, we are left grieving, with unused and useless blame and anger.

Grief triggered by "out of range" targets of a person's blame and anger is commonly seen in the psychological clinic, although seldom recognized as such. More often it is misunderstood as a reaction to residual hurt from those who have hurt the client, rather than as a diminished opportunity to launch and deliver effective blame and anger. As a result, efforts in counseling can be misdirected to the details of how and why clients continue to hurt so much, rather than why clients continue to blame. Blame, without the opportunity to punish and attack successfully is excruciating. It often occurs when people who have been involved in controlling relationships have diminished opportunity for controlling the other person. Their former partner is "around," but no longer living in close proximity. They remain on the "horizon," but are out of effective range.

The Janus Journey: Janus attempts to help a client recover from her destructive grief

Janus's clinical practice, like most, included many divorced and divorcing clients. And like most clinicians Janus soon became puzzled by the lengths that clients would go to in order to harm their ex-spouses. It was not unusual for one party to spend a thousand dollars and sometimes much more in attorney fees in order to force their former partner to pay a few hundred dollars in insurance premiums or to recover a piece of furniture that neither of them valued, but just didn't want the other one to get in the settlement. And perhaps the saddest too-common occurrences were parents who had demonstrated no particular interest in parenting but who battled tooth and nail for physical custody of children.

Janus came face to face with his misunderstanding of his clients' reasons for battling while seeing a middle-aged lady, Doris, who 25 years after her divorce was still battling with her ex-husband. Janus's incredulity at couples spending money, time, and effort at delivering blows to their ex-spouses, when the blows they delivered cost them more dearly than the "punishment" they meted out, had been based on his own simplistic economic view of their behavior.

To him they were merely doing something that was economically irrational. This explanation routinely misled him into attempts to help his clients think about the economics of what they were doing. He rarely succeeded. But Doris's twenty-five year battle didn't seem to fit. She was very bright and certainly rational about money. She was highly organized and seemed to be able to adapt to changes that came along. So instead of going down the same old roads he had in the past—attempts to resolve the emotionality involved so she could act rationally—it occurred to him that such behavior might be viewed as grief. But grief connected to what loss? Perhaps the loss of opportunity to effectively blame someone she had been used to blaming?

Janus asked Doris straight out: After 25 years of weekly battles and angry phone calls following her divorce, why was she still angry at her ex-husband? Did it make sense to her that they may both be continuing *to try to hurt and blame each other the way they did when they were married? Maybe they were both left hanging by the divorce in their attempts to control each other. Maybe they had spent 25 years trying to get the last word that would properly stamp out the resistance of the other to taking on self-blame.*

Doris's quizzical look lasted only for a moment before she declared that was the most ridiculous thing she ever heard. She was damn glad she got rid of him and hadn't regretted the divorce for a moment. Janus replied with the suggestion that our grief fills us with feelings we can no longer carry through on toward those we have lost. He was wondering about why her angry feelings stuck around so long. He told Doris the story of parental grief over the loss of a child and how the parents rescued themselves by realizing it wasn't loss they grieved, it was loss of the opportunity to care for a loved one. Perhaps Doris's and her ex-husband's anger was like that; perhaps they had lost the opportunity to blame each other into submission—to really get the other one.

Doris sat silently for several minutes. Then she tearfully began talking about her hate toward her former husband, how he had abandoned her emotionally when she got terribly sick when their children were very young and she couldn't care for them. Tears alternated with loud cursing at him as she experienced more and more of her rage culminating in the statement that she would give her life to kill him. As she said this her eyes opened wide and she said, "Oh my God! I can't let go of trying to punish him."

Their remaining sessions together were more and more about all human beings' capacity for destruction. They shared stories illustrating how people they knew and they themselves had expressed selfless anger, that is, a willingness to sacrifice our own well-being in order to be destructive to the well-being of another person. They talked about how necessary it is for us to own up to our capacity to be destructive in order for us to have a choice to make—the most important choice we can make about our lives—choosing to develop and listen to our caring and loving self instead of our destructive selves.

Doris was able to rescue herself from herself at last. She later came to see Janus occasionally and they passed the hour catching up on one version or another of their experiences of what they had agreed on when they had ended her regular counseling—that we human beings can be such pathetic creatures.

***

Why we fail to recognize the selfless nature of our caring and hating.

Growing up in a control culture distorts our view of freedom and voluntary living. We naturally come to think that doing as we please for our own ends is what it means to be free. We miss the fact that not only is "doing as one pleases," taken in the sense that others must get out of our way and otherwise kowtowing to us, is a delusion. But unfortunately this delusion is plausible if we have the means to threaten others who are in our way. In other words we miss the fact that our idea of "doing as we please" depends on our willingness and capacity to be destructive.

The "good feelings" we experience concerning this notion of freedom come from our experience of our simple destructiveness. As a youngster, Janus felt terrific and a sense of freedom while destroying the block towers he had built. Since willingness to control implies willingness to make destructive threats—destroy something if necessary—controlling others taps into our capacity to be selflessly destructive. The ideal of freedom that says we can do as we please carries the same natural oomph that loving behaviors carry. It is one way of living voluntarily if we choose to live a life devoid of compassion and relationships that confer upon us our personhood. We would be free, but very alone.

We start out wanting to play games because we love the games. We play with toys because we love the toys. We please our parents because we love our parents and therefore want to see them pleased. We naturally act for the sake of others and other things and derive satisfaction from doing so. But we also have a natural capacity to act for the destruction of others. We destroy toys because their destruction satisfies us. We bite because we derive satisfaction seeing harm come to those we bite. We are capable of both care for other beings and destruction of other beings, and both without regard for what the cost may be.

But all this is hidden from us in control communities. Neither Janus as a young man, or his clients later in life, understood that they grieved because they were *unselfish*, not because they were selfish. Loss looked to them like a loss of something they benefitted from, not loss of their ability to deliver benefit, or destructiveness, to others.

How does this change take place? The key to answering this question is to look at the ambiguity of the nature of control in control communities.

When we are successful in a control community we are exercising voluntary living because we are acting in accordance to our natural capacity for exercising selfless destructiveness—we are "destroying" unwanted behaviors of others out of selfless destructiveness which gives these behaviors the "oomph" that comes with voluntary living.

At the same time we benefit by our success. We are successful in winning and exercising status and leadership in a control community by borrowing from our capacity for threat and harm for the sake of destruction of others. But these efforts get us something more than satisfaction. They get us respect and praise by others—success in a control community. And as children in control communities we are presented with a plethora of examples of success and its rewards, while of course being told that above all we must care about winning them.

Thus, control in a control community depends on threats which are driven by the controller's capacity for selfless destruction, all the while viewing the actions as selfish.

Therefore the default position of the compassion switch in a control community is off for the winners except with close family members and friends. This is why any signs of compassion on their part are viewed as exceptional virtues worthy of inclusion in their obituaries, along with, of course, a recounting of their successes in accumulating status, power, and wealth. Again, viewing selflessness as exceptional testifies to the "fact" that selfishness is expected to rule successful people.

Also, because *shoulds* are viewed as the reason for caring about others in control communities, caring about others is also viewed as selfish. The selfless nature of caring as well as the selfless nature of destructiveness are lost in favor of explanations built on needs and motives with personal well-being as the central view of ourselves and others.

Our misunderstanding of loss shows up as trouble in grief and depression.

Our community-wide misunderstanding about what is lost when we lose someone or something prolongs the pain. The grieving couple in Janus's office continued to grieve because they thought they lost the opportunity to "get" something. They both had been raised in the cultural belief that pain is caused by not getting what one wants or losing what one had. Once they understood that what they were suffering was a lost opportunity to *give* something to a child, they started to recover.

We can do something about finding a new place to direct our vital interests. But we can never restore to the present what is now in the past. A life based on never losing anything would devolve into a changeless frozen void, a life that tolerates no change and therefore by definition has no future.

Janus's clients thought of themselves as needy and pathetic because they were hurting so bad that the hurt must mean something had been taken away from them. They were helped by seeing that they were hurting with love that no longer had a place to go. Seeing opportunities, once again, for the exercise of that love relieved their suffering. In the case of a couple that had lost their child, they asked, and felt they received, permission from their dead daughter to give to another what was to be hers. They were on their way to recovering a sense of optimistic freedom and planned for a family again.

Grieving leaves us with a wellspring of love, compassion, and/or anger and many other feelings and expectations that no longer have a place to flow. Simple grieving, uncomplicated by depression, does not switch off compassion, nor does it shut off destructive feelings. On the contrary, it leaves us with feelings with no place to go. It leaves us with an accumulation of feelings, like rising restless waters against a dam, which no longer have a way to spend their potential energy. It fills us up with the means to do those things which no longer have ends to achieve.

Grieving is our response to the loss of objects of our concerns. Grieving occurs when an object of our loving, our hating, or our liking, is missing. We mourn to one degree or another every time we lose something, big or small—the loss of a loved one who dies or leaves, the loss of food when we diet while still wanting to eat, the loss of a cigarette when we quit smoking when we still want to smoke. We suffer with some degree of grief through many of life's changes.

While grief entails the loss of people to whom we wish to express our love, depression, on the other hand, entails the loss of the ability to feel our love for people who are still with us. We may not even be able to put on an act of loving, without forcing ourselves to do so. We know the words to life but have forgotten the music.

Grieving fills us up with feelings. Depression drains us of all feeling except pain.

Self-control is at the heart of depressive pain.

As we have seen we, as members of control communities, participate in control through gossip and self-gossip. And as we have also seen, control relies on our capacity to act destructively toward someone without regard for their well-being.

Self-control therefore entails our capacity to become destructively engaged with ourselves with lack of compassion toward ourselves. Depressive pain and depressive self-destruction, even to the point of self-murder, point once more to the "self-less" nature of our destructive drive, once it is engaged. Our view of ourselves as selfish and acquisitive sets us up for trouble when we lose clout. Loss of money, loss of affection, loss of reputation, loss of position — all of these become grounds for a charge of failure, and a sentence of obedience to another's control. And it is a sentence which lacks compassion, even for oneself, because it is energized by only one thing—our capacity for compassionless and selfless destruction.

Depression is a self-sentence. A large part of that sentence is the loss of compassion not only for others, but for ourselves. Our feeling tank is empty except for pain. Unlike grief, we fail to feel the love we know or think we have toward people and things we know or think we value. Deeply depressed clients often confess that they know they love their children, but they don't feel that love. The only feeling that they have, that they know is genuine, is pain. Relief from that pain is what they seek, often with self-medications such as alcohol or other anesthetic-acting substances. These "solutions" combine the aims of the two diverse desires for using them—they relieve some of the pain and also destroy. Drinking oneself to death is not just an expression.

Both depression and grief are problematic in control communities. Their problematic nature can be traced to the same source—the nature of control and its effect on compassion. Depression results from the application to oneself of the community's method of control. One becomes a soldier for the *shoulds* of the community; even a soldier against oneself. Self-blame, even self-destruction becomes a way of self-control. Like the police inspector's last action in *Les Miserables*, Javert's suicide, one is willing to execute oneself for being a bad policeman.

Grief, which by itself is absolutely necessary for living and moving on through change, also becomes problematic in a control community because of the nature of control and its effect on compassion. In order to maintain the notion that control is the heart of community order, one must believe that behavior in general is dependent on selfish ends.

Economics is the closest thing we have to a science of control based on this principle, although psychology has contributed greatly. If it is true that behavior is based on selfish ends, then grief must last forever, and compassion is just a smokescreen for getting something one wants.

The title of Richard Dawkins' book, *The Selfish Gene,* is peculiarly unfortunate and misleading. Its reference to selfishness has nothing to do with his argument. The book is about altruism. Bottom line, altruism can be seen as a good thing for survival of some species, especially social species who rear their young. Perhaps it isn't a stretch to attribute his choice of title to the fact that people in control communities, his audience, expect there to be selfishness lurking somewhere wherever any human behavior occurs, including altruistic behavior. The notion of a selfish gene is just silly. Our survival as a human race depends on compassionate care for our children. It is the survival of hierarchical control systems that is dependent on believing that we are selfish.

The facts are that we do think of ourselves as basically selfish and do look for self-serving "real" motivation. This presents a large obstacle for helping people to think otherwise, especially about themselves.

As Janus learned very well in his practice, clients want to know what they "should do" in order to relieve suffering. Because they are already paid up members of a control community, they are actually asking how to control themselves better by being given self-serving reasons to threaten themselves. This is like trying to cure an overdose of heroin by taking more heroin. They want to cure the results of their overdose of self-control and self-blame by yet another regimen of self-control and self-blame.

Some suggestions for achieving compassionate self-guidance are contained in the next and in following chapters that don't depend on self-control involving self-threats and blame.

---

[61] Studies of parenting styles show that authoritative parenting and autonomy-granting parenting are not opposite ends of a continuum. That is, they can co-exist. There is no reason to believe that relationships other than parenting are different in this respect. That is, a very controlling spouse may or may not also be respectful at times. See for example: Silk, Jennifer S., et al. "Psychological Control and Autonomy Granting: Opposite Ends of a Continuum or Distinct Constructs?" *Journal of Research on Adolescence* 13.1 (2003): 113-28.

[62] Freud, Sigmund. *Beyond the Pleasure Principle*. Ed. Ernest Jones. London, England: The International Psycho-Analytical Press, 1922.

[63] Freud, S. (1962). *The Ego and the ID*. New York: Norton Library.

Chapter 18: The Joy Test for Discovering Goals That Keep Compassion Alive

Whither goes thou?

Behavior takes us places. But where? Our habits take us down well-worn paths of tooth brushing, reading, fighting with our spouses, placing our fingers on the right guitar string or on the right piano key. In other words our habits take us many places we have been before. Then there is our self-talk that also takes places we have been before because the self-talk is guided by habit. Depressive self-talk is like that. We have learned to gossip to ourselves the way the control community gossips about "losers."

However we can talk to ourselves in ways that invent stories about where we want to take our lives. We have pointed out that when we are young we invent stories every morning about where we want to go that day. Janus's stories had to do with the woods and the creek on the farm he grew up on. Many of his stories were about exploring new places. At Christmas a young Jack invented stories about pleasing his mother with a present and receiving presents that replenished his toy supply. Maybe he would get an electric train which he could use to go to imaginary places. Or maybe he would receive a set of Lincoln Logs so that he could build buildings that would take him on adventures in an imaginary time and place in the woods, surrounded by wild animals.

As Jack and Janus grew older, it became more difficult for them to decide where they were going and where their habits were taking them. They exercised their imaginations less, and they searched for rules more. Where they were going became more a question of what they *should* do than what they *could imagine doing.*

Finding right directions for ourselves

Full-fledged membership in a control community means one lives with a "conscience" that targets not only oneself, but also others. This means we learn to go where we *should* go and attempt to control others likewise. Because control involves threats, in practice we and others learn more about where *not* to go than we learn where we *should* go.

In the movie *Rebel Without a Cause*, a teenage character, Jim Stark, is played by the iconic actor James Dean. In one of the only three movie parts he played before his unfortunate early death, he portrays beautifully the tragic part of a teenager in search of what he should do. As Jim Stark, he portrays the conflict created by attempting to conform to all the diverse warnings of where he shouldn't go in life and losing sight of any sense of where he wanted to go. Movie viewers feel their hearts being torn when James Dean cries plaintively "Mom, I just... Once I want to do something right!"

Having a should-loaded conscience, while hanging on to one's innocent simple compassion, produces a dissociation between two major parts of who we consider ourselves to be. Am I the one who believes I *should help others* vs. Am I the one who believes I *want to help others*. This two-part conscience sets the table for uncertainty in one's understanding who they really are. This is especially the case for our behaviors that are punished. When one tries to conform to *should nots* of the community the question arises, is the real "me" the one trying not to do what I shouldn't do? Or is the real me the one who would rather do it? Who is the real me? The one trying to avoid my spouse's disapproval by not going out with my friends? Or the one who wants to go out with my friends?

The attempt to swallow whole the conflict between pretending to feel good about doing something and continuing to feel otherwise has been referred to by psychoanalysts as the foundational lie of morality.[64] The lie consists of displaying to an authority agreement and behaviors that comply with their wishes while feeling and acting in private according to the opposite sentiment. It might better be called the foundational lie for obedience.

An obedient dog walks at heel with a loose leash as if he were acting voluntarily. An obedient child pretends to feel happy showing deference to an adult despite feeling and displaying private contempt. Both are acting on a lie that supports the control community within which they live. They are both displaying in "public" a willingness to behave, which in private or other circumstances they do not wish to perform, and don't. The dog, when off the leash and more than a few feet away from the master, is likely to act otherwise than coming to heel. In private or when on the playground with friends, the child is likely to pursue language, thoughts, and fantasies about the adult that are anything but deference. One might rephrase this process again as "out of this hypocrisy the morality of should-loaded ideologies comes into existence."

The child is taught to head for one destination while being observed while secretly still heading elsewhere. While Janus was learning to avoid helping neighbors before helping his own family, he secretly helped them while appearing not to. Despite being taught to avoid looking up girls skirts, he continued to covertly pay attention to any chance occurrence that might present itself. Was he the boy who thought about and took every opportunity to look up girls skirts or was he the boy who demonstrated to others that he wasn't interested in what might be seen there?

Our secrets have been long recognized as a source of unhappiness. People go to confession, clients go to counselors, and friends try to relieve their "consciences" by confessions to their friends. These confessions are likely to be met with yet another layer of *shoulds*.

Some philosophers and many psychologists elaborate on these *shoulds*. They add some "shoulds" to those of the control community or they substitute other "should nots" for the community "should nots" such as "You should recognize what is within your control and what is not." Or they add some shoulds concerning how you may lessen your suffering such as "You should stay in the present" or "You should become aware of your breathing."

Rules only rule when they require obedience.

The reader may immediately recognize the absurdity hidden in a search for rules for getting away from the consequences of living one's life by following rules. It's like asking for a master to run your life in such a way that your life is not being run by a master.

In addition to those mentioned above, the control community promulgates many rules for living, meant to help you with the depression and anxiety that accompany obedience to control. Just let go of it—Stop your whining—Control yourself. These are little different from the "debriefing" Milgram's subjects received who suffered from having "shocked people"—something their simple compassion no doubt rejected.

Milgram's subjects suffered from anxiety and even seizures resulting from going along with "You-should-not-quit" instructions. They thought they were administering painful electric shocks to people who were writhing as if they were in pain. But they were "debriefed." Is there any "debriefing" that would change what they did? Would instructions in minding their anxiety or bad feelings about themselves by "staying in the here and now" or telling them they were being irrational by feeling bad about what they did because they didn't really shock anyone" help them? Could the experimenters have faced telling them that yes, they did a bad thing? No. They were obviously not in a position to tell their subjects, who they had harassed into doing a bad thing, that they are humans and sometimes we humans do bad things.

Yet clinical depression and anxiety problems are treated with instructions one "must obey." Early in his practice, before he took seriously that his clients were likely to have the same problems he had with control, exacerbated by his soldiering against control with control, Janus took the usual approaches to anxious and depressed clients. His efforts consisted of trying to teach anxiety-ridden clients to "stay in the here and now" or trying to teach them that they were being irrational and would "lament" if they think they are in control of things that they had no control over.[65] His efforts met with short term success, but long term failure. The initial success was almost certainly due to the fact that the clients now felt they had discovered a psychologist that knew what ailed them and could tell them what to do about it. The extra benefit of the short term success was that his referrals increased. Concerned family members and concerned doctors referred clients because they were tired of telling them they had nothing to worry about. They didn't know what to do with them and were relieved by changes in the clients brought about by an "expert."

Longer term, the recurrence of client's problems was merely taken as indicating they were difficult patients and required more treatment. The long term failure was almost certainly due to the fact that when failures to do what he told them to do occurred, it re-enforced their belief that they were a bad client and they would need to work extra hard and extra-long in order to fix their broken life. This also had a positive effect on Janus's practice. But it didn't have a positive effect on Janus.

Janus finds a rule that doesn't rule: Teaching clients to consult their simple goodness.

As Janus ridded himself of the control baggage that hid from him his own simple compassion, he searched for ways to help his clients escape along the same path. He wasn't about to commit the cardinal mistake of becoming a soldier for his beliefs in individual self-determination. Instead, he began to rely on the use of stories. He was, for the first time in his life becoming much less critical of religious views and saw the rich lode of biblical stories (religion treated as an imagination-fed ideology rather than as a should-loaded ideology) as a way to be of some help some to his religious clients. He saw that as long as "believers" and wannabe believers weren't soldiers for their faiths, they were doing important work on their own lives in their grappling with their beliefs and spiritual well-being. A couple of clients even included him on their church prayer board. They worried about Janus's church-less life, while otherwise respecting his attempts to be of help to them.

Finally making his peace with religion, freed him to work honestly with religious as well as secular clients. One such client, Ruth, had brought in her teenage son, Bill, who was in the usual difficulties born of disobedient children in school. He saw them for a few sessions and mostly tried to reassure both Ruth and Bill, that Bill was better than either of them thought, and that they had the most important thing teenagers and their parents could have. She and her son still talked openly and honestly with each other. This very fact is what was frightening Ruth. Bill was sharing with her his doubts and feelings about school and adults and Ruth's religion.

They were a refreshing change for Janus, who was use to parents and teens who couldn't have a conversation without it turning into a control struggle. He reassured both of them and emphasized their success at being open with each other. He urged them to keep the door open for communicating without feeling the other was trying to control. Bill could utilize his mother's experience and her input to make wiser decisions if the door for communication were open. Janus's reassurance and advice that they both attempt to "keep the door open" between them, lessened Ruth's concerns and opened for her a door to imagine a good future for them. They terminated their counseling sessions after a few weeks.

A few years later, Janus received a letter from Ruth who had moved with Bill to another city. The letter was a sort of report on how they were doing. But mixed into it was pain. She felt Bill was renouncing religion and she was terrified at the prospect.

Janus's rely to Ruth is below.

The Janus journey: Janus tries to help repair a bridge between mother and child.

Dear Ruth,

Let me apologize for such a tardy response to your lovely letter. I could plead being busy as an excuse, but the real reason for my delayed response is that your letter concerning Bill touched me with its motherly compassion and thoughtful ideas. I have waited to gather my thoughts and feelings until I could hopefully compose a response worthy of your inquiry.

First, concerning your comments on my family, it is true that we tried to raise our children with inquiring minds. But we didn't make a big deal out of their religious beliefs. As to spirituality, it is my belief that this is something of overwhelming importance and is too important to "pass on" to our children before they are old enough to have experienced the trials of living and have the mental tools to commit themselves willingly to some sort of faith that can stand up to the scrutiny of an enquiring mind. What we too often see is either adults who have been inoculated as children with teachings they do not understand and therefore reject for the rest of their lives, or adults who substitute "know it all" beliefs for faith due to their early education.

I take faith, by its very nature to be an act without proof of result. And by its very nature cannot be proven to people. As we come to realize as adults, that we can prove nothing about the future, not even the next second, and acquire a healthy skepticism of what we think we know for sure, it is then that faith and spirituality can find a place in our everyday lives. Every act is an act of faith.

But as I said, faith is an act, and as with all acts it must originate in freedom in order that it be an original creation of the agent actor (us). Your response may be that faith is through God's grace. In my way of thinking, what Christian's call God's Grace is actually the recognition that we cannot have earned all that is good in our lives. That life is truly a gift, and that something cannot be a gift and also be earned. Isn't this what Christmas is supposed to be about? Doesn't it celebrate the creator's gift, a gift that was given without measuring its cost to the giver? Does it make sense to call something a gift that was given by measuring it according to costs and benefits of giving it?

My view is that creation is truly a gift, meaning that there are no motives that can be used to explain the creation of humans and their motives. My objection to present Western religious doctrines is that they attribute natural attributes to the creator of nature. The source of creation cannot have attributes that didn't exist until the creator created them.

But the source of creation and the gift of life and of everything that has ever existed and ever will exist is as mysterious as children's play. The best we can do to explain truly creative behavior is that it is done out of Joy of doing it. To give motives or inclinations or any other familiar attribute to the creator of these attributes is to deny that they were created by "it" or "him" or "her," take your choice. The same may be said of human play, creation, and love. To explain them with motives is to deny that they exist as creative acts by their creators. It is in this sense that Bill may be correct in saying that he doesn't believe in God. That is, any creator which has attributes which we can know other than as being beyond all that we can know.

There is much in religious writings, including the bible that suggests such a view. For example the name of God, "I am I am", makes the predicate into the subject.

But none of this speaks to faith and spirituality. It is my belief that spirituality comes into our lives, not from faith in an eternal God with biblical characteristics, but from faith that giving without measure exists. I am not so presumptuous to believe that I know what the true historical Jesus, or Buddha, or their predecessors, the Egyptians, actually taught. But it seems to me that they all focused on man's ability to create for the sake of creation, and that doing so is Joyful. Not the belief that it will result in joy, but is Joyful in the doing of it. Much is made of human suffering by those who, in my opinion, utilize these religions as a means for controlling others. To me, "the good news" is not "if you do as I say and what I tell you to do, your suffering will disappear in heaven." It is that busying yourself with that which you do without measure will be joyfully done. For me this means that the meaning of my life is the possibility of Joy in everyday creation.

Creating something of value, that is created without measuring its worth to the creator, can only mean that it will be of worth to others, otherwise it wouldn't be of value. This means that it contributes to the wellbeing of others now or in the future. Everything I do and say out of Joy will be there forever, possibly affecting all in the future. This idea is not too different from the notion of Karma in Hindu belief. That the good and bad we do lasts into future lives.

Does all of this have anything useful to say to Bill? I don't know. In case you decide to show this to him, which you are welcome to do, I will say this to him directly.

Dear Bill: Consider in searching for what you do each day the possibility of finding work that you can do joyfully. Here's a search tool for you to use. Search for tasks which you will be able to do without measuring their cost to you or their profit to you. I remember you as being a truly good person. You will therefore find joy from that which you do which accords with that goodness. If you do what you can do joyfully, you will live a good life. If you ignore your capacity to act in ways that really matter to you, you are apt to consider each day to be unimportant, temporary, and totally gone the next day. Many people live "throwaway days" and end with "throwaway lives." Their lives disappears each day and they will not have lived at all once their last day comes to an end. But perhaps that will be of little consequence, because they were never alive anyway. Find joy in your life and your life will be there forever. My best wishes to you Bill.

Ruth, thank you for your letter and I wish you all the best, Janus

***

The Joy Test for our intentions.

Janus's recommendation is the basis of what we will call "The Joy Test." This test is constructed so as to help reveal what one's simple compassion has to say about what one is considering doing.

The joy test says:

- Search for something that is a joy to do without measure of gain or loss to you.

Mark Twain wrote "What work I have done I have done because it has been play. If it had been work I shouldn't have done it." He went on to say:

"Who was it who said, 'Blessed is the man who has found his work?' Whoever it was he had the right idea in his mind. Mark you; he says his work--not somebody else's work. The work that is really a man's own work is play and not work at all. Cursed is the man who has found some other man's work and cannot lose it. When we talk about the great workers of the world we really mean the great players of the world. The fellows who groan and sweat under the weary load of toil that they bear never can hope to do anything great. How can they when their souls are in a ferment of revolt against the employment of their hands and brains? The product of slavery, intellectual or physical, can never be great."[66]

This quote exposes one of the two roots of The Joy Test. Find the work that belongs to you. You own it. It's yours, so its purpose originates from within you.

Twain does not expose the other root of The Joy Test. That root is our simple compassion which by its nature operates "without measuring the profit or loss to ourselves."

Although The Joy Test is a rule, it is unlike rules that function to control our behavior and shut off our simple compassion. It is a way of searching for our simple compassion instead of switching it off. It is a way of answering for ourselves the question of "Whither goes thou?" It calls upon our simple compassion for help in choosing the destinations for our behavior.

A young person who feels they are attracted to medicine can use the joy test in this way: "Is practicing medicine something that would bring me joy without consideration of profit or loss?" If so, that young person has set a destination that includes simple compassion. They have chosen to remain fully human.

If someone is considering becoming a farmer, they can use the joy test: "Is farming something I would find joy in doing without consideration of profit or loss?" If so, that person has set a goal that includes giving not only to the land, but to others. Janus's father spoke to Janus about his goal of leaving the land better each year than he found it. This was such a goal. Caring for the land is an act of simple compassion.

If one is considering working in a store one can apply the joy test. "Is interacting with people and helping them find what they are after, something I would find joyful without consideration of profit or loss?"

The issue that the joy test gets at isn't whether you would or would not take the job without pay. The issue is whether you would perform the job without feeling you were *doing* it for pay. That is, will doing it contribute joy in your life or is it only for payment?

Being Joyful encourages Self-Gratitude.

The reader may have already noticed the relationship between joy and gratitude. We express gratitude to those who have given us a gift we are glad to receive. Giving that gift to ourselves encourages self-gratitude.

Feeling gratitude toward something or someone can clearly not occur if our compassion switch is in the off position. Suppose a child is told to write a thank you note to Aunt Judy thanking her for her Christmas gift. Assume the child feels no simple-compassion toward Aunt Judy, that is, her well-being is of no concern or perhaps the child actively dislikes her, meaning the child actively wishes her ill. Then writing the note will not be an expression of gratitude. It will merely be a performance.

The connection between being joyful over what one has done and self-gratitude therefore implies a good side as well as a drawback to the joy test for finding your destinations

The good side is that if you already experience a modicum of simple-compassion, the joy test will help establish self-compassion. You will be truly grateful to yourself for acts you have performed that provide joy. In other words it will contribute to self-esteem. If you set your destination on teaching because you could do it joyfully, and you reach that destination, you will feel thankful for having set that goal.

However, the big drawback to the joy test is that using it depends upon having one's simple compassion accessible. Most of us who grow up in control communities have somewhat limited access to simple compassion because we have the community's notion of a morally developed conscience. This is highly self-blaming and actually shuts down simple compassion. This will place you in the position of the child who tries to write a note of gratitude to an aunt for whom you have no compassion.

Simple destructiveness can also be "called up" by the joy test. Once one is a soldier for a should-loaded ideology, one can quite joyfully carry out destructiveness.

This means that one must have some of understanding of their natural goodness and have a preference for it over destructiveness in order for the joy test to function as a destination finder that preserves ones simple compassion.

Next we follow Janus's efforts to show how our simple compassion gets tangled up with control community teachings and how this tangled web can be undone

---

[64] Fenichel, O. *The Psychoanalytic Theory of Neurosis*. W W Norton & Co, New York, NY, 1945. In the first lines of Fenichel's chapter on the development of the Super Ego, p102, he says: "The fear of punishment and the fear of losing the parents' affection are different from other anxieties motivating defense. While other dangers demand cessation of the dangerous activity unconditionally, in the case of these fears the activity may be continued in secret or the child may

pretend he feels 'bad' in situations where he actually feels 'good.' (Ferenczi once said in a lecture on this subject: 'And out of this lie morality came into existence.')"

[65] The Greek slave of Romans, Epictetus, wrote in *The Enchiridion* "…if you suppose that things which are slavish by nature are also free, and that what belongs to others is your own, then you will be hindered. You will lament, you will be disturbed, and you will find fault both with gods and men." *The Enchiridion* was not only Epictetus's "Manual" 18 centuries ago, but also the manual for Albert Ellis 18 centuries later. Ellis was arguably the most influential of the cognitive therapy psychologists of the 20th Century.

[66] The Mark Twain quote is taken from **The New York Times, November 26, 1905.** It can be found on the WWW at http://www.twainquotes.com/19051126.html

Chapter 19: Cultivating Compassion toward Others and Our Selves

Fortunately a large reservoir of simple compassion remains active in control communities from which we can develop careful and competent compassion. For example, members of control communities who have children or loved ones who have severe health problems cannot avoid the awakening of some simple compassion in their lives. Both the simple compassion we were born with as well as the careful and competent compassion we learn, help provide us with a map for how to exercise our simple goodness.

However, although the compassion among members of control communities may also be naturally awakened in intimate relationships, it often fades with time. It is often eventually deadened by *shoulds* and *musts* that are aimed at each other. For example, a person's initial naturally occurring and untutored feeling of wanting to help their spouse or partner often devolves into feeling that they are helping because they *should* help. Budding control attempts in intimate relationships eventually wear down the sense of voluntary association and caring that may have been present in the beginning, and the compassion switch spends more time in the off position.

But there are nooks and crannies where compassion remains alive among members of control communities. There is no self-instructed "should" required for the awakening of protective feelings toward helpless infants or small animals or children victimized by a vicious adults. However, the narrowing of control community members' capacity to feel simple compassion to cases of helplessness has important implications. If one's view of those who are "deserving" of compassion are only those who are helpless, think what this view implies for self-compassion, self-help, self-respect, and relationship compassion. How is it that we can help ourselves if we need to feel helpless in order to become an object of our helping?

We tend to view those for whom we feel compassion as children.

We need not perform a psychological experiment to observe that most of us are much more likely to try to help an infant we come upon in a doorway along a city street than we are to try to help an adult found there. As adults we often lose a clear and acute sense of compassion for others, unless they are *as helpless as infants*, whether they are older children or adults. Growing to adulthood in a control community involves replacing compassion with *shoulds*, a process noted succinctly by the line, "When you grow up, your heart dies," spoken by Ally Sheedy playing the part of high school student Allison Reynolds in the movie *The Breakfast Club*.[67] One nearly universal exception to having a dead heart for adults in a control community is their response to helpless children.

The survival of compassion toward helpless beings in control communities affects the nature of caring toward non-infants. Simple compassion gets turned around. We view those whom we are helping as helpless infants even if they are not helpless and not infants. Given that our emotional reaction to children is the exemplar that awakens simple goodness, we are apt to view those for whom we care as childlike. This process, called *infantilization,* has been studied in the treatment of those in poverty[68] as well as in the treatment of the elderly and the homeless.[69] Perhaps a more descriptive neologism than *infantilization* would be *childilization.*

We return to Janus and Nancy to see how a caring conscience can *childilize* even an adult life partner. We also see how this can be overcome, an effort that can be richly rewarded. We return to the story of Nancy and Janus started in the previous chapter. Here the waves created by Nancy's acceptance of her simple goodness envelope her relationship with her husband Jack.

The Janus Journey: Competent love is different for children than for adults.

One day Nancy's appearance and demeanor in Janus's office was so changed that Janus had the impression she was a different person. Her smile went all the way to her eyes. She was dressed more attractively than earlier. After telling Janus that she was beginning to feel like the person he had been saying she was, she eagerly volunteered her story of the last two weeks.

In the previous session they had discussed what it meant to love and care for someone in the sense of valuing their well-being as you would the well-being of a helpless child, but to care for them with a love that was appropriate for an adult. Nancy had spent a lot of time thinking about her relationship with Jack. It kept coming back to her that Jack had remarked on the Picasso painting of a mother and child that she kept in her office, the same painting that Jack had referred to, as the reason he loved her. The picture depicted a helpless infant. Could she have mistaken his meaning? She thought Jack had meant that he saw in her a mother of their children. Could he have meant a mother to him?

Looking back at their relationship, she had reviewed one memorable event after another to see if it fit that framework. It was she who suggested his thesis project while they were still in graduate school. She was the one who pushed for having a baby and who worked as a research assistant, and studied for her prelim exams and passed them while she was pregnant with Susan, all while she was helping Jack through a retake of his statistics prelim. It was she who took the lead in finding jobs at the university where they met Janus. She had proposed that they collaborate on research, so that they could both sink or swim when it came time for promotion.

But, more importantly, she began to see how the nature of her feelings for Jack led to the nature of the "help" she gave him. When their daughter Susan was little, Nancy had even joked that she felt like she had two children. It wasn't a joke, and she knew it wasn't a joke even when she first said it.

She told Janus that she had recently pondered her relationship with Jack over all these years, and she was able to get somewhere for the first time. The reason was that she was able to stop making it a matter of deciding whether she loved him or not. Maybe she loved him, but didn't love him in a way that did anything positive for him or her.

She knew that she wanted someone to love. But over the years she had built up more and more resentment of Jack for being more like her infant child than like an adult. She had thought many times that her resentment came from the fact that she wanted an adult to love her back. Why couldn't he give her that? But that way of thinking didn't seem very satisfying.

Now she saw their relationship in a simpler way. She did indeed love Jack with a love that was much the same as her love for their child Susan. Their well-beings both meant the world to her. But she now saw for the first time that the way she went about caring for them was also much the same; the way one needed to take care of children who are helpless or ignorant or both!

She recounted these thoughts to Janus, and then she told him of her confrontation with Jack. She had told him all of it. It had taken most of a night. It was the first time she and Jack had stayed up talking all night since before they were married.

Jack, instead of being defensive, had come alive. She said it was as if she were observing a time-lapse movie of a blossoming plant. He said he didn't really want her to care for him as if he were a child. But it was the only way he thought he could be loved. Now he could see another path for himself.

As their session neared its end, Janus refrained from any warnings and predictions concerning the work left to be done by Nancy and Jack. Over many years as a counselor he had seen many "leaps into mental health," that were only beginnings of the effort to make long-lasting changes. But it was a good day. He let it be.

***

The competencies required for acting on compassion are like imagination-fed ideologies.

Janus's early experiences with paternalistic caring for others, not just caring about them, were with helpless young animals. Later in life, during his journey toward careful and competent compassion, he learned to avoid paternalistic caring because, aside from care for children when they are helpless, paternalism poisons simple goodness.

Put another way, one may coo and talk baby talk to infants in an attempt to reassure them and perhaps do so. But talking to nursing home patients like you would talk to babies does not reassure them; it demeans them. Attempting to contribute to the well-being of another adult, or of a child who isn't helpless, by caring for them as he would a helpless infant, is more likely to hurt their well-being rather than help it. Janus's simple compassion toward another adult was the same as the compassion he felt toward a helpless child, but he had to find and learn different ways to contribute to their well-being.

Janus's farm upbringing had been a bit confusing on this issue. Certainly taking care of newborn lambs that had been disowned by their mothers was different than taking care of older lambs. Newborns were fed with a bottle. Older lambs were fed with a bucket and allowed to eat grass. But they were both fed and watered. However it would never have occurred to him to feed the older lambs with a bottle. It was just a difference that he took for granted. However, if he had asked his father to tell him how lambs ought to be fed, his father would verbalize this difference. "Feed them by bottle for the first week or so, and then let them eat grass and feed them a little grain."

This recipe for caring need not be treated like a "should" or "should not" like the ones that torture depressed persons. It is a "should" that helps us get to somewhere we want; a healthy sheep. It doesn't say "You should feed lambs!" It is like lines on a map that tell you where you should turn to get to Tulsa. It doesn't say you should go to Tulsa. Maps of this sort can viewed like imagination-fed ideologies. They expand our horizons, but they don't require obedience.

Likewise, saying you should exercise compassion differently with adults than with children does not say you should have compassion toward either children or adults. It says, if you are concerned with the welfare of another living being and wish to help them, whether they are adults or children, you will not get there by treating the person as a helpless infant unless they *are* helpless. It's like saying if you want to help someone learn to play the piano, you will not get there by moving their fingers for them.

Being able to help ourselves is an important part of well-being.

A crucial part of being a person is to view our self as a person. This may be described loosely as being captain of one's own ship or what is more commonly referred to as self-respect. There is hardly anything more important to children than personhood—being welcomed into a community of persons so that they can view themselves as a person.

"I can do it for myself" is an oft-heard statement from people of all ages. You may easily remember how much you desired to be able to drive a car. If you examine your memory, you will likely remember the feelings you had when you were first able to drive yourself where you wanted to go. There was a lot more to it than being able to pick up your friends or get away with going places you didn't bother to tell your parents. You likely remember the sense of well-being that came with being the captain of your own ship. Persons drive cars.

Self-respect is easily endangered by losses that seem to overwhelm one's ability to cope. Therefore competent compassion, not just compassion, is needed for helping others who are overwhelmed with bad things. They are likely to be in danger of losing the feeling of "being able to do it for themselves." The aim of such help can only be to actually help the person help themselves since "not being able to do it myself" IS the problem. If one lacks the knowledge necessary to help others help themselves, falling back on simple compassion helps keep both you and them human. Even if we are unable to help others in other ways we can actively welcome them as companion persons.

Just as it is important to respect others as persons when helping them, it is important to respect ourselves as persons when helping ourselves.

We are to be both the receiver of and the giver of self-respect and we can use that respect as a stepping stone to help reduce our self-blame. This is because respect for oneself as a person carries with it the assumption that we have a capacity for self-help if a dire situation should occur. It's like saying, "I will carry my brain and problem solving skills, such as they are, with me into the future and my decisions can be made then." It relieves some of the pressure for searching the future for threats that translate into the generalized dire self-warning "If I'm not careful and prepared I will make my life a disaster." Self-respect calms us concerning the future and gives us room to examine and maneuver in the present. As Jane Austen wrote in *Sense and Sensibility* two-hundred years ago "I will be calm. I will be mistress of myself."

In the Janus story above, Nancy was able to treat herself respectfully partly due to Janus's help. He told her a story in which she was viewed with respect as a human being with human compassion. She was able to see herself through his respectful eyes. It wasn't a story that convinced her that somehow her self-blame was unjustified. It just helped open a door for her to her own "personhood."

Taking a point of view toward ourselves as full-fledged members of the whole community of persons that one would ever have contact with in the world—a human being—releases us from the non-respectful view of ourselves as helpless infants, even if we still blame ourselves. Self-blame that goes with low self-esteem does not remit until a person is able to live voluntarily without feeling they must be a soldier for a *control* community. However, a helper can contribute a great deal to another person's self-respect by clearly treating the person respectfully, as did Janus in the story he told to Nancy about her simple goodness.

Displaying helplessness in order to get help precludes self-help in control communities.

There are rules for receiving help in control communities. They are the same rules as apply to "inferiors" (children) while interacting with "their superiors." As pointed out in an earlier chapter on the rules of childhood, the rules are Deference, Politeness, Obedience and Refraining from Demands.

The rules for getting help exclude any sign of full-fledged personhood. Quite the contrary, the rules of childhood must be practiced by those seeking help. Helplessness may be seen as having taken on a role suitable for those who are "beggars, not choosers." Its purpose is to spark compassion in those who are otherwise without compassion, because they function in control roles.

A huge downside to having to exhibit helplessness in order to receive help is that we cannot help ourselves because we must view ourselves as helpless in order to spark self-compassion. Therefore self-help already has two strikes against it because, being helpless means one has no credential for being of help. Helplessness *is* the default attempt for getting help, but when directed at oneself, it shoots itself in the foot. One does not expect help from the helpless.

Bridging the gap in time between initiating self-help and reaping the benefit of self-help.

Important changes in our lives are difficult and always involve delays in reaping benefits just because they are hard to make. Self-help for alleviating suffering due to the self-blame that goes with "losses," or more extreme reactions we would label depression, require hard-to-make changes in thoughts about oneself and life events. It therefore requires tolerating a delay before experiencing results of adopting new ways of thinking.

There are many reasons why changing our self-gossip habits to alleviate self-blame is particularly problematic in this regard. For one thing, persons must face many situations in which their gossip habits occur in order to significantly change those habits. Changing one's self-gossip habits in one life context does not produce change in other contexts. For example, work situations involving a supervisor, family situations with a spouse or children, facing expenses that can't be easily met, and so on, may all elicit forms of self-gossip that involve self-blame.

Extinguishing self-blaming self-talk requires visiting many of these life circumstances in order to change self-gossip habits and this takes time before noticeable results occur. Furthermore, in the case of depression, some of these situations may have been previously avoided due to the debilitating effects of depression, and as the depression starts to lift due to some progress in reacquiring a simple conscience or due to the effects of medication, new challenges are encountered upon returning to more usual activities. "Going back out there" entails encountering situations one had avoided while having been living in a state without hope and heart. Recovery from long-term addictions to alcohol or other addictions encounters this problem. It is a truism that an alcoholic, who started seriously drinking as a teenager, must start life again as a teenager once they stop drinking or using. Everything one ordinarily learns through early adulthood about meeting and being with people and relationships must be learned without benefit of a substance.

What one needs to learn, including reducing self-gossip that blames oneself, can however be made into a destination. It clearly passes the joy test—Search for something would be a joy to do without measure of gain or loss to you. Using the test to establish extinguishing self-blaming talk is a step forward for self-compassion. So we can establish it as a legitimate destination.

So how can one get there? The joy test helps us to establish the destination of reducing our self-blaming talk. But it doesn't tell us how to get there.

The first step is to recognize that one can enjoy the journey to joy.

Here again, we can utilize stories told by others who learned to utilize their problem solving skills to make their journeys enjoyable. Henry David Thoreau chronicled such stories in Walden[70]. For example he showed us his simple arithmetic for deciding how to go to a nearby town; by rail or walking. He explained to a friend who thought he ought to save money so that he could travel by train why he should walk instead. *"The distance is thirty miles; the fare ninety cents. That is almost a day's wages. I remember when wages were sixty cents a day for laborers on this very road. Well, I start now on foot, and get there before night; I have travelled at that rate by the week together. You will in the meanwhile have earned your fare, and arrive there some time tomorrow, or possibly this evening, if you are lucky enough to get a job in season. Instead of going to Fitchburg, you will be working here the greater part of the day. And so, if the railroad reached round the world, I think that I should keep ahead of you; and as for seeing the country and getting experience of that kind, I should have to cut your acquaintance altogether."*

Thoreau showed us a map for getting satisfaction while on the way to a more satisfying goal. One needs maps such as this one for getting to the destination of reducing blaming self-gossip and opening up gratitude. No doubt there are many such maps and we will suggest some of them in chapters ahead.

The character Pollyanna in a story written long ago provides one such map. In the next chapter she will show us how a different appoach, The Glad Game, can aid us in actually finding the destination which The Joy Test established. Pollyanna uses the connection between gratitude and compassion to show us how to change our self-talk about our disappointments and losses.

---

[67] The whole interchange is:

> Allison Reynolds: When you grow up, your heart dies.
>
> John: So, who cares?
>
> Allison Reynolds: I care.

IMDb includes this quote among many others from the movie at
http://www.imdb.com/title/tt0088847/?ref_=ttqt_qt_tt

[68] See for example Bloom, Leslie Rebecca. "'I'm Poor, I'm Single, I'm a Mom, and I Deserve Respect": Advocating in Schools as and with Mothers in Poverty." *Educational Studies: Journal of the American Educational Studies Association* 32.3 (2001): 300-16.

[69] See for example Whitbourne, Susan Krauss, Sarah Culgin, and Erin Cassidy. "Evaluation of Infantilizing Intonation and Content of Speech Directed at the Aged." *The International Journal of Aging & Human Development* 41.2 (1995): 109-16.
Also see Hoffman, Lisa, and Brian Coffey. "Dignity and Indignation: How People Experiencing Homelessness View Services and Providers." *The Social Science Journal* 45.2 (2008): 207-22.

[70] Thoreau, Henry David. *Walden.* South Bend, IN, USA: Infomotions, Inc., 2001. 45

Chapter 20: Changing Our Self-Blaming Gossip with The Glad Game

It is easily observed in everyday life that what we think about affects not only what we do, but also our moods and feelings. Angry thoughts lead to angry feelings. Angry feelings lead to attacks. Thoughts of reclining calmly on a sundrenched ocean beach lead us to feel relaxed. The position of contemporary clinical psychology mirrors this observation. Our thoughts make us miserable or happy or productive or irritable.

Similarly, the story here is of self-blaming thoughts—self-gossip— that not only shut off our simple compassion, they lead us to feel miserable and to cow-tow to authority. Our self-gossip literally turns us into soldiers against ourselves in the service of community control. It renders us helpless, but obedient to authority, when we lose ground in the games of clout.

As we have seen, helping ourselves, when we feel helpless and defeated, is problematic. As paid up members of a control community we regard our need for help as a state of helplessness. How can I help myself if I'm helpless?

This makes changing our self-gossip when we experience bad

things very difficult for us.

Enter the glad game described by the character, Pollyanna, in the book *Pollyanna*, by Eleanor H. Porter in 1913.

The word Pollyanna came to have a negative connotation in everyday use. In 1960, Janus's college dictionary described a Pollyanna as a "blindly optimistic person." A half century later a Pollyanna still means "A person regarded as being foolishly or blindly optimistic" as the Encarta Dictionary's first definition says. This meaning does not square with the original story of Pollyanna. She was a child who attempted to find something good about bad things that happened to her. She was not blind to what had happened and she certainly wasn't foolish. She was not unrealistic and blindly optimistic when she tried to find something to be glad of when pains, disappointments, and discomforts entered her life. On the contrary, she is an exemplar for using an imagination-fed ideology.

The everyday use of the word "Pollyanna" implies that we are being unrealistic if we do not lament our misfortunes in addition to experiencing them. On the contrary, the belief that suffering should be amplified by lamentation—a view rejected by Pollyanna—seems the more unrealistic approach to bad things that happen in our lives.[71]

One might more realistically ask, why would our culture persist in using the word Pollyanna as meaning blindly optimistic? Perhaps the answer lies in the fact that our culture fosters control communities which depend for their successful operation on the view that if bad things happen, the realistic view is that you caused it to happen. It is helpful for successful people if poor people blame themselves for being poor.

As we shall see, self-amplification of unhappy events in our lives serves a purpose: it supports the cause of obedience in control communities.

The glad game instead of the sad game.

A story from the book Pollyanna[72]:

"For the land's sake, Miss Pollyanna, what a scare you did give me," panted Nancy, hurrying up to the big rock, down which Pollyanna had just regretfully slid.

"Scare? Oh, I'm so sorry; but you mustn't, really, ever get scared about me, Nancy. Father and the Ladies' Aid used to do it, too, till they found I always came back all right."

"But I didn't even know you'd went," cried Nancy, tucking the little girl's hand under her arm and hurrying her down the hill. *"I didn't see you go, and nobody didn't. I guess you flew right up through the roof; I do, I do."*

Pollyanna skipped gleefully.

"I did, 'most—only I flew down instead of up. I came down the tree."

Nancy stopped short.

"You did—what?"

"Came down the tree, outside my window."

"My stars and stockings!" gasped Nancy, hurrying on again. *"I'd like ter know what yer aunt would say ter that!"*

"Would you? Well, I'll tell her, then, so you can find out," promised the little girl, cheerfully.

"Mercy!" gasped Nancy. *"No—no!"*

"Why, you don't mean she'd CARE!" cried Pollyanna, plainly disturbed.

"No—er—yes—well, never mind. I—I ain't so very particular about knowin' what she'd say, truly," stammered Nancy, determined to keep one scolding from Pollyanna, if nothing more. *"But, say, we better hurry. I've got ter get them dishes done, ye know."*

"I'll help," promised Pollyanna promptly.

"Oh, Miss Pollyanna!" demurred Nancy.

For a moment there was silence. The sky was darkening fast. Pollyanna took a firmer hold of her friend's arm.

"I reckon I'm glad, after all, that you DID get scared—a little, 'cause then you came after me," Pollyanna shivered.

"Poor little lamb! And you must be hungry, too. I—I'm afraid you'll have ter have bread and milk in the kitchen with me. Yer aunt didn't like

it—because you didn't come down ter supper, ye know."

"But I couldn't. I was up here."

"Yes; but—she didn't know that, you see!" observed Nancy, dryly, stifling a chuckle. "I'm sorry about the bread and milk; I am, I am."

"Oh, I'm not. I'm glad."

"Glad! Why?"

"Why, I like bread and milk, and I'd like to eat with you. I don't see any trouble about being glad about that."

"You don't seem ter see any trouble bein' glad about everythin'," retorted Nancy, choking a little over her remembrance of Pollyanna's brave attempts to like the bare little attic room.

Pollyanna laughed softly. "Well, that's the game, you know, anyway."

"The—GAME?"

"Yes; the 'just being glad' game."

"Whatever in the world are you talkin' about?"

"Why, it's a game. Father told it to me, and it's lovely," rejoined Pollyanna. "We've played it always, ever since I was a little, little girl. I told the Ladies' Aid, and they played it—some of them."

"What is it? I ain't much on games, though."

Pollyanna laughed again, but she sighed, too; and in the gathering twilight her face looked thin and wistful. "Why, we began it on some crutches that came in a missionary barrel."

"CRUTCHES!"

"Yes," Pollyanna said. "You see I'd wanted a doll, and father had written them so; but when the barrel came the lady wrote that there hadn't any dolls come in, but the little crutches had. So she sent 'em along as they might come in handy for some child sometime. And that's when we began it."

"Well, I must say I can't see any game about that," declared Nancy, almost irritably.

"Oh, yes; the game was to just find something about everything to be glad about—no matter what 'twas," rejoined Pollyanna, earnestly. "And we began right then—on the crutches."

"Well, goodness me! I can't see anythin' ter be glad about—gettin'

a pair of crutches when you wanted a doll!"

Pollyanna clapped her hands. "There is—there is," she crowed. "But I couldn't see it either, Nancy, at first," she added, with quick honesty. "Father had to tell it to me."

"Well, then, suppose YOU tell ME," snapped Nancy - almost.

"Goosey! Why, just be glad because you don't—NEED—'EM!" exulted Pollyanna, triumphantly. "You see it's just as easy—when you know how!"

"Well, of all the queer doin's!" breathed Nancy, regarding Pollyanna with almost fearful eyes.

"Oh, but it isn't queer—it's lovely," maintained Pollyanna enthusiastically. "And we've played it ever since. And the harder 'tis, the more fun 'tis to get 'em out; only—only sometimes it's almost too hard—like when your father goes to Heaven, and there isn't anybody but a Ladies' Aid left."

"Yes, or when you're put in a snippy little room 'way at the top of the house with nothin' in it," growled Nancy.

Pollyanna sighed. "That was a hard one, at first," she admitted, "specially when I was so kind of lonesome. I just didn't feel like playing the game, anyway, and I HAD been wanting pretty things so! Then I happened to think how I hated to see my freckles in the looking-glass, and I saw that lovely picture out the window, too; so then I knew I'd found the things to be glad about. You see, when you're hunting for the glad things, you sort of forget the other kind—like the doll you wanted, you know."

"Humph!" choked Nancy, trying to swallow the lump in her throat.

"Most generally it doesn't take so long," sighed Pollyanna, "and lots of times now I just think of them WITHOUT thinking, you know. I've got so used to playing it. It's a lovely game. F-father and I used to like it so much," she faltered. "I suppose, though, it—it'll be a little harder now, as long as I haven't anybody to play it with. Maybe Aunt Polly will play it, though," she added as an after-thought.

"My stars and stockings! HER!" breathed Nancy behind her teeth. Then aloud, she said doggedly: "See here, Miss Pollyanna, I ain't sayin' that I'll play it very well, and I ain't sayin' that I know how anyway; but

I'll play it with ye, after a fashion. I just will. I will!"

"Oh, Nancy!" exulted Pollyanna, giving her a rapturous hug. "That'll be splendid! Won't we have fun?"

***

Clearly, contrary to the popular use of her name[73], Pollyanna was neither blind nor unrealistic concerning the undesirable things that came her way in the story. She acknowledged "the other kind" of things throughout the book. These painful events which are depicted in the story as having been severe both before and after the incident in this story. She did not focus her concern on the pain of these events. If you were feeling discomfort while a dentist worked in your mouth, Pollyanna would tell you to find some other part of your body that feels good to focus on and be glad that doesn't hurt too.

The bottom line is that The Glad Game kept Pollyanna's compassion switch wide open, both toward others and also toward herself. But how does it do this?

Gratitude limits unpleasantness and keeps compassion alive.

Pollyanna's glad game does two things:

- The glad game interrupts the tendency to magnify unpleasantness of what has happened. These magnifications of bad news are a signature of both gossip and self-gossip.

- The glad game keeps compassion alive through an imagination-fed ideology—the practice of searching one's imagination for gratitude.

Pollyanna's glad game shuts down the magnification of unpleasant thoughts and feelings by changing the subject. It's as if you were talking to a neighbor who asked "And did you hear about the burglary down the street?" And instead of taking the bait, you replied "Yes I heard. Speaking of that family, isn't that a great color they used to paint their house?" You acknowledge the "bad" news but immediately move away from it to something the neighborhood can feel good about. You move the conversation away from blaming gossip which switches off the compassion switch, to pleasant conversation that keeps the compassion switch on.

In the case of the glad game, the conversation is going on within you. It is you that moves away from your own self-blaming-gossip to self-talk that keeps the compassion-switch on by awakening gratitude. The most common disapproving self-talk which the glad game interrupts is about having to suffer unpleasantness. Suppose we are disappointed. We then tend to not only feel disappointed, we tend to disapprove of having to feel disappointed. The glad game also interrupt this way of magnifying unpleasantness Pollyanna practiced letting go of her disapproval of being disappointed.

Not approving is different from *dis*approving. She didn't approve of not getting a doll for Christmas. However, with her father's help, she avoided magnifying her disappointment with disapproval of what had happened, by instead searching for some way to approve of what she *did* get for Christmas.

Pollyanna's fictional but wise father taught Pollyanna that it is painful enough to feel pain, severe or otherwise. She need not make the pain worse by adding the view that it is bad to feel pain. She could help draw her attention away from discomfort by seeking the comfort of finding something she could feel glad about.

The glad game is a way to restore our well-being when it is injured by our disapproval of what has happened to us. Our disapproval of injury further injures our well-being as a person, over and above any pain, suffering, or injury done to our bodies or our feelings. When we disapprove our misfortune, we add lament about the world. We treat nature as if it is an enemy. We then have two problems to deal with: the suffering, and nature as a powerful enemy.

From a self-gossip point of view, disapproval of an event is a form of attack. "I shouldn't have lost that game!" Attack by its nature shuts off compassion. It starts our preparation for punishing ourselves with even more self-blaming gossip. A vicious circle of self-blaming-gossip feeds on the disapproval of things that happen in our lives.

Second, the glad game keeps our compassion alive. The habit of searching for something to be grateful for qualifies as an imagination-fed ideology. It is an ideology because Pollyanna learned to turn to it without thinking why. It is an imagination-fed ideology because it helps her search her imagination. It keeps compassion alive because gratitude toward something or someone is incompatible with attempting to control it. Try to imagine giving thanks, real thanks, to someone for helping you in a time of fear and pain. Can you even imagine wanting to control them while experiencing your gratitude?

You may also remember looking back on your own behavior and feeling really good that long ago you decided to do something that has turned out well. Perhaps you just had a baby and are holding her for the first time. Your self-gratitude for going ahead and deciding to have this baby blots out any trace of attempts to control yourself through self-criticism.

Adding disapproval of pain to pain is a membership requirement in a control community.

Disapproval implies that things should have been different. When we add our disapproval to painful events in our lives, we are saying and thinking, "Bad things just shouldn't happen." We are appealing to a should-loaded ideology concerning our lives that says something like: "Good people, people who are members in good standing of the community of good people, are entitled to a life without reverses."

But of course events that lead to suffering do occur. When they occur in a control community, the grounds of disapproval shifts to: "I'm suffering; therefore I'm not a full-fledged—"good"—member of my community. I feel bad, therefore I must *be* bad." Disapproval of our suffering turns into our self-demotion as a person. We turn suffering into an injury to our well-being as a person.

Our control-community thinking tells us that a bad thing is something that should be avoided because we are punished for doing bad things. We are punished for doing something we shouldn't do. For example, fouls committed in a basketball game are bad because they

218

violate rules. They can be especially bad and may be punished accordingly. But fouls are only especially bad when they are thought to be intentional; an outcome of a choice to do something bad.

In reality when we lose money or get sick or don't get the Christmas present we wanted, we may have made an incorrect choice when we invested, or overworked, or misjudged what Christmas would bring. But we didn't do anything bad. Pollyanna's father knew better and taught her a different ideology all together. Instead of the should-loaded view of life of a control community, she learned the imagination-led view of the glad game.

It should be noted that the social science literature contains a research on "The Pollyanna Principle" which refers to a related but different phenomenon. Some people have a tendency to give precedence to pleasant events by listing them before unpleasant events when they make lists. This has been labelled "The Pollyanna Principle.[74]

The stubborn myth that loss always results from bad choices.

In control communities the everyday use of the words good and bad are often used to describe behaviors that lead to success or failure. In a control community one would say that betting to an inside straight in poker was a bad choice *only* if that choice led to losing. But in reality, it is actually a bad (i.e. uninformed or incorrect) choice, whether or not it wins. It is an incorrect choice even if you succeed in filling the straight. But people commonly say it was a good choice if you filled the inside straight and it was a bad choice if you didn't. This betrays the reason we view Pollyanna's thinking as unrealistic, even dangerous.

- Outcomes that are undesirable or painful tend to be viewed as a result of something we did that was bad and outcomes that are desirable tend to be viewed as a result of something we did that was good.

Control communities depend on obedience. It is dangerous to authority for people to believe that incorrect behaviors can lead to desirable consequences, or outcomes of correct behaviors can lead to bad consequences. Danger lies in the possibility that well-off people might not be deserving of the status they are afforded and poor people might not deserve the low status that they are afforded.

The language of obedience says if you are good, good things happen, and if you are bad, bad things happen. That's the way discipline is supposed to work in a control community. Therefore good things happen to good people and bad things happen to bad people. These beliefs form the foundation of a control community, causing us to believe that it is unrealistic to view pain, discomfort, or injury, as anything other than bad—not just unfortunate or painful, but bad.

Probabilities are problematic to control-community thinking. They feast upon the illusion of complete determinism. Underlying and supporting this illusion is an illusion of a world, even a universe that consists of a cascade of events, each absolutely controlling the next through absolute causation. This illusion removes the possibility that any creature including human beings could possibly be the authors of their own behaviors. Therefore we are determined to be good or bad before we are ever born. Life is just a process of finding out whether we are a good being and therefore privileged, or are bad and therefore full of sins for which we can and should be properly blamed. Much more on the illusion of absolute causation is presented in the last two chapters.

Contrary to this illusion is the view of most of modern science where a probabilistic world is assumed where actions have only a contributing influence on consequences. In the real world, actions can be correct while producing unwanted results, even suffering. No doubt Pollyanna would see this immediately. The fact that huge numbers of people don't see this is shown by the huge appetite for gambling in control cultures despite the fact that the good choices are made by the house or the state or large corporate-owned casinos.

The lamentation of "bad news" and celebration of "good news" in control communities is reinforced by the gossip of close family members. They hang their heads in shame after bad news concerning one of their own is discovered. Distant family members shake their heads in an accusatory manner at that "branch" of the family. The bad news can be anything from bad grades, or failure to be accepted at a prized college, to a family illness. Even events such as being the victim of an illness or a robbery or a rape may be echoed with disapproval throughout family and acquaintances. The victims somehow may have brought these things about.

Janus became familiar with several patients who kept their cancer diagnosis secret from community "friends" because they felt shame over having cancer. The focus of many members of the community, including sufferers themselves, is on the "bad news" that is not supposed to happen to good people. What it does is sustain the suffering that goes with it, in the form of self-blame, a simple truth that Pollyanna learned at an early age from her father. Disapproval of suffering does not make pain go away; it makes it worse and longer lasting.

Labeling our discomforts allows us to interact with them.

We don't just disapprove feeling discomfort; we *actively* interact with it. We call it by a name, a name that becomes a diagnosis of our suffering. "Feelings of being disrespected." "Feelings of being ignored." "Feelings of mistreatment." "Feelings of inferiority." Yes, even "feelings of depression." These are all labels given to our suffering. We label our sufferings so that we can actively grapple with them. They become personality traits instead of passing pains and discomforts.

Most of us diagnose and label our suffering in an attempt to subdue it. We show our "mistreatment" that we dislike it. We treat it as if it is a misbehaving visitor. We actively use our disapproval to try to correct its behavior. Janus had labels like "feelings of failure," "feelings of defeat," and "feelings of rejection" for suffering. These well-kept labels were reinforced and elaborated when they were attributed to Janus's early experiences when he traced them back in his lengthy psychotherapy. He missed entirely the reason for their importance in his adult life. They were familiar labels he gave his adult experiences that served to keep alive painful instances in his childhood. Until he could give up his disapproval of painful experiences, Janus had been unable to let go of his attempt to conquer his past suffering.

Disapproval of suffering because of "mistreatment" at the hands of a spouse stays around for years. Couples keep it handy, like a favorite walking stick with which to beat their spouse, while they relive for the thousandth time the same pain. We keep our disapproval of the suffering we felt when we were "ignored" by a parent. We keep it close to our heart to beat their memory with, while of course it makes fresh cuts in our heart.

You, the reader, will recognize that we, as well, use many of the labels for suffering in this work. We have used them in order to kick them out the door. Hopefully we have opened windows to alternatives to suffering named by these labels, instead of ways of grappling with them and keeping them around.

Pollyanna's glad game can help us on the way to living a life according to her father's observation—once is enough for experiencing each adversity.

---

[71] One lone journal article could be found in the psychological literature that suggests that the glad game could be helpful for the practice of "Positive Psychology." See Levine, Murray. "Pollyanna and the Glad Game: A Potential Contribution to Positive Psychology." *The Journal of Positive Psychology* 2.4 (2007): 219-27.

[72] From *Pollyanna*, "Chapter 5: The Game" by Eleanor H. Porter

[73] See online dictionary, Encarta, Pollyanna:
http://www.thefreedictionary.com/Pollyanna.

[74] The "Pollyanna principle" has been seen to be mildly correlated with happiness. See Dember, William N., and Larry Penwell. "Happiness, Depression, and the Pollyanna Principle." *Bulletin of the Psychonomic Society* 15.5 (1980): 321-3.

Chapter 21: Individual Freedom

Exercising individual freedom in a control community is tough. We encounter plenty of daily gossip that mocks and/or pillories those who don't behave in accordance with our communities' should-loaded ideologies. The hallmark of individual freedom is unpredictability, not predictable acquiescence to other's expectations, or even to one's past habits. Regaining a sense of individual freedom, of voluntary living that we had as young children, is difficult.

We return to Janus. This time he is working with a particularly unhappy person who is suffering from being on community probation, both literally and socially. The work they do together helps his client to understand how he got where he is and the wonderful opportunities open to him.

The Janus Journey: Janus helps Sherman take the lid off the box he's in.

Sherman drove below the speed limit on the interstate. He was in no hurry to reach his sentencing hearing for securities fraud which was

to take place at the Federal Court House fifty miles away. Sherman went over the sentencing possibilities for the nth time. He hadn't slept a wink over the past twenty-four hours and during that time his lawyer's words of encouragement about him having a good chance to escape prison time, with a sentence of supervised probation, had become improbable to him. Fear gripped him with iron straps, making every movement an effort. He pictured the judge looking down on him, castigating him, and sending him away from the reassuring presence of other civilized people and into a place where everything was laid bare—his life, his fears, even his body—to predators.

His fear ebbed slightly as his thoughts turned to suicide as a way out. Each overpass along the interstate was supported by cement columns inviting him to instantly end his suffering. The choice was attractive. He sped up, wanting to maximize the inertial forces in a crash. He examined each bridge as it passed, trying to pick one with an approach that offered the best prospect of a fatal accident.

As Sherman's plan came together he realized that his fear was returning. What if he failed to die? Could he actually carry through with his plan? Would he start off the road surface and then veer off with a last minute change of mind and only succeed in causing a bad accident? He saw a sign that said he was within two miles of his exit. "I can't even do a good job of killing myself!" he thought.

Sherman told this story to Janus a year or so later in his first counseling session. He had been spared jail time, as his lawyer had predicted. His wife had divorced him and he had managed to get a factory job from an acquaintance, a fellow country club member and occasional golf partner in his former life, and now one of the few who still acknowledged even knowing him. The wages were low. He discovered that his fellow workers were mostly down and out people whom his "friend" could hire at low wages and who wouldn't quit or organize a union because they had no alternative employment. Sherman thought he knew how his "friend" had become so successful.

Sherman lived in a rented room and ate one meal a day in "a greasy spoon" within walking distance of his room. He rode a bicycle to work. Mostly he spent his time being depressed, writing sad songs and playing them on his acoustic guitar. Fortunately, his landlady liked to hear him play and even encouraged him. She sometimes fed him a sandwich and a couple of beers on a weekend afternoon.

Sherman had no money for counseling. He came to see Janus because an acquaintance of Janus's was occasionally dating Sherman and was worried about him. She prevailed upon Janus to see him a few times by offering to pay him a nominal fee. What she didn't know was that Janus was already convinced to go along with the arrangement by his curiosity. She had described Sherman briefly, but what caught Janus's interest was her description of him as highly talented in music and the arts. This seemed to Janus to contrast with what she told him about Sherman's business background and what had been his devotion to money and status before his legal difficulties.

Sherman, on the other hand, only came to see Janus because his friend "sold him" on seeing what Janus had to offer, even though Sherman viewed his unhappiness as inevitable part of the price he was paying for his indiscretion. Sherman had tried various antidepressants and sleep medications prescribed by an old friend in private practice. This friend supplied the medications out of his drug sample stock. They helped Sherman function, but so far only as a person lost at the edge of a former life, within sight of the "normal world," but without a path to re-enter it.

After four or five sessions in which he had told the story of his "temptation," his marriage, and some of his early years as an adopted child, Sherman appeared for his next session looking especially downcast. He said he was hardly sleeping and he told Janus, "Hey, you're a nice guy and all, but I don't see how you can help any of this. I had a good thing and I screwed up. There's nothing you or I or anyone can do to change that. Maybe if I find a way to move away from all these people I knew before, I wouldn't feel so bad. But I don't know how I can swing that. For one thing there's my probation and my job which is part of it."

Janus asked, "Doesn't a lot of the hurt come from the way you are now treated and the role you play in your community vs. the way it was before? You can't let go of wanting that back no matter how hard you *try?"*

Sherman replied, "Well, that's about it in a nutshell."

Janus let a minute or two go by and then said, "I'll let you in on a secret, Sherman. Nobody or no event can hurt you in the way you hurt unless you let them."

Sherman came awake and for the rest of the session showed some spontaneity, something Janus had not seen before. Sherman kept saying, "You mean the way I feel around my old business and social acquaintances is something I'm letting them do to me?"

Janus could see Sherman's hope begin to come alive. Sherman didn't yet know how he could do it, but he began to feel he had more freedom to build a future than he had felt in years. (Continued below)

***

Sometimes bad things are the best things that can happen to us.

Sherman was given an opportunity to start again on a path to a sense of freedom and well-being that he had not experienced since he was a young child. Janus didn't say it to him, but he viewed Sherman's trouble with the law, and the shunning that resulted, as the best thing that could have happened to him. The energy-sapping and paralyzing effects of his depression prevented him from a serious pursuit of his former economic and social position within his control community. A return to his former social, business, and status-seeking life would not be the worst thing, but it would be a shame for Sherman to waste his opportunity for finding a voluntary life.

What Sherman was about to realize was that what he took as natural—feeling compelled to seek a high salary, big house, and community status—was only natural in the sense that he lived in a control community where these were the common threads that determined one's position in the community pecking order.

It had never occurred to him that he could find a life that could feel free. Freedom had always meant doing something that was not allowed and therefore must be kept a guilty secret. Freedom meant going wherever his feelings happened to take him. For Sherman, freedom meant letting his desires manage his behaviors. In his eyes stealing and cheating were just riskier versions of freedom. They just involved more guilt.

On the other hand, doing what he thought he had to do, accumulating and protecting his status and power, were Sherman's respirators, keeping his sense of well-being alive. What he had taken to be his flight into "The American Dream," was in reality a compulsive pursuit of an improved position in the control community pecking order.

But Sherman's precarious flight had crashed. He now occupied a place in the community pecking order where he was always in serious danger of *being* pecked. The level of threat posed within the control community pecking order had increased dramatically. He was constantly on guard for situations that required demonstrations of deference toward others who were in more powerful positions lest he might step beyond his designated lowly position and lose even the job he had. His self-talk, consisting of self-blame and hopelessness, helped keep him "safe" from stepping out of line.

Sherman's unhappiness had succeeded in "keeping him in his place," as a demoted person in a control community. Sherman still cared about the control privileges of status, and was therefore enough of a community member to be counted in the census of the community, but little else. Besides, he would work for low wages.

Sherman's loss of status was triggered by the discovery of his criminal act. His story might be discounted by the reader because he was a criminal and the reader may conclude that it doesn't apply to them. But the presence of Sherman's story here has nothing to do with the particular trigger for his loss of community position. The issue for him is what that loss of position produced: his hopelessness and depression. This result went far beyond the legal consequences of his actions. The result was an injury to what he considered to be his well-being. Janus's job was to help Sherman see that his well-being wasn't injured at all. Quite the contrary, he was given a chance to get back his life, a life that had been lost long before his legal difficulties, if only he would take it.

Money loss and loss of employment are common triggers for depression and hopelessness. The loss which was suffered need not involve anything criminal or problems with job performance, as it did for Sherman. Whether financial related losses are the "fault" of the person or of the economy or other events outside the person's actions, they are still quite capable of triggering depression.

It is easy to see the connection of financial reverses to loss of standing in the pecking order of control communities. Caring about obedience makes obedience-based pecking orders possible and stable. Money is the handmaiden of control, meaning financial reverses cascade people downward through the obedience pecking order. The paralyzing effects of loss of money or position tend to keep people "in their powerless place," once they lose their jobs or their "fortunes."

One's lowly place in a control community requires one's assent.

Janus had said to Sherman, "No one or no event can hurt you in the way you hurt unless you let them."

Sherman immediately responded to this, as do many unhappy people, understanding right away that it opened a door that had been long closed: the door to hope. He did not yet grasp that in order to stop the hurt, he would need to understand what he hoped for. Then he would have to come to terms with whether he really wanted what he hoped for, just as Janus had done years before and still continued to do. Did he hope for the house because of the status of the house; or as a place for comfort and shelter? Did he hope for a job for the sake of doing something he valued or for the status and money it afforded?

Sherman realized that whatever the source of his suffering, it had something to do with his feeling un-free. That is why he and others who are unhappy, often instinctively appreciate the freeing implications of Janus's statement that they don't have to allow events and people to make them suffer.

In order to get to that place of freedom from the bondage of involuntary living, Sherman would have to answer the question, "What is the nature of this suffering I feel?"

Sherman finds a real person buried under the ideology of childhood.

Janus counsels Sherman continued:

In following sessions, Sherman and Janus talked a good deal about different kinds of suffering and hurt. They developed an informal scale of suffering. They agreed that at the top of that scale was an experience that both of them had observed in their communities. Both had known women who had married early in life and limited their educations in order to have children only to be trapped in marriages to abusive husbands. These women were trapped because they felt they had no way to support their children. They continued to be demeaned or otherwise abused. But worst of all, they often saw their children suffer at the hands of their husbands' abuse. They felt they had to watch their children suffer while feeling it was their fault. This was what resonated with both Sherman and Janus—watching someone you love suffer while feeling it is your fault.

Sherman and Janus agreed that in terms of suffering, these women were in the worst of all possible positions. They were attempting to help their children while feeling that what they had done caused their children the suffering that they witnessed helplessly. Sherman described this phenomenon in detail and understood the awful pain these women experienced. Hardly any kind of suffering is worse than seeing one's children suffer or to fear for them while feeling one is responsible for that suffering. This became Janus's and Sherman's exemplar for "real suffering." It was a ten on the suffering scale.

Janus had asked Sherman whether he felt that kind of pain. Sherman thought for a long time and finally said, "Yes, I think so."

Janus replied, "I imagine that you took a long time to answer because you couldn't find a reason for feeling that way." Sherman did indeed feel the terrible suffering that goes with "real suffering." But why? What was his real concern that could possibly seem as serious as that suffering that goes with seeing one's children suffer? Janus let this issue stew and addressed another issue he had let slide in their sessions together.

Sherman, from the beginning of their sessions, was apt to use a good deal of their time gossiping about various members of the community that had once accepted him, but now held him at arm's length. He told stories in an artful and entertaining manner that Janus actually enjoyed.

Janus knew that he couldn't let this continue, both for Sherman's sake as well as his own. It wasn't good for either of them to gossip about others, and furthermore, Sherman's recognition of why he did this could be a helpful path toward his understanding of his suffering. This proved to be not only true but crucial in Sherman's path to change.

Janus's chance came one day when Sherman started a session with a raunchy locker-room story from his past, concerning the seduction of one of his friends' wives by another friend while at a drunken country club party. The deed was consummated on the fifth green and the story was told by Sherman in his typically engaging and theatrical style. There were sidebars about grass stains that needed plausible explanations and clever allusions to various hazards, golfing and otherwise, that had been avoided.

After the story, Janus said, "Suppose we rewrite the story. Suppose it took place in Salem three hundred years ago. Let's imagine that they played golf in Salem, but otherwise had the same laws and should-loaded ideologies that Salem had, that led to witch trials, adulterous branding, and all. Suppose your story took place there, except that the couple was discovered on the fifth green and the woman was charged with adultery and convicted. Suppose she somehow got off with just branding an A on her forehead. I know I'm mixing up times and places and stories here, but it's just a story."

Sherman was silent for a couple of minutes and then looked up. "So you're saying that I'm that woman. And just as I was tried and convicted by the community standards, so was she. Except it is me judging and convicting her by laughing and gossiping about her to you, making her the target of a humorous story.

Sherman continued, "I suppose your version of the story is closer to the truth of the matter. I can imagine what would have happened if it had become public gossip. She would have felt real suffering, just like I do now.

"But why this kind of suffering, this kind of pain? Why not just shame or feeling bad because my friends act differently toward me?"

As he answered Sherman, Janus began to feel compassion rising within himself in anticipation of Sherman's pain that he thought he was about to trigger. Janus spoke quietly.

"Sherman, remember how we described real suffering, the suffering that comes from watching your child in pain while feeling that you were responsible for causing the suffering. Remember that picture and let your suffering wash over you at the same time. As you let the suffering come, you will start to feel yourself to be more childlike. Let yourself go on. Let yourself be both that young person and the adult you are. You are here in this town watching your child being shunned by others, knowing you are the parent who did the act for which your child is suffering and you are also the child watching your parent suffer from watching you.

"Feel yourself not only as a child, but as your child. Remember how you were expected to act and feel when you went before the judge? Wasn't that you as a child appearing before the judge? Think of how your former friend, who is now your employer, expects you to act and feel now. You have told me that it wasn't just gratitude that he expected. It was something else. That something else, Sherman, is to behave in the manner expected from you as the child you once were."

As Sherman started to weep, Janus continued quietly. "Suppose your sentence had been to send you to a clinic somewhere, and change you back into a child. You are now that child living in a town of grownups, a town where you used to be a grownup. Well, that was your sentence, except the clinic is right here in this community. Your friends and you yourself administer the social hormone every day that transforms you into a child: 'Act powerless and make no decisions of your own.'"

Sherman looked at Janus with wet eyes. "I can't believe it. That's

231

exactly how I feel. Like a pitiable child. And I feel both. I feel the child's helplessness—bondage, as you put it. And I feel an awful pity for my helpless self. I just can't believe it! My God, I'm feeling lighter!"

Janus also felt Sherman's burden starting to lift and smiled. He went on in a more conversational manner. "You see, Sherman, you and many of us learned to be players in an ideology we might call 'the ideology of child persons and adult persons.' We learned to be soldiers for this ideology when we were taught how to be children. It is a kind of ideology that prescribes the behaviors, feelings, and ideas which are required of children and adults. I call this a should-loaded ideology. This ideology tells its members how to behave. In this ideology the opposite of "adult" is "child." The should-loaded ideologies of children and adults has many important rules, the most important of which are adult persons should control child persons and child persons should obey adult persons.

"Sherman, the long and short of it is that you are living a life in which you are acutely aware, every day, of yourself as a child in bondage. Your loss of status and power belonging to full-fledged adult persons in your community has demoted you to child person status. You suffer fully as much as if your children were put into slavery where you could not reach out to help or intervene, but were always aware of their daily treatment. Their hopelessness and helplessness would be yours. And you feel responsible for the whole thing.

"You feel like a helpless child without a parent to guide or protect you. You, the adult person, are as powerless as the child within you and must merely stand by and experience the fear mixed with hopelessness that comes with lack of power and status in the 'grownup world.'

"Sherman, there are only two possibilities that I know of to escape the kind of suffering that you feel. One is to somehow regain your standing as an adult within the ideology I called "child persons and adult persons." This is what you spend a lot of time trying to imagine. Somehow you would need to get rich or famous enough to demand the deference of those who now shun you. You would ride to the rescue, as a powerful adult, of your child within. You would be back where you started, having to defend your status at whatever cost, lest you lose your

'adult' credentials again.

"The only other possible path that I know of that would take you out of the misery of depression is to walk away from the ideology that connects power with freedom. The ideology of "child persons and adult persons" says that you aren't free to choose, to live your own life, unless you accumulate power necessary to control others. That is an illusion. It isn't true and therefore it gives you an opening.

The fact is there is another entirely different and more accurate view of personal freedom. It is the view that the act of choice requires no expenditure of power and therefore requires no power. It only requires making choices. That's a path worth your consideration. Others have taken it before you. Recently the civil rights movement took it when they found they had choices that didn't require power. Mahatma Gandhi helped millions of people to free themselves with no more than that teaching them that they could choose to disobey. Others have taught the same thing long before he did in one form or another, including some stories in the Christian Gospels, and also stories told by the Buddha.

"We can discuss this path if you wish. It is easy to find, but difficult to follow. You have already discovered that path by just now experiencing your suffering for what it is. You began feeling lighter as if a burden was lifting when you began to see that your feeling of helplessness is connected to your agreeing to be helpless. But I imagine that feeling better will tempt you to return to the control community to seek power, as if it were freedom, once again. The danger of leaping out of suffering can be that you find yourself in mania, a state of exaggerated power and energy.

Your good feeling makes you feel powerful again, so why not practice the game of control? You will find you can't do that without loading up again with the burden you've worked to put down. Change of that sort takes practice.

"If you wish to persist in following the other path out of depression, the path of voluntary living in which you exercise choices to pursue that which you believe to be simply good, you will need to give up your role as critic of others. When we drop out of our control communities we

must not continue to function as a part of their control system. We need to give up gossip, even very well-done gossip, such as your stories. It tears down others and it lies in wait for our own transgressions. These ricochets of our gossip then become self-gossip and strip us of our grownup status and leave us powerless and obedient like the "good child" in the ideology of child persons and adult persons."

Sherman flew out of the session that day. Over ensuing sessions after he had first put his toe in the water of freedom, he worked at becoming more consistently familiar with swimming there without the "support" of status, power, and money. He also became less and less predictable to Janus. He was less apt to try to please. He didn't talk when he had nothing to say. He explored ideas out loud without embarrassment or defensiveness. They were just thoughts and meant nothing unless he decided to act upon them. Janus took these changes as a very good sign, a sign that they were ready to end their sessions.

***

Fully human people are not very predictable because their important behaviors are less controlled by robotic habits. Sherman was becoming less robotic. In addition he was able to experience joy in love, work and play.[75]

Over the years, Janus had come to realize that behavioral and clinical psychologies aren't about fully human behaviors. Being fully human means we act freely. If human behaviors were entirely predictable, psychology would be the mother of all sciences and arts. Then, because human behaviors are predictable, and science and other disciplines are human behaviors, instead of attempting discoveries in physics, architecture, or even psychology, we could concentrate on predicting those discoveries.

That psychology could predict what psychologists will discover produces a paradox, one which brings down the whole edifice built on behavioral determinism. The solution to that paradox is that psychology is not about what people who are free do. Psychology is about what people who are un-free do. They repeat. Or more precisely, psychology is about what we do when we let tendencies and expectations of others command our decisions, particularly habits that run important parts of our life. Janus's job as a psychologist was finished when that part of Sherman's life reduced its destructive influence on his freedom as a human and he had become a freer and more humane person.

---

[75]Firestein points out an early statement by Sigmund Freud on termination: "In one of his 'Introductory Lectures on Psychoanalysis' (1917), Freud refers to the neurotic individual's return to health in terms of 'whether the subject is left with a sufficient amount of capacity for enjoyment and of efficiency' (p. 457). This appears to be the origin of the familiar maxim for assessing mental health in practical terms according to the subject's capacity to love and to work and basing one's judgment regarding termination upon such an appraisal." See Firestein, Stephen K. "Termination of Psychoanalysis of Adults: A Review of the Literature." *Journal of the American Psychoanalytic Association* 22.4 (1974): 873-94.

Chapter 22: Outing Control Communities' Biggest Secret: Freedom Exists

The survival of control communities depends on keeping secrets about the nature of being a full-fledged human, about the illusion of control, and about the nature of freedom.

Three secrets that must be kept in control communities.

1. It must remain a secret that the function of social status and power in a control community is control of others. It must remain secret that success means the achievement of that power—winning at games played for clout. Lost in this secret is the fact that compassion dies with the exercise of control. Supported by this secret is the illusion that status and control are not needed for our individual freedom and well-being.

2. It must remain a secret that we can only be a well-being (fully human) if we choose for ourselves what to do. This includes choosing whether or not we will obey a command. In a control community children are taught to surrender their choices to others and to the *shoulds* of others and that freedom comes with achieving clout. Lost in this secret is the fact that we can choose for ourselves, even in the face of control. "Your money or your life." requires a choice. In fact obedience is always a choice. We don't need permission or power to choose not to obey an authority, or to choose goals and means to get to those goals.

3. It must remain a secret that freedom exists. Our lives need not be strictly determined by rules of nature or man. Our freedom is predicated on being able to search our imaginations for a future that we wish to work toward; a future that only our choices can make real.

Of these three secrets, the third one still needs elaboration in this work.

A common view is that in order to possess freedom, one must be isolated from all contact, that is, one must be autonomous. This view was taken to its logical conclusion by B. F. Skinner, one of the two most influential psychologists of the 20th century.[76] The argument is that our stimulus histories fully determine our behaviors. In other words, in order to truly choose our own behavior, we must be free from all influence originating from the world. Put in the language of this work, according to Skinner and other strict behaviorists, the author of our behavior is our environment, not us.

One problem with Skinner's argument is that it assumes its conclusion as one of its premises. That is, the argument assumes strict determinism. He and many other behaviorists work on the very assumption that a science of psychology must be strictly determined by preceding events. If you start with the assumption that we are strictly determined by our environment it's not hard to prove that we cannot be free from events that completely control us. From there it not hard to conclude you can't be free without being autonomous.

But suppose, we live in a probabilistic world instead of a deterministic world. Then autonomy is not required for individual freedom. As has been noted, psychology and her related social sciences including economics are the only "sciences" that still hold on to the notions of complete determinism.

What is required for freedom is not autonomy, but for us to make some contribution to our own behaviors. That contribution is the capacity to be unpredictable. Imagination provides us with a tool for escaping from the tendencies that can otherwise be used to predict and control us.

Searching for alternate "stories" of how the future might differ from a predicted future is always available to us, regardless of what the prediction may be. Escape from any given arrangement of stimulus control can be provided by our search of imaginary futures which provide alternate contingencies in general, not just aversive ones. We may *seek freedom* by searching our imaginations for alternates to arranged consequences and alternative behaviors just as we may *seek escape* from arranged aversive punishers. We are literally free to imagine stories that have never been told and a world that has never existed.

We can use our imaginative capability, in particular, to become unpredictable to those who wish to control us. Being predictable to predators is a poor strategy for survival and it is not surprising that we might have some tendency to utilize our imaginations to aid us in being unpredictable to anyone, including psychologists. So-called "Protean behavior," is named after the ancient Sea God, Proteus, who was compelled to predict the future if you were able to capture him, but escaped capture by changed his form instantly. Protean behavior (meaning unpredictable behavior) is found in many species.[77] [78] [79]

Another Janus story shows us how he viewed the connection

between human freedom, predictability, and a searching imagination. It is from a diary he kept of his thoughts and appears there after many years in private practice. Its title is evidence that he thought that issues concerning freedom, humanity, control, and compassion were likely to remain unresolved for a long time. The reference to the year 2112 was likely a reference to an album recorded by *Rush* entitled *2112*, words and music by Geddy Lee, Alex Lifeson, and Neil Peart. See the lyrics here.[80] Those who are familiar with Ayn Rand's book, *Anthem*, will see a striking resemblance.

Here is Janus's note from his journal.

A note to a behavioral psychologist in the year 2112.

In your relentless search for environmental designs that produce "desirable" behaviors, what is the difference between your controlling me with threats and controlling my environment? On the one hand, you order me to do X with a threat of what would happen if I don't do it. On the other hand, given your vast knowledge about how I behave, you attempt to engineer my environment so that it will cause me to do X by rewarding me only if I do as you plan. You are either demanding my obedience with a threat or you are controlling my behavior by manipulating my environment. Isn't the only difference between them that your threat gives me a choice as to whether to obey you, while your behavioral engineering, if I'm unaware of it, doesn't readily supply me the choice to escape your control?

Now suppose I were as aware of your environmental designs and your intentions for my behavior as I would be aware of your threat. Isn't there a possibility that I might just search for an alternative future scenario and surprise you, just as I might ignore a threat made by you? I might just decide that I don't want your control in any form and hatch a plan to avoid it. If you cling to your deterministic empiricist ideology by claiming you wouldn't tell me what you had in mind, so I wouldn't "feel" controlled, then I have some questions.

What strange version of determinism says that prediction and control must be secret in order to be correct? If that is your view, then *haven't you admitted to yourself that my discovery of this secret would introduce <u>in</u>determinism into my behavior? It would seem then that deterministic psychology only works when it isn't understood by those who are its target. Doesn't this mean that those who are aware of psychology are exempt from its predictions? And isn't that how tyrants have always ruled—by keeping choices for themselves while controlling the lives of others?*

* * *

Our well-being is dependent on the degree to which we are whole, and are distinct from others; not separated from others, but distinct from them. When our behaviors and feelings are dependent on what we are told they should be, we are not distinct, nor are we whole. Instead we are extensions of others. Our parts—our feelings, our thoughts, and our behaviors—do not work in harmony. This is why choosing for ourselves—freedom—contributes to our well-being. It is also why we are likely to rebel against control even when that control is well-intentioned. B. F. Skinner believed that we only rebel against control when it is aversive. Our theses here is that we rebel against prediction and control because they threaten our well-being as a whole and distinctive being—our well being.

Choices make us whole

We are influenced by those around us. These relationships are critical to us. But there is a big difference between influence and determination. Where the "decider" is located, there lives the whole person.

As members of a control community, when loss demotes us, our borders become less distinct and we are not whole. We are less sure who we are or who is responsible for what we do. We are apt to treat others, even ourselves, in an inhumane manner because our obedience blinds us to what we are actually doing. "I'm only reporting to the authorities as I was told to do." Like characters in a Milan Kundera novel, we do not see the horror we cause by our complicity with authorities until we see the bodies of neighbors lying in front of us.

This happens within us as well. When our self-control takes the form of an absolute and unforgiving authority we lose even self-compassion. Failure, even the prospect of failure, then brings vicious self-attack, sometimes even suicide.

This is true even of young people as they learn the role prescribed for children by control communities. The should-loaded ideology distinguishing childhood from adulthood does not serve children's well-being. It serves authoritarian organizational structures. Predictability is necessary for control and is therefore necessary for authoritarian cultures. The practice of self-blaming among community members is necessary for control on a large scale. It is also characteristic of depression. For this reason it may be conjectured that depression is likely to be observed with high frequency in authoritarian cultures among both children and adults.

But whether or not depression in its clinical form occurs frequently when authority and ideology run things, involuntary living is the norm as a way of life in authoritarian cultures for those who fail to achieve superior status. Authorities tend to be intolerant of the unpredictability of individuals who act with freedom.

As Janus observed concerning Sherman, when he became less predictable, Janus didn't see how he could help him further as a professional psychologist. In fact this was a sign to Janus that Sherman no longer needed his help. As freedom from the bondage of the control community made Sherman less predictable, it also made his life more voluntary.

Once a person has come down on the side of freedom, compassion, and being human, there is nothing to add concerning how another person should live.

When you are compassionate and human, you will be free. This means your life is yours to create.

---

[76] Skinner, Burrhus Frederic. *Beyond Freedom and Dignity*. Knopf/Random House, New York, NY, 1971.

[77] Edut, Shahaf, and David Eilam. "Protean Behavior Under Barn-Owl Attack: Voles Alternate between Freezing and Fleeing and Spiny Mice Flee in Alternating Patterns." *Behavioural brain research* 155.2 (2004): 207-16.

[78] Jones, Katherine A., Andrew L. Jackson, and Graeme D. Ruxton. "Prey Jitters, Protean Behaviour in Grouped Prey." *Behavioral Ecology* 22.4 (2011): 831-6.

[79] Miller, Geoffrey F. "Protean Primates: The Evolution of Adaptive Unpredictability in Competition and Courtship." *Machiavellian Intelligence II: Extensions and Evaluations.* Cambridge University Press, New York, NY, 1997. 312-340.

[80]

http://www.lyricsfreak.com/r/rush/2112_20119899.html?zvariant3=1&utm_expi d=19763888- 0.KUHVg3T2QeiocjiamVO__w.3&utm_referrer=http%3A%2F%2Fsearch.side cubes.com%2F%3Fcategory%3DWeb%26p%3D1%26st%3Ddn%26q%3DRush %2B2112%2BLyrics

Chapter 23: Moving the Control Community Culture toward Voluntary Living

What is the opposite of a control community? What is a community like that fosters voluntary living? What sort of community helps us keep simple compassion in play, fosters cooperation in place of control, and helps foster fruitful relationships? And above all, what is a community like that validates Joy as an objective in human activity in place of pleasure? Can a form of government produce these things?

It is a given that millions of people have sought more joyful and voluntary lives by overthrowing their governments, sometimes even their form of government. It is also a given that they tend to bring involuntary living along for the ride in the form of their desire to replace control by others with control by themselves. Slavery, subjugation of women, and a privileged oligarchy have often been the companions of new governments and new forms of government. Having a chance at the "good life" has meant "making one's way to the top." Equality has meant that more people have a chance at achieving privilege. The American Dream is about upward social movement; the achievement of status and clout. "He *rose* from poverty to be a pillar of the community. Only in America."

All of these points can be hotly argued. But one point that cannot be seriously questioned is that attempts to bring voluntary living to individual members of a community by means of government action are futile. Government has a very different function. If it works well, it will protect its citizens from each other and from outsiders. This in no way protects them from choosing to attempt to control others and themselves by the means that lead them into living involuntary lives.

All of these points derive from one simple fact: political freedom is not the same kind of freedom that is achieved by living a voluntary life. There is certainly nothing wrong with political freedom. Living a voluntary life is certainly easier in a politically free community. We must all find ways to protect ourselves from people who are predators and government can help us do that. But living under a well-functioning government that also keeps its nose out of individual behaviors which don't harm others, does not produce the kind of freedom and joyful living that we have described here as voluntary living. So, if not government, what sort of change would foster this kind of freedom?

Cooperative individuality (without joy)

In an earlier chapter, Janus's father introduced him to a simple story of voluntary cooperation among boys playing in the woods, which preserved their individual dignity and self-determination despite being governed by only one of them. They needed to find a lost knife before dark. They managed to organize their search into a cooperative venture. One boy was in charge of assigning search jobs for each of them, not because he somehow had more clout, but because someone had to divide up the work, and it didn't matter who did it as long as he did it efficiently. No one participated involuntarily. They merely agreed to a plan in which each of them had a different role. This little story represents an ideal for voluntarily living in communities. But where's the joy?

His father's use of the story was in the context of teaching him that he had responsibly at home and these responsibilities were shared among family members. There was no ambiguity about the fact that his father expected Janus to live up to those responsibilities. The story was about dignity, individuality, and cooperation. But it wasn't about joy.

In our search for cultural change that would lend itself to individual freedom and away from a culture of control and blame, we must start with joy as our guiding star.

What does joy look like and does it really accompany compassion?

Charles Darwin, arguably one of science's most astute observers, published *The Expression of the Emotions in Man and Animals* soon after the *The Origin of the Species*. His chapter on Joy begins with the following description.[81]

Darwin's description of joy:

"JOY, when intense, leads to various purposeless movements— to dancing about, clapping the hands, stamping, &c., and to loud laughter. Laughter seems primarily to be the expression of mere joy or happiness. We clearly see this in children at play, who are almost incessantly laughing. With young persons past childhood, when they are in high spirits, there is

always much meaningless laughter. The laughter of the gods is described by Homer as "the exuberance of their celestial joy after their daily banquet." A man smiles—and smiling, as we shall see, graduates into laughter— at meeting an old friend in the street, as he does at any trifling pleasure, such as smelling a sweet perfume. Laura Bridgman, from her blindness and deafness, could not have acquired any expression through imitation, yet when a letter from a beloved friend was communicated to her by gesture-language, she "laughed and clapped her hands, and the colour mounted to her cheeks." On other occasions she has been seen to stamp for joy."

***

His description unfailingly associates joy with interaction with loved objects or persons. Compare Darwin's description to the author's notes describing a woman's behaviors when she first catches a glimpse of her loved one in the airport returning from a deployment in Iraq.

"Upon seeing her loved one, woman's mouth opens wide, her right hand goes to her chest with mouth and eyes open wide while she starts high pitched repetitive screams. Both of her hands go up to sides of face, mouth wide open, while screams continue. Her hands come down in a chopping motion while she starts jumping up and down still screaming, while smile starts around her still open mouth and still wide open eyes. She runs to the soldier, with arms outstretched, screaming and smiling and laughing, and throws arms around him."

One can imagine using these descriptions of joy to teach an actor how to play the part of a joyful person on stage.

A fortuitous set of observations made in the early 1800's show the joy of a child in relating to a loved object. Both the source of the observations and the child's loved object which produced joy are unusual enough to belie any notion that compassion and joy have their origins in morality or any form of controlling authority.

In 1800, a boy appearing to be about twelve years old, emerged from the woods in Aveyron in the south of France. He was presumed to have spent at least seven years of his youth fending for himself in the woods. He was taken to Paris and eventually spent several years with Roch-Ambroise Sicard, an early careful observer and student of human behavior.

The boy has been referred to over the years as the wild boy of Aveyron, although Sicard gave him the name Victor.

We take the following description written by Sicard from *The Wild Boy of Aveyron* by Harlan Lane.[82]

Victor's story: His relationship to the weather brings him joy and longing.

"...for example, when observed inside his own room he was seen swaying with tiring monotony, turning his eyes constantly toward the window, gazing sadly into space. If a stormy wind then chanced to blow, if the sun suddenly came from behind the clouds brilliantly illuminating the skies, he expressed an almost convulsive joy with clamorous peals of laughter, during which all his movements backward and forward very much resembled a kind of leap he would like to take, in order to break through the window and dash into the garden.

"Sometimes instead of these joyful emotions, he exhibited a kind of frantic rage, wrung his hands, pressed his closed fists to his eyes, gnashed his teeth audibly, and became dangerous to those who were

near him.

"One morning when there had been a heavy snowfall while he was in bed, on awakening he uttered a cry of joy, left the bed, ran to the window, then to the door, going and coming impatiently from one to the other, and finally escaped half-dressed into the garden. There, giving vent to his delight by the most piercing cries, he ran, rolled in the snow and, gathering it up by the handful, devoured it with incredible eagerness.

"When inclement weather drove everybody from the garden, that was the moment he chose to go there. He went round it several times and finished by sitting at the edge of the pond.

"I have often stopped for hours with inexpressible delight to consider him in this situation, to note how all these spasmodic movements and continual swaying of his whole body diminished, subsiding by degrees and giving way to a more tranquil attitude; to observe how his face, vacant or grimacing, imperceptibly took on a decidedly sad or melancholy expression, as his eyes clung fixedly to the surface of the water, while from time to time he threw in some debris or dry leaves. When, on a beautiful moonlit night, the rays penetrated into his room, he rarely failed to waken and go stand in front of the window. There he remained, according to his governess, for part of the night, motionless, head high, his eyes fixed upon the moonlit landscape, carried away by a sort of contemplative ecstasy, whose silence and immobility were only interrupted at long intervals by deep breaths nearly always accompanied by a plaintive little sound."

***

Victor's behaviors described in Lane's work describe nicely the joy exhibited by someone when they have compassionate contact with an object of value. In this case the valued object is the natural surroundings he has "grown up with." Clearly Victor had no human teacher for these relationships. Victor's joyful relationship with nature is reminiscent of the poem written by Friedrich Schiller, *Ode to Joy* which was incorporated as a choral by Beethoven in the last movement of his 9th Symphony. Some translated lines from *Ode to Joy*[83] that resonate with

Victor's joy when they are heard with Beethoven's magnificent music are:

> All creatures drink of joy
> At nature's breast
> Just and unjust
> Alike taste of her gifts,
> She gave us kisses and fruit of the vine,
> A tried friend to the end.

The enhancement of joy is the business of individuals and cultures, not governments.

Government governs. It can certainly govern in ways that increase or decrease individual suffering. But they have little to do with producing joy which accompanies individual wholeness and distinctiveness that unbinds our compassion. Constitutional governments with defined human rights can make voluntary living much easier, but they can't legislate joy.

Conversely, individual sovereignty is something that cannot be taken from us by government authority except by individual torture and extreme pain, unless we concede it. Hence the joy that accompanies it, is mainly our own business.

Although government has little to do with people's willingness to hang on to their compassion, individuality, and the joy that accompanies well-being, culture when understood in a certain sense has a great deal to do with the presence of joy. Culture has a lot to do with the formation and maintenance of control communities and could possibly be a vehicle of change in those communities.

The word "culture" has had many meanings and interpretations. It is a central concept in anthropology and to some extent in sociology.

Here we use the word culture to refer to the predominant moral attitudes of a community. An attitude in its most literal sense refers to the position one is in. Just as the attitude of an airplane can be nose up on its approach to landing, a person's attitude on approach to a black person can be nose up, in the sense of approaching with a superior attitude.

Moral attitudes are the moral positions one takes "going into" interactions with people and valued objects—children, white people, black people, fat people, a sunrise, a painting, a warm blanket , one's self, etc. We also have moral attitudes toward building designs, green space, oil spills and so on. Anything we approach with a sense of it being good or bad, valuable or worthless, important or unimportant is a moral attitude.

So cultures, in the sense of the word used here, consist of the predominant ways that community members have of approaching people and things that involve moral evaluations. Culture is the sum total of a community's attitudes about good and bad. This includes the community's attitudes toward education, arts, race, gender, obedience, and religion. All of these contain attitudes that are parsed into morally good and bad categories.

Using the language of culture, we can speak of control communities as having a culture of control and obedience. Which is to say, their members approach each other with an attitude that it is good to achieve and rule, and it is good for failures to obey plus of course many subsidiary attitudes.

Is it possible for compassion to spread within a control community?

Understanding what the compassion switch is and how it works can be good for members of one's community. Changed attitudes of individuals can help the community change toward compassion to the extent that individuals achieve simple freedom and experience the joy that accompanies compassionate contact with objects that *they* value. They become a source of change from within control communities. How can this happen?

One thing that Joy has going for it is that it is infectious. Laughter is infectious. Enthusiasm about something is infectious. Energetic movements accompanying appreciation of someone or something is infectious. These are all signs of joy. When they accompany cooperative activities that preserve the individualities of those involved, we have demonstrations of cooperate individuality with joy.

Cooperative individuality isn't enough. Janus's father gave him an exemplar of cooperative individuality—the cooperation of family members performing individual tasks according to their talents. But this example contained little or no joy. However, later in life, Janus recognized other examples that he was exposed to that *did* expose him to cooperative activities that involved individuality and joy. He and his father loved to play music together—Janus on the piano, his father on the violin. They would play square dance music in the living room for hours from scores his father had accumulated, both remaining animated to the point of exhaustion. Later Janus sang in different choirs, some quite mediocre. But one, a boys' choir at a summer camp for choirmasters from boy's choirs throughout the country, was a truly joyful experience which he never forgot. His experiences with playing and singing music with others became his later exemplar for how to teach and how to recognize a good teacher. He taught with enthusiasm and made learning a cooperative adventure in discovery and mastery with his students.

Example has an advantage for changing people that control does not. It doesn't try to control, so it doesn't elicit counter control. Janus found himself relying on stories more and more as he became more experienced as a counselor. Stories of people in grief and their misunderstanding of grief as selfish loss that paralyze them, were his vehicles for helping grieving people. Stories of loving competently that depict different ways of caring for infants and adults were his vehicles for helping people trapped in a punishing relationship with a spouse who treat them the same as they treat their children.

Examples and stories containing examples told with animation can change attitudes. So they can change cultures. It is highly plausible that romance literature, which depicted women who actually married for love instead of property for their families helped change attitudes. It was widely read by millions of women over the last 200 years in the West and helped to change women's attitudes toward equality marriage and eventually women's rights. So-called romance novels are being read by millions around the world today. Would it be a surprise if attitudes toward sexual pleasure might change?

When movies and radio, and then television, stopped depicting black people as shuffling idiots, it had to have had an impact on listeners and viewers who expected otherwise.

Dear reader, please do not think this is an advocacy for *should* and *should nots* and a recruitment for soldiers in the cause of policing stories. We have come too far together to make that mistake. We are not suggesting that we construct should-loaded ideologies for hiring teachers, raising children, or establishing a government program for funding the fine arts. Again, cultural change is about individual attitudes. Change in culture will come about as the sum total of changes in individual attitudes.

We are merely pointing out that examples of freedom together with joy, like individual imaginations, can free people. Putting imagination and stories together, stories about imagined change can help create change in the culture of control communities.

We can help ourselves maintain our compassion by attending to our own attitudes toward failure and obedience by actively seeking stories of people who love their work and love to be with one another and/or with valued subject-matters. We can actively avoid entertainment that glorifies violence and playing for clout. As our attitudes change, we will find ourselves looking less and less at sports scores and stories of mayhem. We will be drawn more and more toward circus-like entertainment, and humor that is based on childlike ingenuousness instead of humiliation and shock. We will be drawn more toward people as values and less toward people as valuable to us. And above all we can demonstrate Joy whenever we are having compassionate contact with any object or activity we value.

And oh yes, our idea of fairness will gravitate away from just "equal treatment under the law," although that is important. Our idea of fairness will grow to include "Everybody we meet or know about counts or nobody counts." And we will learn to include our self as one of those who count.

---

[81] Darwin, Charles. *The Expression of the Emotions in Man and Animals.* University of Chicago Press, Chicago and London, 1965. P 196-7

[82] Lane, Harlan. *The Wild Boy of Aveyron.* Harvard U Press, Oxford, 1976. P112-3

[83] See this link on WWW. http://classicalmusic.about.com/od/romanticperiodsymphonies/qt/Beethovenjoyt xt.htm

About the author:

Carl Semmelroth's interests span both philosophy and psychology. He received his doctorate in psychology (personality and developmental) from The University of Michigan in 1969. His BA and MA were in philosophy, also at Michigan with emphasis in Logic and Ethics.

Carl's training, research, and clinical interests touch on topics of interest to both psychology and philosophy—perception, information processing, measurement, and personal ethics. He was awarded a post-doctoral associateship by the National Research Council which allowed him to spend a year at the Bureau of Standards. His interest in the importance of measurement and classification systems and their relationship to perception and information processing spans many issues in psychology as well as philosophy. Accordingly his publications concern reading and language, sensory and measurement issues in color science and vision in general, issues in diagnostic "name calling" involved in psychiatric hospitalization, college teaching, and child discipline. (He served as an expert on child discipline on child discipline for Child.com answering readers' questions.) His four books on anger have been well received in the US and are also published in several foreign languages including Arabic in Saudi Arabia and Indonesian in Indonesia. Among recognitions he has received he is proudest of a "Civie" which he received in 2004 from Americans for More Civility for speaking out against violence in sports.

He has been in private practice in Michigan as a psychologist since 1975.